Alexander Chisholm

The Bible

In the Light of Nature, of Man and of God

Alexander Chisholm

The Bible
In the Light of Nature, of Man and of God

ISBN/EAN: 9783742809872

Manufactured in Europe, USA, Canada, Australia, Japa

Cover: Foto ©Lupo / pixelio.de

Manufactured and distributed by brebook publishing software (www.brebook.com)

Alexander Chisholm

The Bible

THE BIBLE

IN THE LIGHT OF

NATURE, OF MAN, AND OF GOD,

ALSO IN ITS ESSENTIAL RELATIONS TO THE
RELIGIONS OF THE WORLD.

BY

REV. ALEXANDER CHISHOLM,

Boglashin, Glen - Urquhart, Inverness.

VOL. I.

TO THE CALL OF ABRAHAM.

Are there more Gods than one?
There is but one only,
The Living and True God.—*Shorter Catechism.*

The Lord, He is the God; the Lord, He is the God.—*2 Kings xviii. 39.*

INVERNESS: A. CHISHOLM.
1891.

(All Rights Reserved).

PREFACE.

THE Bible is constructed like the subjects whereof it speaks. These are God, Nature, Man, God. God is first and last and, throughout, All in all. It is a Revelation and Representation of these, or of the absolute appearing in the relative, of the Divine Being in His self-manifestations. It comes forth from the Spirit All Father-Son as nature and man do; and has its Plenary Inspiration and Infallibility from and in the Spirit. Its holy men of old speak as they are moved by the Spirit. It is thus also fitted for its purposes, as to the all-man all-world, and as to God in both (2 Tim. iii. 14-17). The writer can truthfully and thankfully say that he got more of real instruction and true knowledge, in early life, from his godly parents, Alexander Chisholm and Marjory Fraser, than he ever yet got through all other means put together. It is his decided duty and great pleasure to add that the members of the family, Hugh, a girl who died in infancy, John, Margaret, Duncan, Mary, and he (the youngest), were of incalculable help to each other in receiving and mutually imparting the same. The religious Authors who have exercised formative influence on his mind are Thomas Boston (Fourfold State), Bishop Butler (Analogy), and Dr John Owen, Prince of Expositors. How he came to see the essential structure of the Bible is too mysterious and delicate here to describe; and may be equally unnecessary for the Reader to know. He is eagerly anxious that he and the people should come as much as possible to know the Bible in all that it is and speaks of, as understood and written by the sacred writers themselves; each to know his God and his duty, to know God and Jesus Christ whom He hath sent, which is everlasting life.

A. C.

April, 1891.

THE BIBLE

IN THE LIGHT OF NATURE, OF MAN, AND OF GOD;

ALSO

IN ITS ESSENTIAL RELATIONS TO THE RELIGIONS
OF THE WORLD.

IN the beginning God created the heaven and the earth. By faith we understand that the worlds were framed by the word of God, so that things which are seen were not made of things which do appear. It is more than assumed, it is asserted, that the universe is created by the power which it manifests; omnipotence of the absolute, self-existent, eternal, and unchangeable Being; an assertion which comprises the full meaning of the theistic view in the Christian sense of the Father doing all things in and through the Son by the Spirit, or the Father doing all in, through, and by the Son, and the Father and Son doing all by the Spirit. The ultimate evidence of the being of God is the correspondence between the mind in man and the mind in nature; nature manifests mind, and mind interprets nature, each as correlative of the other; and so it used to be said that the Spirit's work and witness in the heart is the greatest and ultimate evidence of the existence of God. There are ever kept in view, both in word and work, the ideas of substance and personality, and of fatherhood and sonship, in some respects resembling the same as realised among men; three persons in the order of Spirit, Father, Son, in one nature; farther than this the theistic view needs not be said to have more generalised truth to contain. The steps in the round of modified departure from, and return to, this central truth, have a certain order, marked more by measure and gradation than nature and kind. From monotheism, with three in one, is often a straying into tritheism, that each of the three is a distinct and separate God; next is henotheism, or each of all a God; then polytheism, with its partially generalised personalities; thence to pantheism, in which the personality is viewed as becoming one with the phenomena; and, lastly, atheism, which means a negation of all religion, except towards oneself, as the remaining

1

God for and to himself and others. Atheism, in a less aggravated and personal form, sometimes assumes the existence of space, matter, and motion to be adequate causes of every appearance; and, in one of its mildest forms, it holds that no sufficient evidence of the existence of God has yet been furnished. It is unnatural to man, and the remaining step is the return to the starting point of the one living and true God. Monotheism is natural to man and to all things ; and it underlies all those other isms, even in their darkest and strongest forms and imports In infidelity there is a denial of, or disbelief in, Christ being a personal manifestation of the Deity, or such manifestation having ever been made or being possible.

Between God and the heaven and the earth the connection is causal; He is the first cause; He created them in the beginning. That everything that happens must have a cause, and that there is not an infinity of secondary causes are the two indisputable postulates of all philosophy. It lies at the basis of human intelligence that the ultimate reality is a being with omnipotent and eternal causal energy ; the laws of nature are an expression of volition ; and the whole course of nature or world process is, in its existence, a continued act of will; while, in its content, it is a logical course or process. The will requires an end for some reason ; and that implies that both the will and the end are reasonable. Power, or force, presupposes will to exercise it, and intellect and righteous mode or law to give its exercise intellectual fitness for just action and end ; and yet will presupposes power to exercise it. The exercise of will and intellect in the region behind and beyond that of subject and object, as known in the relative, may be difficult to form into thought or formal act of the mind, because it does lie in that region, and because of the difference between the absolute and the relative ; yet it is in that region that the will and the intellect, and all else, have their real and essential power and force ; our life is hid with Christ in God. Intellect does need an object in order to its exercise and operations ; it does need the distinction of subject and object for its exercise, just as consciousness needs the same, in the relative ; but both have their higher existence and exercise in their essential relation to, and radical being in, the absolute. Its intuitions are wider, its reasonings fewer, and its affirmations larger, as its power is higher or greater ; and there is every ground to conclude the existence of a self-existent, infinite, and eternal intellect. The union of will and intelligence with power is manifested by the whole universe, as well as in idea; and the universe may be a necessary end of the divine activity or contingent.

The relative presupposes the absolute, on which it depends for its essence and existence, and to which the whole series of relative realities point and tend; the relative is a modification of the absolute and infinite, its phenomena veiling it yet manifesting it ; the absolute is a reality and a reason beyond analysis; universal being is organic, with an aspect of finality as formed with a system of definite directions, not an inflexible monotonous mechanism capable of analysis by mere process of reducing complicity to simplicity and special law to general law. Correlation is not existence; a thing is not explained by merely tracing it back to its rudimentary forms, and by exhibiting its growth. The nature of the power of the ultimate reason transcends intuition and is beyond imagination; in essence it is unknown and unknowable; yet it is manifested through phenomena to our consciousness; and what is made manifest is interpreted by the intellect in its cognition by perception and reflection. The primary fact recognised or revealed by it, in the relative, is the distinction between self and non-self, a distinction which is accompanied by the idea of moral obligation. The source of this obligation lies in what is beyond the physical, and on which man is dependent. There is a supreme power over all, and a law of righteousness in the moral order of all, throughout the universe; and this power and this law are recognised by the human mind as those of the ultimate personal reality, and such as ought and must be submitted and conformed to. The human intellect discerns and testifies that the ideas of truth, justice, goodness, and beauty, faintly and dimly reflected in itself, do belong to an order of principles existing in the absolute as anterior and superior to the relative in which man finds himself. By a law of its being it is compelled to refer the complete realisation of these ideas to the ultimate reality; and, having this reality manifested to it through consciousness as law, which is another name for reason and righteous will, wherein consists personality, it is naturally led to view this reality as the highest and central personal object of all desire.

Mental phenomena, equally with external phenomena, manifest the ultimate reality as law, to which they add the further revelation that the reason is true and right, that the law is just and righteous, that the will is ethical in the character of reason and righteousness, and that the person is good and holy.

There is also a noteworthy manifestation of the ultimate reality by necessary truths, as axioms of ethics, self evident and unchangeable and independent of experience. In man the Ego testifies of itself that it is something which is one, identical, permanent, rational, volitional, and free; and his belief in the unity of it rests on his being able to appear to himself at all, not on his appearing to himself as such a unity. While the ultimate personality contains within itself the conditions of its existence, the ideas of being, substance, and casuality in personality are somehow transcendant and incomprehensible to us; and while reason and liberty in Him must be in essence and in truth, they are so in a way and form unknown to us. The existence of the perfect Being, and that He is the supreme active cause and Ruler in all things, may be difficult for us here to reconcile with such a world as ours is, with its guilt and misery; but the solution of the terrible problem may be in the nature of things passing through a course of formation and improvement from the lowest to the highest, in their relations and interactions as things of the relative as one whole, and in the relations of the absolute and the relative with each other, in Him in whom they all exist, in whom they are renewed, and in whom they are perfected, all in one, Christ.

Though we cannot know the universe in its origin or beginning, yet there can be no true and valid objections to theism and the world's creation by divine agency from science and forms of the laws of consciousness. Physical science knows nothing of the cause which formed the first cell of any creature, how that cause developes there from the organism, and how it creatively rules its evolutions; but the facts of science compel the mind to infer an ultimate reality with a superhuman intelligence; not an abstraction or notion of a being, but a being with aspects or attributes of independence, self-existence, infinity, and eternity. The Bible does not contradict the facts of science and philosophy, of human experience, or of universal natural religion. Let it receive the justice of careful, intelligent, and prayerful examination of its statements and contents; let it speak out its own meaning in its own way; and it will make known to us the truth we need to know and we ought to accept.

Evolution presupposes creation, or the pre-existence of what is evolved. Both in creation and in evolution there is activity, and also passivity; the one in the subject, the other in the object. The self-existent is self-active and self-passive. There is a derived self-existence in the created or evolved, with a derived self-activity and self-passivity. Being implies oneness of what is, with an envelopment, or involution, on all sides, of what is not, or of non-being; and development, or evolution, is the coming, actively and passively, of the one out of that envelopment, or involution. The envelopment, or involution, as non-being, in relation to and contact with being, implies a form, as crust or shell, in which being meets with non-being, where they forever inter-act and co act, where they forever give themselves each unto death to the other. Here being is forever giving itself into nothing; but in and through becoming nothing, it ever becomes being, it ever washes and purifies, renews and resumes itself; it ever decays, dies, and disappears, and it ever revives, reappears, and grows. On all sides of it, and of all its parts, cells, or atoms, this is so.

The point common to both, that of being-nonbeing, is like a point with a zero-like circle, a centre and its circle; while the centre being is three in one; and the circle is a corresponding three in one. Its out-motion puts one half of the circle to the one side, and the other to the other; each forming into a circle with a centre-being, and both together forming a son-being, a son-bud, or some son-form, as in plants and animals. Its first out-growth is its three in one from one to four, its next from four to seven, and its third from seven to ten, which is its normal three parts in one; making ten, with four special being-nonbeing points of one, four, seven, ten. These four specially creative points imply three in one in each, or twelve; but the tenth, as a new starting point, is as the first, making a one-ten ending-beginning point forever onwards, with an inner fourth and seventh of like form and meaning. At the shoulder point of every out-growth there is ever being formed this being-nonbeing point; containing the sum-substance of the past for a new onward growth, for fruit, food, or seed. Such is the case in the smallest cell and atom, and upwards in gradation to the highest formation in earth, animals, and man, in the twelve signs of the zodiac, and all else. So did the Creator, Himself, appear to act in creating the heaven and the earth; and so does He ever act in all His works of heaven and earth, and all their host. This is the Bible's spirit moving on the face of the waters; this is the sacred Om of the heathen nations; this is the halcyon nest of the waters of chaos brooding the beginnings of creation. The absolute thus appears to have this incidental self-being-nonbeing working Om; existing, or having being, in and out of being-nonbeing, forever outgoing in to and fro, descending and extending, movement, respiration, and circulation, in the relative, in all its ten whole, and ten form gradation of parts and points.

In the revolutions of evolution the first point is for ever passing into the fourth, the fourth into the seventh, the seventh into the tenth, and the tenth into being the first again. When the first is becoming great-grandfather, the fourth is becoming grandfather, the seventh is becoming father, and the tenth is becoming sons or children; this is seeing one's children, and his children's children, to the fourth generation. Every ending-beginning may be correctly termed the beginning as to the point, part, period, dynasty, or that to which it stands as beginning: and the sum-substance of essentials and elements, principles and laws, and all else, is taken as already created, eternally existing, or eternally being created and eternally having being, all in one om, to be newly evolved in renewed being, and all thereto pertaining. What preceded thus passes into being the succeeded, with variations and distinctions difficult to recognise. Whether the earth has passed through the course of changes, correctly taken in the number and order of three in one, or into and through a fourth, as nebulous ring, gaseous spheroid, liquid spheroid, and solidified earth, may be legitimately and profitably studied in the light of what is or may be known of other heavenly bodies, of such distinctions as in some respects still true of earth, and of the laws and facts of its constant and periodic changes in actual course. It is remarkable that the same numbers and order obtain in the theory of meteors into comets, comets into suns, and suns into cooling planets, passing into and through the fourth into externally solidified crust form.

Earth is inner and cultivated land, the holy land, as distinct from ground, the outer uncultivated, and common land. In all the changes that the earth, or nature, undergoes, it holds true that matter and force are eternally changeless in quantity; nothing is lost, nothing is annihilated. The varied phenomena of nature are produced by modes of motion which are interchangeable; and matter passes from one state into another, but with no absolute loss in the process. Beginning's primal power is the eternal power, ever working in unbroken oneness and undiminished quantity; manifesting its divine character and origin in the uniformity of its laws and the circularity of its modes; in short, that it is The One in all that is. This Divine Personal Spirit gives form and fulness to the earth out of being without form and void; without increasing or diminishing the absolute quantity of matter or motion. In the process of doing this there is an unbroken and endless chain of link-like oms, making one circle, or whole om, through the whole scale of being; all in a natural, systematic, and scientific gradation from the smallest and faintest form and throb of the om's inner one and outer form of the smallest beginning cell to the full form and sum-contents of universal being. The one of the om is the infinite and eternal spirit, and the circle is the external form of the universe, and of each part and point of it. Its gradation is from the smallest atom and organism to the universal system of systems in one full form and contents

Spirit, whatever and however it is or may be in itself, is, in our present ultimate knowledge of it, and at least relatively, a simple unity. The creature, physically considered, is a changing mode of motion in a transient form of matter; but both the motion or force in motion, and the matter, have a gradation of existence and relations onwards from the first, and outwards from the inmost being in the eternal, self-existent, and creative spirit. Various opinions have been formed and entertained respecting the origin of the human soul; that of the creationists' being, that it is created by a fresh act, for each new body; that of the traducianists, that it is engendered by the parents and transmitted like the bodily characteristics; and that of infusionists, that it pre-existed elsewhere, but is infused into the body at some given moment; while the transmigrationists think that it previously inhabited the body of some other man or animal, which doctrine is a development of the preceding or third opinion.

Life's gradation is the Divine Spirit, the human spirit, animal life, and plant life; the lowest appearing first, the next higher thereafter, and so the rest in order, on to the Spirit who is invisible, yet manifested in all. A triad of dynasties, each of three in one, or into a fourth, may be taken as the nebulous ring, the gaseous spheroid, the liquid spheroid, and the solidified earth; when the earth, in its solidified state, may be taken in relation to the continued form of these three into one, Okeanos, and moving on, under Chronos, Zeus, and Christ; making one clear triad, each into and through a fourth, with Christ as rising from the dead at the eighth point of resurrection or head part of glory. From beginning's opening out in the creation of heaven and earth, the onward gradation's four points are the first day's light and firmament, the fourth day's light in the firmament, the creation of man, and man's passage through the Garden into new life; the sons-begetting process being from the Garden to the Deluge. Under Zeus, or Abraham, there are Abraham, Isaac, Jacob, and Joseph. How they are formed into twelve is shown in Jacob's family of twelve sons, with the feminine side in Dinah. The Chaldean triad of Triads, put into one triad of one man triad, like Jacob's sons under Joseph, are, Ana, Ea, Bel; Sin, Shamash, Raman; Nindar, Maruduk, Nergal; Nebo, Belit, Ishtar. Special distinctions need not here be dwelt on.

Created objects are classified in Scripture in the order and gradation of their creation: an order and gradation for ever and everywhere kept among all objects; any exception proving the rule. How far the existing classifications by scientific men agree with this of Scripture cannot be but very partially noticed in this work. Scientists mark such natural distinctions as between the inorganic and the organic; the former necessarily demanding the attention and study of the naturalist of whatever character, but specially that of the geologist and mineralogist; the latter demanding that of all, but specially that of the biologist. The subject is taken as being the characteristics of organised bodies as distinguished from, or compared with, unorganised bodies. The way taken to ascertain these is by an examination of their chemical composition, form or shape, arrangement of parts, mode of increase, and periodic or cyclical changes. Order and number of elements and parts, both in progression and proportion, enter largely into these characteristics. Every living body possesses the power of absorbing or inserting into itself certain congenial materials from without, and of assimilating the same to itself as food for its preservation and growth. It constantly gives out and drops away the decayed or dead portions of its substance. It has the power of begetting or reproducing its like. It is also an advance of the inorganic body. It possesses the substance, and is subject to, and affected by, the physical and chemical forces and laws of the inorganic; but it is more, and possesses more than the other. It is living, and possesses energy in a sense peculiar to life; it has a measure of power of self-acting, towards self and non-self, within certain limits.

The laws of Arithmetic are well applicable to the standard of human existence. It is natural that they should be so; for they enter into, and are essential to, the nature of all being. Among all nations the Deity has ever been known and acknowledged as one, The One; yet also as three in one, The Triune, or the Divine

Trinity in unity. The three persons, Father, Son, and Spirit, imply and suppose each other, as do the pronouns, I, Thou, and He. The one Spirit cannot be Father without being Son, nor Son without being Father; nor can the Spirit, in being Father, or Son, or both, cease to be still the Spirit, as the third person and common in and to each and both. The Son is the only begotten in the bosom of the Father; the eternally being begotten of the eternally begetting Father; the one eternal Spirit eternally self-existent, self-begetting, self-being-begotten, self-acting, and self-passive Spirit; implying all being and all relations, all law and all life. Scripture represents the Father and the Son as addressing each other with the first and second personal pronouns, and as speaking of the Spirit and the Spirit as speaking of them; but it does not represent the Father nor the Son as speaking to the Spirit, nor the Spirit as speaking to them. In every work and every act no one person of the three acts without the other two. There is order in their existence, their relations, and their work.

God is light. All things were in the eternal and universal Om in the beginning. In the evening-morning first day is the Almighty fiat, Let there be light. The sun, moon, and stars appear out by the fourth day. Man, created in God's image, is one personal sum of all; and through the Garden he and Eve re-appear as gods knowing good and evil. Light has thus the natural stages of three in one, or into and through a fourth, and so have all things. Face contains a summary expression of a person or thing. The Spirit's moving on the face of the waters, is His begetting, in the original state of the elements, the creatural beginnings of the ideals and types of things in His own mind or in Himself. It is the original of the Ancients' representation of one beholding himself in a well or watery mirror, falling in love with the reflected self, and dying of love for it, passing through death into new life in the creature in begetting the creature. It is done, as all things are done, in the Son, as given in love for the world, the whole kosmos as whole and each part to the lowest atom. It is a continuation in the creature of the being begotten sonship God is love in self-begetting as in the Son, in begetting creatural self-reflection in every created being, and self-image in full-form man. The same is continued in nature and man begetting; all which is done by God as love and in love to Himself and to all; and all which teaches that man ought so to do all things in love to God, to himself, and to his neighbour as to himself, and in gradation throughout nature. It implies the true spiritual and natural religion of living, moving, and having being in God. Man's response is in seeking God's face to be begotten in him, to appear in it as God's image subjectively, and for ever to enjoy it as objectively made known. This is strongly essential to the soul's ever livingly everlasting desire and yearning for immortality. The existence of God and the immortality of the soul are here together in the unbroken chain of connections, and in nature, character, and action, in life and through all change and all death into life of all life

The waters here signify the first out-spreading of the Spirit's elemental work ; the two sides, like the two first and opening leaves of a plant, spreading out each to its respective side. It is one firmament, one heaven, one outer side ; the inner part being continued as the more secret and sacred part, and its other side as the begetting side. The spirit continues in the outer side as Elohim ; in the inner and begetting part as Jehovah who is, and who was, and who is to come ; ever coming and becoming, Father, Son, Father, Son, forever. At every tenth point transition passage, the sum-total of the outer is absorbed with that of the inner, purified, renewed, and carried on in further growth or some form of advance ; more easily seen in the onward course of the work.

The phrase evening-morning is a form of the universal creative Om of ending-beginning, darkness-light, death-life, nonbeing-being, oldness-newness, nothing-all, of endless evolution in endless revolution ; never-ending force in self-preserving and self-propagating circle of influences and forms of action and relations. Concentration of inner powers and energy into mid-line of force is implied in every motion of mind and body, and shows marked prominence in some motions more than in others ; a fact well worthy of study, and easily known and understood. These evening-mornings, like all other things, exist in triads ; and are, therefore, here and through scripture so treated. The first is from one to four, the second from four to seven, and the third from seven to ten, all formed into one sum man triad, with a self-younger as Father-Son, for ever and in all relations. Here there are only seven expressly stated, three in one twice, only two triads. Man is created at the seventh point, but does not come to manhood till his fourth point, which is the seventh of the animals and the tenth of the plants. At this level the full-form creation of ten points in the outer or physico-plant nature, the middle part of which is peculiarly the work of the second triad of days from four to seven, and the third or head part is the manhood sum of the whole occupying, as sum-total and representative form and substance, the part from seven to ten. The three parts of this head-sum are the face, containing the five senses, touch, taste, smell, hearing, and sight ; all in the sixth sum of that of preservation, in hunger and thirst, and all desire for all means and manner of action and enjoyment conducive thereto ; all also in sum for propagation in begetting and rearing offspring. The second part is in the mid-head part, or cerebrum, answering to the body mid-part of from four to seven ; and the third part is in the cerebellum, or lesser brain, which is beneath the back part of the cerebrum. The brains two lateral masses, called cerebral hemispheres, are each divided by deep depressions into three lobes, the anterior or front lobe, the middle one, and the posterior one. This back part seems to be the seat of the intellect, the oraculum in the most holy place; and here is the inmost secret and sacred place of the all creative begetting Om, of the Divine Spirit and sum-total substance and form of all things, as at the beginning, the eternal and all-comprehensive ending-beginning. Full manhood is thus in three parts in one, or ten points in one, all being Om.

The Greek term for man is Anthropos, composed of ana, up; trepo, I turn; and opa, eyes; formed up in gradation of all things in all steps and stages to the highest and most heavenly part, the eyes, the intellect, as most God-like, and expressing—I so view all and work all and in all, the perfect man (Christ) being All and in All. The a is their first and father letter, Alpha; the n is the inner closing-opening or producing consonant letter, as in ana up, and in the Chaldean God Ana; t is hard d, but softened by h into ha forward sound (as in the Gaelic tha); the o is the om vowel; p, as emphatic b, andicates giving more of the hos or os son sense, as in Joseph. They have a phrase—aeon ton aeonon, age of ages. The a is as already noticed; the e is the vowel letter marking the outer line, as it does also in Hebrew with l as in El; the o is the om vowel; the n is as already noticed (as b is the labial form as in Abba); t holds the place of the hardest form of d of man-name, Adam, as in Japhet, and Het, and Het-ites or Hit-tites; and the on is repeated in the third word, as Genitive (begetting) plural form of beginning all things by, of, out of, and from the nominative singular one inner on, or labial om (including any number of inner on's). Man is thus the man, or the father son man, of the age of ages; and, for the sake of brevity and convenience, may be called the Aeonic Man. It should be carefully noticed that the inner is not from the outer; but that the outer is from the inner. Man is not from the ape, or from anything else, but from God in the inmost om and oraculum place and sense. The outmost is from its next inner, in gradation to inmost man; who is, in the inmost, most original, and highest sense, of and from God in eternal begetting sense—man is the Son of God—Christ is the Son of Man, the Son of God. Buddhism has the all-comprehensive and all-expressive maxim, that a man is born into the world he has made. There is a self-made sense true of all things. The inner line of force makes a surrounding world for itself, in moving on and recomposing itself at every transition point, modified examples of which are in the effect of early training, in one's conduct, in making a dwelling-place, in home-making of beasts and birds, and, indeed, in all activities in all things. It is also pre-eminently true that a man is made by the conditions, influences, and circumstances of his being at birth, and any, and every time. But in the highest and most proper sense, all things are of God, who is ever in necessary, creative, formative, and renewing contact and inbeing relations with all things.

The work of creation is given in the order of each respective evening-morning day. The first-day work is spoken of as being the production of light, the division of it from the darkness, and calling the light day, and the darkness night. In the second day's work is making a firmament, thereby the waters above are divided from those below, and the firmament is called heaven. The third day's work is in gathering together the waters under heaven into one place, the division thereby into dry earth and seas, and calling them earth and seas. The three days' work, up to this point, are here summed into earth, one form of three kinds gradation of plant life, grass, herb yielding seed, and tree yielding fruit. In the fourth day's work lights are spoken of as being in the firmament of heaven to divide the night from the day ; to be for signs, and for seasons, and for days, and for years ; and to be for lights in the firmament of the heaven to give light upon the earth. These are the twelve signs of the zodiac and the great milky way. Then follows what is said of the sun, moon, and planets ; God made two great lights, the greater light to rule the day, and the lesser light to rule the night ; the stars also—these last being the planets. And God set them in the firmament of the heaven to give light upon the earth, and to rule over the day and over the night, and to divide the night from the darkness. The sun is the head-sum of these lights, and the moon is the feminine side of the same. Venus is God-like, the om inner being of them, ever acting in Father-Son begetting, renewing, sustaining, and working all, as to all persons and things, in all conditions, circumstances, and relations. The fifth day's work is as to water and air life-productions. Let the waters bring forth abundantly the moving creature that hath life, and fowl that may fly above the earth in the open firmament of heaven. And God created great whales, and every living creature that moveth, which the waters brought forth abundantly, after their kind, and every winged fowl after his kind. Here the Om-form production is called the waters ; the productions are the moving creatures that have life, divided further into fishes and fowls. Higher forms succeed in mid-part gradation ; and they are to fill the waters in the seas, and to multiply in fowl forms on the earth. It is in the open firmament the fowls are to fly. The sixth day's work is in the production of terrestrial living creatures proper. God said, let the earth bring forth the living creature after his kind, cattle and creeping thing, and beast of the earth after his kind. And God made the beast of the earth after his kind, and cattle after their kind, and everything that creepeth upon the earth after his kind. All production is out of the universal Om by God, in all gradation and relations. Now, when man is being made, the Om is in the terms us and image ; let us make man in our image, after our likeness. In being so made, man is also plural ; and let them have dominion over the fish of the sea, and over the fowl of the air, and over the cattle, and over all the earth, and over every creeping thing that creepeth upon the earth. So God created man in His image ; in the image of God created He him; male and female created He them. Each creative or begetting act is performed in the double character of masculine and feminine; the Divine One of the Om and a relative counterpart form for the feminine side circle of the Om. In the first verse there is God as the one, and the term beginning is the feminine side; He created in the beginning. God and the beginning are together one; I am Alpha and Omega, the beginning and the end, the first and the last. The creative act is a self-act by the one self-existent Being. It is much the same in the third verse; God said let there be light, or let light be: God, in begetting intercourse with light, producing that light; and that light, in the same begetting intercourse with God, begetting itself, God also producing Himself in it; or God-light, as masculine and feminine, producing this God-light. This is the Egyptian god-goddess, Neith or Ne-ith, the self-begetting and all creative inner being of all beings: commonly paraphrased in the words, I came from myself, or I eternally come from myself. It is the divine inner being, eternally self-begetting, all-creative and self-begetting, in all gradation, from the light in its lowest and smallest form and sense to the human intellect in God's image; from the God-beginning Om form and sense to the same of the end; the beginning and the end, as the one of the first and of the tenth, being the same; and so through all the world of worlds and the age of ages. It is the Athenè of the Greeks; a, from; theos, God, or thea, goddess; and nao or neo, I beget, or I am born in being self-begotten, in brief, the self-begetting and all-begetting God-Goddess. It is Ishtar of the Chaldeans; the Ish, or Isha, being like the same in Hebrew for man and woman, and the second part, tar, for the one inner principle of nature. It is the Bible's Jesus, the eternal, universal, and all-creative Om word; in whom is the all-life that is the light of men, as men of the ages and comprehending all world beings; who was in the world as its inner and all-filling being, who made it, and who lighteth every man that cometh into the world. The outward object taken for it is the planet Venus, the Greek Aphrodite, whose relative position, orbit, course, and influences, bear peculiar resemblances to the six days' works. The fourth is what the ancients called the mysterious number four; because it is the first number through which the three in one pass into being a new or renewed three in one up to the next mysterious number seven. The three in one from seven to ten make the third of the triad of triads, written one and a zero, which together make the Om form of the universal and all comprehensive circle and one, or the all-one, within it. At this point is the end like the beginning, at which the beginning goes on anew, ending-beginning, ending-beginning, for ever.

The firmament spoken of is not the outer infinite space where the system of systems of heavenly bodies exist in one whole space, and each in its respective part space; but that between the waters above, and those below. All things have been created in the same way; but here the account is specially of this earth and of what relates to it in its immediate vicinity and connections; and the range of these and of the space occupied by them is widening as they are produced up to the Garden state. This firmament is called heaven, as the high place.

Every beginning has ending as the oldness which it puts off and away; so that this ending is to it as night is to day, darkness to light, non-being to being, death to life, and such like in all changes. Thus it is always an evening-morning, and ending-beginning creative act by the self-existent, eternal, omnipotent, and omnipresent Being. This creative act has the zero and one, the cell or radicle, or Om form of the eternal one being, whose act it is. It has the Father-Son, two-one, or three in one of Trinitarian relations, in and underlying all forms through all changes. Protoplasm and ozone are the lowest known forms of material substance, the ozone being more related to liquid or sea and sky, and protoplasm more to earth or solid matter. They must be two forms of the one that is common to them both, possibly the ether, which must be the Omic one of the first and tenth, and of all between. The one must be in the self-being and the self-being must be in it all.

The self-being is to this whole one in all its forms, as the human spirit is to the human body as the representative epitome of things; the human spirit having its first and last, or ending-beginning, and all through in highest sense and form, in the intellect as essential epitome. Such phrases as let there be, let the earth bring forth, are fiats of the self-being, passing on actively, and passing through all forms of being; and they imply the self to self sense of that fiat, continued in the onward and outward gradation of things, as they are being created and evolved. This self to self, self of self, and self from self sense is essential to what is said in the words, bring forth, yielding seed, yielding fruit, after its kind, and emphatically in the words, whose seed is in itself. The ending-beginning sum of it and of all is in the words, let us make man in our image, after our likeness. The same epitome is carefully and briefly put into the summary repetition of, and it was so; what in itself is so is the It, the He, the Being; what is in gradation of variation of form is what it is becoming; and both are the eternal Father-Son of all things, of the All in All. The eternal self-energy of the Eternal Being manifests itself in the constant and persistent ending beginning force and motion of that Being's intelligent and just will; a causative force effective in some particulars and in some not; in some permanently effective and in some only temporarily so; visibly permanent and effective or only invisibly so; just according to the eternal purpose, character, and ways of that intelligent, just, and good-will manifested in the nature, laws, and forms of all beings. Gradation belongs to force and motion, causation and effectiveness, permanence and visibility, in common with all other things; and all that gradation, and all to which it belongs, are from the Om sum of perfection and of all else. Visibility has a peculiar and prominent relation to the second or middle part, from four to seven, for itself and for its co-existences, overlappings, and surroundings, of the other two parts of from one to four and from seven to ten.

2. The very shape of arithmetical figures was intended, and is fitted to indicate the natural meaning and use of numbers in nature, and particularly in all forms, relations, and manifestations of all beings. The Om has been already noticed; it represents the sum-total of all things. From one to six the number of strokes, or short lines, is the same with the number indicated by them. Six is made of six short lines with the opening to the right, and denotes the number six with an opening forward into a third triad. Seven's upper line is the transition line at the shoulder and neck place, and its downward line is the sum of the lower and mid-parts in one sum-substance passing through. Eight is the human figure come out of his creative transition seventh line; and is the purification and circumcision place, denoting all the six points of the six days having passed in sum-substance through the seventh, or circular circumcising neck point, into creation's head-sum man of all ten points in one universal Om, of nature, man, and God. Nine is the zero of ten with the one of all entering into it to form the one-all Om, which is ten in one and zero in front. The one of ten is taken as the last, that is the whole, of the past, and the first, that is the whole of the future, both in the eternal present tense of being in I am, paraphrased into, I am Alpha and Omega, the beginning and the ending, saith the Lord, which is, and which was, and which is to come, the Almighty. The tenth and eleventh are, therefore, counted as one, as containing all in one Joseph, of Jehovah will increase and multiply, will give more, all more, and evermore. But what will be given in the next ten, and every ten, is not a new, or another God, man, and nature, not another Absolute and another Relative; but the same infinite, eternal, and unchangeable, and universal Being, of whom, and through whom, and to whom, are all things. It is the one Spirit in the one Om, the one Joseph, the one Jesus, re-creating, renewing, and re-begetting all things; in the twelfth, the Joseph double self into second self Benjamin, both as one self-existent and self-begetting, in God-Rachel, Zeus-Athenè, Joseph-Asenith, sense, of I come from myself. It is the full form triad of triads in one triad, or into, and through, a fourth, a seventh, a tenth-last-first, an eternal ending-beginning Father-Son begetting and being begotten one three in one Om. The alphabet is also shaped in imitation and indication of natural forms and figures, intention and purposes, numbers and their import and use.

In mathematics the Om first form is the point, having position but not magnitude, but having all magnitude in the inner all one; and that one coming out in the one mid line, which may have, and actually has, its Om in any and every point as the centre of the universe and of every thing therein existing; and which may be drawn from any one point to any other. Nature and the Bible mathematically agree, and are one in themselves, in man, and in the whole relative as the region of the self-acting and self-manifesting of the absolute one eternal Being. Everyone can examine, ascertain, and verify this for himself, at anyrate up to the fourth proposition of Euclid's mathematics. Though Alexandria was Euclid's native place, there is a fourth point, and there is a fourth proposition, difficult for any, unless in the light of the nature of things, and not less for a Hamite, an Ishmaelite (man-ass), an Arab, to get over, namely, the line differentiating Ham from Shem and Japhet, placed across the mysterious fourth point. The Egyptians might not eat bread with the Hebrews; for that is an abomination (an unnaturalness) to the Egyptians.

The heaven and the earth are the omic and aeonic form of the all one of things in the beginning; that of the whole universe, that of every system of worlds therein, that of every world in every system, and that of every thing in each world and all worlds. God as the All-One in the all Omic Zero brings forth the heaven and the earth. As the beginning is feminine towards God as the One in the creation of the heaven and the earth, so is the earth, as without form and void, and having the face of its secret place, in the sense of feminine secret parts, the deep, hid under darkness for covering or veil, as on the face of the bride. This Om is like a deep well, the well of the waters of creation into created being and life, as the opening of the absolute out into the relative. Waters here, and in such connections, signify the original substances of things in their elemental sense and state. As the face of man, or of any being, is the summary means of communication between the inner and outer world, in all inner and outer being and meaning, so the face of the waters, in this all omic secret place, means the seed elements of creatural beings; and the moving by the spirit on this omic face is the spirit's begetting intercourse for the production of the earth in form and being. So is Jesus, Himself, conceived by the Spirit in the womb of the Virgin Mary. The letter m is the emphatic closing-opening form of the closing-opening letter v, as in Eve, the mother of all living; d, as in Adam, is the inner hard form of v, and thus the v is the well-form or feminine of the d one form, as Eve is of Adam. The Hebrew, like the Gaelic, has bh, dh, mh, with their Gaelic sounds. The feminine is the Om mother of all living; the other is the man-father of all living. D repeated becomes r, and changes Adam into Aram, which put with Abba into one word makes Abram or Abraham. The m, taken as emphatic of v in Eve, and put with r, as the repeated of d in Adam, gives Mara, or Miriam, the feminine of Abraham, and of Aaron. So the Spirit's omic work here is the same as in man's creation and Adamic dynasty, in the Abrahamic dynasty, and in Jesus and the Christian dispensation. Being's lowest form of outer covering is non-being, and it forever exists in self-being and self-motion, putting off and on the relative as its outer garment, gradually from the lowest non-being form, through all kinds and measures, again to non-being re-being. The nearest to non-being is darkness and death, the next remove is in a measure of light and life, and so on through all gradation in the whole scale of being. The omic contact of the relative with the absolute is the secret place of the Most High. In creating and evolving the relative, the absolute must have an omic form, or feminine side, in begetting intercourse, with which it produces the relative by self-action in that omic form. The eighteenth Psalm says—He made darkness His secret place; His pavilion round about Him were dark waters and thick clouds of the skies. All force acts in to and fro motion through an omic ring, or a number of rings in a sheath-like line of least resistance. The omic ring is three in one, in which there is a triad of triads, or ten points into one whole and a new beginning twelfth. It is all days in one day of all works in one creation whole. So it is put in the fourth verse of the second chapter—These are the generations of the heavens and the earth when they were created, in the day that the Lord God made the earth and the heavens

Aeon is that which has the eternal absolute in its inner being; with the eternal form, which the eternal absolute takes in the relative, for its outer body form. The letter a is the first-last father-son vowel with the Omic vowel o as feminine through the whole mid-line; and the letter e is the vowel passing out from the fourth point in and along the outer line, with the vowel i in the outmost or last syllable, as in Elim. So a e are the dividing point at the fourth point, showing full form and sense of the lower part; a e i show the full form of the whole; and hence a e i mean, all always, which together with on (being) give Aeon, the all always Being and Form. Abba is father; Adam is man, who, being repeated in begetting a son, becomes Aram, meaning man-father; so Adam becomes Father Abram, in the Abrahamic dynasty. In an inner and deeper sense and sound is the ch, sounded deep down as in the Gaelic cha; the less deep and loud letter in which the ch man comes to dwell is the c, or ca, as in Cain, Cainan, Canaon, Isaac; and so cha, or ca, indicates son and possession, or man-son in possession. The guttural sound of d is dh, as Adhamh in Gaelic; and that of e is e h, as in the Gaelic cha; while bh is sounded like v. Thus ca or cha being the inmost son-form of man, and actually begotten, the Adam becomes father in Aram, and grandfather in Abraham (expressly said to mean great-father, that is, grandfather). In the next begetting of the Adam (man) is like the seventh point or creation point of Adam, and he becomes renewed and circumcised great-grandchild, to begin the Abba (father) again, and repeat the d into r, and so on in ever forward sense of a, the ending-beginning in all and in each step. The name, person, and time, of Abram, signify that the Adam, or man, has become, in the Aeonic dynasty sense, a grandfather on earth. The first Father, at first and in the higher and proper sense always, is God, Adam being, in fact and as genealogically traced by Luke, the Son of God; the second is Adam, or God-Adam; the third is Abram, or God-Abram; all making three in one God-man, to pass through the fourth point passage into the next point of open and onward course. But, while man is produced, in his son-sum of lower part, at the fourth point, it is at the seventh point that he is produced in his son-sum second part, or son-sum-substance of lower and mid-parts, into the third of from seven to ten. Correctly and appropriately the first letter form in the word Chaldea is ch, or cha, the l is for El, the d for man as in Adam, the e for the out-splitting, and the last a for the whole as passing in the Om o and one of a, into Abrahamism; as the chaotic state of things at the beginning pass

	Abracadabra	
	Abracadabr	11 a's
30 a's	Abracadab	4 b's
13 b's	Abracada	4 c's
7 c's	Abracad	4 d's
5 d's	Abraca	3 r's
11 r's	Abrac	—
—	Abra	26
66	Abr	11
	Ab	—
66 + 6 of every new form's place = 666.	A	37 + 36 = 73
	11 steps	73 + 4 sacred points
	10 in (1)	= 77.

a
cad
acada
racadab
bracadabr
Abracadabra
bracadabr
racadab
acada
cad
a

Form of cone and of world.

into all-very-good creation. The d in Adam now comes to its last form in t, as the substance of Chaldeanism comes out in and with

Abraham in Lot; the sum-substance of which being El-o-t, or El-Adam as old passing into the renewed state or dynasty. The term for man now is Ish; the I being the one, advanced and more heavenly form of a i, the sh being in Hebrew of three in one Aeonic form, and with cha, bringing out the inmost form of Godman from the lowest depth and highest height of Being in earth and heaven. These, put together into one, give Isaac, or Ishaach, which is Iah-ish-acha, or Jehovah-man-all. Isaac has his lower part in Ishmael (man-ass, or man-lower-part), and his division into two in Jacob as inner and Esau as outer. Isaac now becomes father, hence the name Jacob, or Jah-ish-aae-abba; Abraham becomes grandfather; and Jacob is the Aeonic Son. All this retains the father-son form and sense of the past; but it takes the advanced fulness of character implied in the Jehovah-ish-aach, which is formally expressed and actually realised in Joseph, as father-son sum of all in three in one parts, and twelve in one point. Ab, or Abba (father), and all the rest are carefully put together, and conveniently expressed in the word Abracadabra, as given in the foregoing triangular and conical forms. It shows the to and fro, backwards and forwards, decreasing and increasing, states and movements of things, by having a letter dropped off in each point of descent and decrease, and a letter put on at each point of ascent and increase. It briefly and beautifully, concisely and connectedly, shows the all changes of all things; as are also very fully and affectingly given in the Chaldean Ishtar's descent, in the Egyptian Osiris, in the Greek Dionusos, and in the Balder of North Europe, &c. Though the letter a is the only vowel used in it, the vowel o is really the one employed, for a is made of o and i, as the one Om in all existences and actions, all forces and forms, and all else.

Om mani padme hum are the sacred words among the Buddhists, which so far correspond to the Abracadabra, and form the Buddhists' Paternoster for all occasions and all things. The most sacred canon of the Hindus and the ritual of the Parsees are supposed to be little understood by their priests, and much less by the people; whence it is difficult for foreigners to interpret, both the ritual and the canon. That such important matters should be so, may have arisen, partly, at least, from such selfish motives as keep the breviary of the Roman Catholics in a language not understood by the people. These mysterious words are sometimes printed or written on long scrolls of paper, which are wound within a small brass cylinder. The writing is often on many parts of the paper, in Aeonic connections, and the cylinder is caused to rotate on an axis, each revolution of the cylinder counts as a prayer, as if the words were repeated by word of mouth, and is in imitation of the Aeonic revolutions and changes in one's course of life, and that of the whole world. They are the three in one, or fourth, in eternal duration of universal and omnipotent being; they are the self-existent and creative inbeing of all Aeonic formations; and their revolution in evolution is the turning of the wheel of the all in one excellent law. The absolute seeks to discover the one in the Om, and does ever succeed in finding that one, by ever going into it in begetting intercourse, and that one is itself. So every creature seeks to find the inbeing builder of himself, and goes into the Om and Oms of his whole course of life to find it ; and that builder he finds to be himself with the real sense of the Divine Being in him. To act in the natural way of the excellent law is the way thus to find the divine inbeing ; in living in, and with whom (as Enoch's walking with God), is to be saved in life, and finally to cast off one's building or tabernacle, and to attain to Paradise, the ultimate and first Nirvana Om of pure, perfect, and happy being. In short, the Om mani padma hum are the three parts into one, or fourth, or ten points, or one, four, seven, ten, in one ever ending-beginning being. They are so in all motion, in the Tora or Law, in the Lord's Prayer and all formations. One to live and act in such conformity to this as to become himself in the sense of the original first cause self is to find the true self, the first, last, and all self of the inmost and universal being, with corresponding blessedness and glory.

It is a Platonic doctrine that, in the generation of all things, intelligence and final causes precede matter and efficient causes. The same is taught in the Vadic Hymns. Scientists, equally with Christian men, recognise and teach that life precedes material organisation. Four different terms have been employed by the Greeks to distinguish the four, or three in one, parts gradation in the human frame : soma, as the lower and outer ; psuche, as midpart ; pneuma, as third part ; and nous, as the finest and fullest sum, and nearest in spiritual nature to being divine. In the New Testament these words are translated—soma, body ; psuche, soul ; pneuma, spirit ; and nous is mind in the highest and sum-substance sense. It has already been repeatedly noticed, and is everywhere implied, that each outer form appears before its next inner form ; and that the outer is made by the inner, not the inner by the outer. Each outer is a second-self form, self-reflection, and self-manifestation as the relative is of the absolute. The original and first second-self is non-being, into being, as in let there be. The next is the highest and lowest, the first and last, form, namely, darkness, as first covering of the creative Om into light. It is through the face and the senses in the face that the intellect has communication, in sum, with the outward world. Face of the deep denotes that the deep Om has all the senses, and is in a mature state for the spirit to act on in creative and begetting intercourse ; and its nuptial veil of darkness, the well-fitting and the only available one in the actual state of things, is on it for the occasion. Then the face of the waters denotes the same in respect to the seeds of creation ; and the moving on the face of the waters denotes the actual intercourse taking place. What is here stated is continuous ; it all goes on now and ever ; it is the all begetting and being begotten process in one act.

Naturally and historically the first part of all and any production appearing in the issue is the highest part of the head. Descent in all things always precedes ascent; no one has ascended into heaven but He who came down from heaven, the Son of Man who is in heaven; so is it in all nature, in all man, and in all God's ways and works. Every kind and measure of a different way have always and rightly been regarded as unnatural and of evil omen; not according to the all very good way of the all very good spirit and Om. The oldnesses of the past are put off and away in every new creation, begetting, and renewal; and all oldnessses are here summed in one word, darkness, and all newnesses in the one word, light. The Spirit with His one Om of all Oms is the creator and begetter of all things implied in that which is most like Himself, Light, and that all Light is the creature of the Spirit with the one all Om, saying let there be light and all in it as one sum being, out of the preceding darkness as one non-being.

What first appears in light is the firmament in, through, and along which things exist, move, and have their being. This firmament, by creation and according to the nature and necessity of eternal order and constitution, lies between the above and the below, and between the north and the south; and its to and fro motion is in the main between east and west, south and north, down and up, but also in all directions. Its lower part is in the sea, its opening division at the meeting of the surface of the sea with that of the dry ground, its middle part on earth, and its third or head part in what is called the open firmament, the sky or airy firmament. Each part is also a firmament in itself, so is each formation, of whatever kind or magnitude. It is the high place.

The tenth point is the same as the first point; the hairs on the head are as the grass under and about one's feet on the earth; and both the hairy scalp and the grassy surface of earth are respectively the first part to appear in nature's outcomings. The eyes are the first of the organs of sense to appear. Birds in moulting, and other animals in casting their outer covering, begin to do so at the head and foreparts; and the young of all come forth head foremost. Falling on the face is a common phraseology through the scriptures, betokening the putting off and away of the old face of outer oldnesses in an act of renewing intercourse. The production of light is the work of the first day. From one to four it is comparatively undivided and indistinct from the darkness, till the appearance of the sun, the Om eye of day, and of the hills and hollows, and of distinct body configuration of creation's parts and points, plants, birds, beasts, and man, as in the hundred and fourth psalm. Every Om's creative act of production is the day of that production; therein it has its creation and being, its type and measure, and duration, and its distinct division and separation from the darkness and the other days. The bounds of every being are like the waters at first, as to beginning, ending, and all around state; a state of non-being being, ending-beginning, old and new; it is from the same creative Spirit and Om that it comes and goes, as to itself and its all; and these ending-beginning waters it has above and below, east and west, south and north, and all around. Every being is so situated, like the great milky way, and this world's great line of empire from east to west, with its human frame-like shape, its course of sun and seasons, its zodiac signs and stages, its breath and breathings and begetting beings, its changes and passages through heavens and hades, its north and south and all-around seas, ever dying and ever living, a distinct being, yet one of all and with all beings in one Being, wherein it lives, and moves, and has its Being. This firmament God calls heaven : it is heaven ; in it the Most High hath His abode ; God who dwells in the high and the holy place, yet also with him, and in him, who is humble in heart and contrite in spirit. God does more respecting any and every being than saying, Let there be, let be, let (do so and so) ; there are the phrases, the Spirit of God moved, God divided, God called, God made, God set, God created, God blessed, I have given, God ended, God rested. There is more than the possession and out-putting of energy, the exercise of force, the setting something in motion. Energy, force, and motion have laws of causation and relations, order and regularity, type and form, facts and fitnesses, implying the omnipotence and omnipresence of the all and infinite intelligence and will of the eternal and supreme Being, who is All and in All as to all things. In Him they live and move and have their being. These all wait upon Thee that Thou mayst give them their meat in due season. That Thou givest them they gather ; Thou openest Thine hand, they are filled with good. Thou hidest Thy face, they are troubled ; Thou takest away their breath, they die, and return to their dust. Thou sendest forth Thy spirit, they are created ; and Thou renewest the face of the earth. The glory of the Lord shall endure for ever; the Lord shall rejoice in His works. Every blade of grass and every hair of every disciple's head, everything from the smallest and slightest motion in the Spirit's work of moving on the face of the waters to the one universal motion and movements of universal being, is under the constant care and ceaseless working of the All-Father in heaven.

In the evening-morning third day are the gathering of the waters into one place, the appearing of the dry land ; and the earth bringing forth grass, herb yielding seed, and the fruit tree yielding fruit after his kind, whose seed is in itself, upon the earth. Hitherto the whole world Aeonic formation is in its watery or first part state. The light spoken of is the dusk and dawn, or evening-morning light, together in one, as tenth and first points in one, or at the first or Om out-coming point, as in the early morning ; the second part light will appear at the fourth point ; and the third part state with man. The first or lower part of the firmament is with the mid-line of the lower part of earth which is to continue under the waters ; the second part is the open firmament which is to be occupied by the dry land, with seas to south and north and all around, also by the atmosphere and living beings, as insects and birds and the clouds ; and the third is the space which is the pathway where the sun, moon, and planets move along the Zodiac. Every begotten being has from its beginning a head cover like the first kind and form of its beginning. Each sprout-like icicle that shoots out of the ground grows up and melts or drops down with a small quantity of earth on its head The head-sum of everything tells the tale of its who or what, and its whence and whither; dust thou art and to dust shalt thou return, yet the spirit shall return to the God who gave it—vanity of vanities, yet eternal reality. The Chaldean pictures represent the lower part of the full Aeonic formation, as in man, as a sea-being with form and scales of a fish, in allusion to the lower part of the world being thus and continuing thus in the sea. The dry land is called earth, and the gathering together of the waters is called seas ; both terms are Aeonic ; the difference between earth and common land is made clearer and more distinct in the second chapter.

Plants are spoken of as being brought forth by the earth, as are also its kinds of living creatures in the twenty-fourth verse ; while sea and sky animals are spoken of as being brought forth by the waters. Plants are classified into the tripartite kinds of grass, herb yielding seed, and fruit tree. Plants, taken in their natural state and improved by cultivation, pass through the transition stages of the one, four, seven, ten, into varieties like species. This shows the importance of cultivation ; but shows also the immutability of natural laws, and the mysteriously creative and renewing character of the transition points of passage. The races of varieties thus obtained are perpetuated with perpetual cultivation ; but when allowed to grow wild, and scatter their seed in ordinary soil, they will, in time, lose their improved character, by steps and stages, as in Ishtar's descent, down to their original state and type of natural species. An instance of these remarkable changes, and of home interests, is in the improvement and reversion of the Brassica obracea, which, in its wild state, grows on the sea-shore ; but which, under proper cultivation, passes through the transition points into the varieties of cabbage, cauliflower, brocoli, savoys, and curled greens. Its first change is in being formed into a heart or globe, as in ordinary cabbage ; corresponding to the typical Om shape of the earth and all things, and appearing anew, as is here said of earth, let the dry land appear. It now begins to bring forth its new plant forms through regular transition stages, in accordance with the fiat, let the earth bring forth grass, herb, tree ; and anon it appears as cauliflower, and brocoli, with flower-stalks become thickened and shortened, and other peculiarities. It is unnecessary to follow out these changes here; the forms effected are well known; only it may be added that the curled form of the greens variety is supposed to arise from the cellular tissue, parenchyma, becoming largely developed between the vessels, and perhaps marking the limit of effective improvement and the line of distinction between plant and animal life. Similar changes are produced by improvement in cereals, as in wheat, barley, oats, and such-like, which are supposed to be races of varieties of wild-state species now unknown.

SECOND PART.

The fourth day's work is given in the verses 14-19, both included. And God said, let there be lights in the firmament of the heaven to divide the day from the night; and let them be for signs, and for seasons, and for days, and years; and let them be for lights in the firmament of the heaven to give light upon the earth; and it was so. And God made two great lights; the greater light to rule the day, and the lesser light to rule the night; He made the stars also. And God set them in the firmament of the heaven to give light upon the earth, and to rule over the day and over the night, and to divide the light from the darkness; and God saw that it was good. And the evening and the morning were the fourth day.

The order of creation is preserved and continued in the continued act of creation; so that what it is now is what it was at first and is at all times. To know what it is now is to know what it was at first and is at all times. The gradation in order and relations now is what it ever has been. It is so in all matter, or all the substances that affect the senses as occupying space, nebulous, gaseous, liquid, and solid; states which the component parts of matter take according to the relative strength and effect of the forces uniting them, and the energies disuniting them. It is so in the relations of the smallest particles, whether as molecules, or mechanical and combined units, or as disunited and free atoms in the form of chemical units. Even in the primordial element, or the farthest back state in which matter can be conceived of by the human mind, as one-all matter, there must be order of two polarities and a middle state common to both, like subject and object, and their common state in consciousness, in the intellect, in the will, and every three in one state; whatever that one element may be, as ether, or whatever else. Combination of particles takes place in definite proportion of weight and measure, and according to the periodic law of advance by sections and overlappings; the elements being seldom found in a simple or free state, but in a compound of two, three, or four, seldom more.

The sun is formed on the universal Omic principle; the nucleus appearing like a gaseous mass of inconceivable heat or heat causing power, next the photosphere and chromosphere, lastly the corona. The spots of the sun are in Aconic relations. The law of speciality and intensity is a part of the law of variety in unity, suited to all origin, adaptations, and ends. Different figures of growths in nature are caused by the different forms of the motion of force. The circular shape of the Om point and cell is necessarily related to the centre and circle of any thing and all things, such as when the major and minor axes are equal, and the foci and centre coincide; and is to be seen in the shape and revolutions of beings or objects. Beings shaped straight, or erect, present the direct out-going or growth of the Om centre in midline direction; and is to be seen partly in everything, and most prominently in man's erect and upright creation. God made man upright in mind and body. Spiral motion is a combined form of the forward and circular motions; and is found in many things in heaven and earth. The ellipse is a curved line, in oval form, such that the sum of two straight lines, drawn from two points within to any point in the curve, shall be always the same; the two points being called the ellipse. In conic sections it is formed by the section of a cone by a plane. When the plane cuts the cone parallel to the base, the section is a circle; when through both sides obliquely, it is an ellipse; when parallel to the side, it is a parabolla; when the cutting makes a greater angle with the base than the side, it is a parabolla; and when the plane passes through the vertex, it (the section) will be a triangle. The three in one out-growth of the Om makes a pyramidal formation in stages like the Assyrian Ziggurat, with a head containing the representative sum-substance of the whole growth. Ziggurats had the number of parts and points in the structure, growth, or formation intended to be represented; and essentially the number was three in one parts and ten points, as in creation here and in the creation of any natural beings. It was sometimes called the house of the mountain. So scripture says, the mountain of the Lord's house shall be established upon the top of the mountains, and be exalted above the hills, and all nations shall come to it. Psalms fifteenth and twenth-fourth, and fifth chapter of Matthew, refer to this Aconic and Omic mountain. Among the Greeks it was Mount Ida and the Olympia. The Assyrians called it also the Mountain of Countries; because it is the world prominence of the Aconic line and seat of empire, and has its gradation throughout the whole scale of being. The hills and hollows on the surface of the earth, and the ruggedness (however small) on natural objects, and very specially the circular marks on the sun's disc, and that of the moon, are natural forms of the universal Om. Fixed stars, or suns, alternately expand and contract their rays, showing a periodic to and fro alternation, like other things. Zodiacal light has also its times and seasons; appearing as a faint luminosity in the sky, visible in the west, immediately after twilight in spring, and in the east, towards the close of autumn, before sunrise, being very distinct in tropical regions.

In all formations there must be some contraction and expansion, and a passing through a transition point into further expansion or an alternation of contraction and expansion at one central point. In comets, the head, which is a luminous Om or nucleus, surrounded by diffuse light, called coma because resembling hair, represents the contracted and absorbed Om form, and the tail the expanded body leading to or from the head or Om sum; the tail being frequently bifurcated, as opening into two at the fourth point, and sometimes opening out into more branches. Nutation shows a necklace-like form of the Om in the circle which the earth's pole describes round the pole of the ecliptic; a waved or undulating circle, supposed to be caused by the action of the moon on the protuberant parts of the earth at the equator; and a motion which accompanies the motion called precession. Precession of equinoxes makes a change equal to one degree in seventy-one years, or thirty degrees in about two thousand years. It is an instance of the universal Aeonic movement.

Time has to do with the measure of motion and action, as well as with the duration of things; it is the Om season in which a thing is being done, evolved, brought forth or to pass, or having being. Everything has its time and season. Besides annual periods, there are plants whose flowers exhibit diurnal periods of opening and closing. This led Linnaeus to arrange a number of such into a floral clock, in which each hour of the day was marked by the opening of some flower. A measure of light is in every measure of motion of the ether, and is with ether in all motion pervading all substances and through all space. Light, as being the work of the first day, is the outmost, and in it things appear from the first day to the fourth. Its intensity is as the square of the distance, so it is again in fourth point distance stage the work of the fourth day. Its day form is a three in one parts of morning, mid-day, and evening, in ten or twelve double parts of gradation of all its forms and measures of intensity, from earliest dawn to latest dusk; the mid-part, from four to seven, being the height of day, having the sun for head-sum representative of all light, as man is head-sum representative of all creation. Light is also within, passing through the Omic parts and points of physical and plant forms, plant and animal life, animal and man's higher parts life, with peculiar relation to intellect, and an overlapping of things in outward gradation. Light in its first full and undivided state is white, as it is in coming from the sun. When passing through its natural gradation of colours, it presents seven distinct primary colours, as in a prism and here in creation work; these colours being violet, indigo, blue, green, yellow, orange, red. It should be noticed that its white and full form is again reached in man, with a peculiar relation to intellect; while it is in the same full form in the sun from the fourth point, which is light's own seventh point. When it forms into part combinations, as in halos and the rainbow, red is innermost ; showing a correspondence of gradation, as here in the relations of warm-blooded animals. On the same principle the diffusion and reflection of light by the air, transmitting it obliquely, present a ruddy illumination of the sky and the clouds, sometimes at sunrise, sometimes at sunset. The gradation of absorption of light, passing from a heavenly body through the atmosphere, varies with the difference of altitude or elevation, above the horizon, at the usual rate of one, four, seven, ten, or one, four, eight, twelve, sixteen, twenty, &c., both which are really the same. In the production of things from the beginning to the fourth point, the ozone and the protoplasm, both in themselves and their place in the creative work, are in comparative concealment and confinement ; but at the fourth point the ozone is openly connected, under the sun, with the creation work of sea and air, while the protoplasm continues in special connection with the ground, or earth and its production work in their natural state, and with the earth in the sense and work of cultivation. While ether and light, ozone and protoplasm, have each and all so great and important parts in all first and all continued creation, the creator is not any or all of them, but the personal and eternal God, the All Father-Son, All in All. Ozone has continued work, in comparative outwardness, in plant life above ground, also in sea and air life, while protoplasm has its work more concealed in the under-ground part of plants and in the cultivation of the ground as earth. The creative inner and all-where omnipresent and omnipotent Being is Jehovah increasing and multiplying, and passing on in all beings to increase and multiply. Works of ozone and protoplasm are carried on, at all times, in the various operations connected with the changes that take place in all things, specially in those of the preservation and propagation of plant and animal life, just as expressed or implied here in these works of creation.

And God said, let the waters bring forth abundantly the moving creature that hath life, and fowl that may fly above the earth in the open firmament of heaven. And God created great whales, and every living creature that moveth, which the waters brought forth abundantly, after their kind, and every winged fowl after his kind ; and God saw that it was good. And God blessed them, saying, be fruitful, and multiply, and fill the waters in the seas, and let fowl multiply in the earth. And the evening and the morning were the fifth day.

In every day's work there is a three in one implication of let there be, let the earth, or as here, let the waters bring forth, and that it is God that does it all, and all very good. Immediately all things are of, from, and by God ; of His own will, self-will, and self-action. This self-being, this self-will, and this self-action, are, as far and as much as possible, imparted to whatever is made ; so that what is farther made is in a secondary sense of, from, and by the things already made. Still, He as God is common to both and in both respects; so that by Him as the eternal Spirit and Father-Son, or in the Son, are made all things that are made. In every step there is a further form of Om act of creation and evolution into a further formation, in an immediate sense. There is the use of the already made as the Om conch, in which the creative act takes place. The head-sum substance of the made is absorbed in the creative act, or intercourse, to pass, in a renewed and refined kind, together with that which is being evolved from within, into the new formation or creature. While this substance of the outer or already made, is taken with the inner which is being evolved, there is from and by the Spirit that which is common to both, as the Spirit Himself is common to both. Corresponding to these are the germ and sperm in begetting intercourse, together with what by the Spirit's special and higher work is common to both, all making three in one being. Ozone and protoplasm are present in the germ and sperm; and they together become one with that which is common to both, as their higher and real being, as that which is in immediate and eternal relation and union with the Spirit, and that which is the one substantive all of the worlds, after its, or their kind. The coming forth of the newly made, or newly begotten, puts the already made, in its immediate relations, into the place and relation of father, or immediate progenitor, the next outer into that of grandfather, and the next into that of great-grandfather. This order in these relations and changes is ever kept and marked in nature. Plants exhibit it in foliage and flowering, in root and stem, and all else. Trees have their three in one duration of leaves. The leaves of some cease to perform their special functions when the bud is completed, and are deciduous; some continue until new ones come forth next season, and are annual; while others continue for several years, to three stages back, and are persistent. That plant life is naturally and closely related to animal life must be well known to everyone. But what the nature and closeness of that relation are, what in the one passes into the other and becomes an essential part of it, and how all life is one though ever being distributed through all gradation in all sorts of variations, for ever closing and opening, ending yet beginning in and through that ending, are not and cannot be so easily or so well known. In the original Om and root, all things are one. That one is three in one, which, in the on-going and out-going of the endless course of all possible existences, is infinitely and endlessly repeated and distributed in orderly gradation of relations of unity in variety, of successive and co-existent forms of beings; the same substances and the same laws being in the same eternal unity in the same eternal variety, of the ever changing ever the same whole one of all ones.

There can be nothing in the effect but what was previously in its cause, sum-cause, or cause of causes. It cannot become a cause, or produce a new effect, without turning on itself. In turning on itself it is active towards itself as passive; and it actively, through or with itself passively, or by passive and active self-intercourse, produces itself anew. Self-existence implies all existence, and self-reproduction implies all-reproduction; and both imply all in all. This self-one underlies all things, and is the inmost being of and in all things. Becoming new, or being new, implies having passed from old being into distinct new being, a father into a son, a cause into an effect. The father-son and the self-one of each, which is the self-one of both, and is common to both, are the one self-one, both in the father-son and all distinctions, and as underlying all distinctions. It is the self-one, three in one; the self-existent, the eternally-begetting being begotten all in all. The same self-begetting being begotten self-one is ever passing into being self-son, in which it is also father, the previous self-fatherhood becoming self-grandfatherhood; and so backwards and forwards, and all ways in all relations and distinctions. All this self-oneness in all self-distinctions and self-relations is essential to all being; and implies that all beings, whatever their distinctions and varieties may possibly be, are one self-one.

3. The relative is the sphere of the outgoings and incomings, the descending and ascending, the all motions, movements, and manifestations of all beings in all gradation and relations of having being, as the lower and the outer of the absolute; it is the begetting second-self, couch, and counter-part of the absolute. So are the absolute and the relative co-related. So it is said of Eve in relation to Adam, in the sense of mother and father of all being, "The man is not of the woman, but the woman of the man. Neither was the man created for the woman, but the woman for the man." That which is lowermost and outmost appears as such; it is of and for its next inner and higher in part and whole; it is derived from and is rooted in its inner and higher, and continues to be so through all its duration of its distinct existence; and in head-sum substance it returns to it in onward and upward gradation of being. So it is in all things within the relative as relative, and so is the relative in relation to the absolute. Everything is in contact with the absolute, yet in gradation of relations to each and all of all beings in the relative; or the relative, in each and all of its beings, as distinct and as one whole, is so in contact to the absolute; and it both contains and is contained in the absolute. Thus all things are co-related and co-united in root and fruit, stem and branch, distinctions after their kind, and all else. Dust, as original elements, they all are, and to dust shall they return; of God they all are, and to Him they all go. So it is as to man, the representative sum total of all. Everything in the Bible, in man, and in nature indicates and vindicates the truth of these statements. Union and interdependence, amid all disunions,

separations, and severances, apparent imperfections, anomalies, and inconsistencies, and all incidental oppositions and kinds of evil are everywhere. The substance of fire, air, earth, and water, as an ancient classification, pass through ceaseless changes, from one being and class of beings to another, throughout the whole scale of beings—all according to eternal order and law.

Protoplasm and ozone pass through absorptive, digestive, and renewing changes in advancing stages and parts, steps and points, in the process of preservation and propagation in plant life. In like manner they pass through a like course in animal life. Physical forces and substances are ever being absorbed into plant formations, and through them, or they, into animal formations. Plant forms indicate, among other things, the manner in which the course of these processes is conducted. Organs of nutrition assume forms according to the functions which they have to perform in the economy of plant life. This is seen in root, stem, and leaves. The part of the common axis, or stem, which is underground, is its descending part, or root system; the other, or ascending part, is the stem system; and the life of the whole and its processes have two kinds of relations—the one to earth and protoplasm, the other to heaven and ozone.

Type and kind hold true of everything in its whole connection and course of being, of nature, colour, character, and contents; varying in the cells as in the plants, in such forms as crystals of lime and phosphoric acid, air, and oily matters, wax and fat, sugar and starch. From one to four and from seven to ten, or at the ending-beginning of every thing, as in the fruit and seed, cell and underground state, ozone and protoplasm have more of oneness, and hidden form and action, than from four to seven, when the ozone is more in the open firmament, with its outward forms and states of being. Still they are everywhere distinct in themselves and their work. Plant life is so nearly akin to animal life that of some formations it is difficult to say to which life they belong. Nature's co-existences are so evolved and arranged that outer formations overlap their inner. Animal life is produced on the fifth and sixth days, or from the fourth day to the seventh or eighth. Plant life is produced on the third, which is therefore its first; and from its third, which is the first of animal life, it overlaps the animal life, whose seventh is on the level of the tenth of the plant life, and the fourth of man. It should be carefully observed that there is no life-producing work on the fourth, or on the first or tenth, which two are regarded as one and mostly the same in ending-beginning sense. What is specially to be dealt with in these mysterious numbers is light, or God as the original, creative, and renewing source, and omnipotent, personal, and begetting energy of all. So is it as to the seventh, which is also pre-eminently the day of God's rest, self-refreshing, and rejoicing in His works. These works are summed in man, who, as head-sum of all things, shares with all and as the sum of all in that rest, self-refreshing, and rejoicing of God. At these sacred points and passages things have a kind of peculiarly composite and common-looking character and expression, which are transitional, and make them somewhat more difficult to distinguish the one from the other than at other points and times.

The closeness of relation of plant life to animal life at first, or from one to four, is much hidden. In the out-growth from the Om seed and cell the spongicle is the type of the lower part, and the leaf is that of the upper.

Life in plant and animal is an undeniable fact; but what is the life of plant or animal is difficult if not impossible to say. Every thing is somehow like and somehow unlike all other things; and what in any thing lies beyond the point or line of all distinctions, or must be taken isolately as such, or only related to its zero, be it Ishtar or essence, is, as such, more for the capacities of consciousness than for forms of thought, of senses, and of language. That certain forms of matter exhibit a tendency, in certain conditions, to pass through a definite course or series of changes, in a determinate order, or sequence, does not make known what the life in these forms is. As the laws of the conservation of energy and matter, and of the course of changes and sequences of events, are the method by which the First Cause conducts His works and governs the universe; so, on a lower scale, are the laws by which and according to which all life and motion possess and engage themselves in the being and work of the same universe. Life can be traced to the lowest form of cell life, in size not more than the fifty-thousand-millionth part of a cubit inch, and multiplying such minute forms equal in number to the whole world's human population in a few hours; but what it is in itself is at every point and in every form unknown. It can be traced to that clear, colourless, and structureless something called protoplasm; and from it, through the whole scale of world formations, from the most minute fungus to the stateliest plant and animal; yet everywhere a rigid definition of it is impossible. Though every living thing has its life in that protoplasmic compound, and has it as means of nourishment; yet both the life and the protoplasm are distinct, and each the effect of the true and original cause of both, t.ie Divine Spirit, the real cause of matter, of life, and of mind in all creation. The vitality of every spore, cell, and seed is from and by that Spirit; and so is the creation of the cell itself, whether by a single and simple act for each individual and each species, or by a process of work and development, or by both. Science can and does tell much of the indications, manifestations, and circumstances of life, but nothing of its essential being, or its origin, unless in the Bible way of reference to the work and way of all creation by the Spirit as in this chapter. Atoms may possess life energy of kinds and gradations; but, if so, it is because of the Spirit's presence and creative work in them and about them. The sun is in some respects the source of light and heat, both which are essential for plant and animal life; but the originator of them is not the sun, but He who is the originator both of the fourth-day sun and of them, and of all light, and life, and all else from the beginning, or all ending-beginning of all being. The sun, in shape and meaning, is one, and possibly the leading one in our planetary system, of the many summary Oms, which are outward forms and symbols of the universal organs of creation and of the great and hidden marvel and mystery of life. Among the ancients the doctrine taught was that the spirit dwelt in every Om point, in light such as of which Scripture says that it is inapproachable and full of glory; that He was the author, fountain, source, and creative and begetting cause of all created or creatively begotten beings; and that His presence and work were in seven, or ten, otherwise twelve points gradation of Oms, frequently, as in the Book of Revelation, called the seven spirits, or Om-days as in this chapter. Everything thus produced has its Oms for dwelling-place and preservation, and for re-production in co-relations with the spirit and all co-existences; and in each case, and for each purpose, it goes out, or down, or both, through its allotted course, all in the spirit, and the spirit in it. The Spirit's Father-Son form of being, presence, and work in it is its prototype and creatural realisation in parts and forms of being. In its evolution and gradation each advanced step contains the substance of its lower, outer, and past, together with what is its next inner and higher being, the summary and essential form and characteristic of it, as in itself, and as distinguished from all others.

Motion implies change; and a measure of descent and ascent, of out-going and in-coming is true of every formation, during its course of existence. Activity, of some kind and in some measure, is everywhere. Form also, of some kind and in some measure, is necessary to every existence; varying from the distinction of being from non-being to the most composite, complicated, and complete organisation. Substance, life, and form, are ultimately traceable to the spirit as the living, creative, and formative cause. Of all forms and means of being and having being it can be said, they are the land which the Lord thy God giveth thee. Life may have a number of steps in its gradation of forms before the lowest point at which it is known to us in protoplasm; that so-called physical basis and medium, through which life is known to be brought into relation to, and to be manifested in, the external world; that chemical compound, which, in a sense secondary to that of the formative work of the spirit, is capable of forming any structure the most complex, yet does not differentiate into such distinct parts as necessarily constitute organisation. Like other things, it is subject to the laws of gradation; the number of its composing elements being four, nitrogen, oxygen, hydrogen, and carbon; and the number of conditions apparently connected with its life being about the same, free oxygen, water, a certain measure of light and heat varying between the freezing-point and a hundred and thirty degrees (Adam's age of manhood), and other materials of necessary life-sustaining use. Conditions of life, as externally manifested, are secondary to those of life's hidden and immediate relations to the spirit in these hidden conditions. Not only is this so in the earliest stage, or steps, of the means of propagation, but also in all stages; a fact well known in the case of many plant seeds and animal ova. Wheel-animalcules (Rotifera), so highly organised as to possess a nervous system, organs of sense (even vision) and reproduction, mouth, stomach, and alimentary canal, are found in continued possession of life in the absence of all or some of the secondary or external conditions, or in a state susceptible of resurrection. These minute beings may be kept in a dried dust state, and seemingly quite lifeless, and thereafter restored to their former activity and vigour by the application of water, or of the absent conditions. There is something more in every vital phenomena than forces and principles merely chemical and physical; that something is difficult to know in itself and its relations and contact with the creative, life-going, and life-sustaining spirit. Digestion, nutrition, and reproduction, have not been and cannot be explained by what is merely chemical and physical. Nature, the Bible, and mythology, agree on this point, as on other matters.

Some kind and degree of life are present in every thing; yet at a certain stage or level of gradation there are characteristics by which is recognised the distinction of living and non-living; and so, again, there are characteristics by which the living are divided into plants and animals. At their higher levels these plants and animals are, in a general manner, easily distinguished, by such marks as the animals possessing, and the plants not possessing, a nervous system and organs of sense, a stomach or internal means of receiving and digesting solid food, and the power of voluntary change of place. But, at the lower levels, and in the less highly organised, the distinctions between the two divisions are more difficult to determine; and hence, at these levels, a closer comparison and greater care are necessary for correct reference of individuals to their appropriate places in the respective divisions.

No animal life is spoken of before the fifth day; or until after the production of plants, and the appearance of external and formal means of light and heat, as is the sun. Accordingly, the food of plants is fluid or gaseous, as both they and it belong formally to the period from one to four; and the food of animals is the protoplasmic compound, elaborated by plants, and so ready-made as means of nutrition of animals by oxidation, or process of burning, by which the contained energy is made to pass into the living tissue of animals. Animals thus appear on the fifth-day level, and so in natural relations to plant work, light, heat, and all means necessary for its distinct existence and maintenance.

Proteinaceous matter, or substances, of protoplasm, exist in forms fit for and used in plant life, previous and preparatory to the compound state of it which forms a basis and means for animal life. Water, ammonia, carbonic acid, and some proportion of certain mineral salts, are the inorganic compounds which form the food of plants, and which they unburn or deoxidate, under the influence of sun-light, into the unstable and organic elements of food. While the substances in food for plants and animals are, in themselves originally and always the same, the higher nature and level of animals require and necessitate that they should be raised from their food-state for plants to that of animals, and this is done by the laws, modes, and processes of the vital chemistry of the plants. This process, or work, is completed through the plant fourth-point transition change, by which the compounds of ozone and protoplasm are fully fitted for animal life in all gradation. These formations which outwardly mark this transition passage, are, in some respects, distinctly plants, while, in other respects, they are as distinctly animals; such as certain fungi which are plants, yet require organised compounds, as animals do, for their nourishment. There are well-known organisms exhibiting at one period of their life an aggregate of phenomena which appear to be of distinctly plant nature, whilst at another period to be as distinctly animal, the change from the one to the other taking place through their fourth-point passage. The most obvious characteristics are those of external form, or outward configuration, but no absolute distinction of this kind exists between plants and animals. Some plants, as vaucheria, the protococcus nivalis, and others, are, in their embryonic state and form, possessed of cilia, by which they swim, and bear so much resemblance to infusorian animalcules as to have been for sometime taken as belonging to that division of the protozoa, the cilia being anticipating marks of transition to animal life as about formally to appear. The sponges and many of the protozoa, which are decided animal formations, also retain so much of the nature and form of plants as to have often been, and even still to be, taken for plants. The flustra, or sea-mat, among the molluscoida, is frequently regarded as sea-weed, and many zoophytes, as corals, sea-shrubs, and hydroid polypes have been for sometime described as plants. Internally plants and animals are composed of molecular, cellular, and fibrous tissues, and are, therefore, similar in internal structure. In chemical composition, both plants and animals contain representative compounds differing, not in kind, but in proportion of the same to each other. The hydrated starch of plants becomes glycogen, secreted by the liver of the mammalia; the cellulose, a compound so characteristic of plants, is found in the outer covering of the sea-squirts (Ascidian molluscs); and the green-colouring compound, chlorophyll, also strongly characteristic of plant nature, is found, in a rudimentary or normal form, in animals of the infusoria and the coelenterata. Power of moving from place to place is generally distinctive of animals, but many plants, some in their embryonic, and others in their mature form, possess this power by cilia, such as those characteristic of so many of the lower forms of animal life; many of the lower plants, such as the desmids, and diatoms also show that power through life, while many animals in their adult condition become fixed or attached to some foreign object. These changes occur at their natural levels; they mark the points at which the new steps of the creative work and evolution takes place, and the beginning and measure of the overlapping of co-existences, and they show the descent and outgoing everywhere for places, means, and works of new creations, maintenance of life, and propagation of beings. Plants and animals are nearly allied everywhere; and at every point of transition passage the closeness of that alliance is much the same as at the first point of disunion, departure, or separation; the distinctions between adult and open formations of repeated growths, as a tree made up of repeated shoot-growth, being more apparent and easily observed. The balance and relations between protoplasm and ozone, as between all things whatsoever, is as if ever being disturbed, yet ever being preserved. Action and reaction by plants and animals, as to ozone and protoplasm, are also as to earth and atmosphere, and as to each other as divisions and individuals, in food, reproduction, and common activity. Production of free oxygen characterises plant reaction on the atmosphere; production of carbonic acid characterises the reaction by animals upon it—the plants decomposing the carbonic acid and retaining the carbon, to the setting free of the oxygen, while the oxygen is absorbed, and the carbonic acid is emitted by the animals. Action and reaction are indeed universal.

Physiology comprises a triad of parts or departments, namely, functions of co-relation, of nutrition, and of reproduction. Morphology also comprises a triad of departments, namely, histology, under which minute tissues are investigated, embryonic development through changes prior to mature character, and anatomy, which is concerned with the shape, structure, and arrangement of parts of maturely developed beings. Distribution is as to the relations and conditions in which beings are being placed. Throughout each and all of these, Omic and Aeonic order and arrangement, forms and functions, relations and gradations, substances and laws, are present in all unity and variety, culminating in man as representative summary or cosmos. It should be borne in mind that the most invariable mark of ascertained distinction between plants and animals is in the proportionate and graduated nature of the food used respectively by each, and in the results of its conversion as used. The real and essential distinction between plant life and animal life is in the latter being of a higher nature than the other, and so is it in respect of food and other things; the grades of plant life being in the Omic third-day creation work, and the grades of animal life being in the creation work of from the fourth to the seventh. The same law of distinction holds in the gradation of plant life taken by itself, and in that of animal life taken by itself; all in accordance with the gradation in this chapter and throughout Scripture and throughout universal nature. The number of primary differences is the number of these Omic days of creation, namely, two triads, each being three in one, or into and through a fourth, with the third as summary in man. The teaching of science is in agreement with this. All known animals are found to be constructed on six plans, or morphological types, and on corresponding six degrees of physiological division of labour or specialisation of function. So that every animal is found to be, by natural gradation, a resultant of these two tendencies, the morphological and the physiological.

The animal kingdom comprises these six types as so many sub-kingdoms, all the members of each agreeing with each other in being formed on the same definite type of structure, and differing from each other in the grade or level of their respective organisation, and corresponding specialisation of function. They are named Protozoa, Collenterate, Annuloida, Annulosæ, Mollusca, and Vertebrata. The gradation of each being and of all beings in one, in the outer form without inwards, is the gradation from below, behind, or first level upwards or onwards, and the process of evolution is in the gradual out-bringing or out-growing, in outward or upward gradation, of the being, in the order of its inward gradation, each inner coming out before its next inner. Its original type holds true of it, in all its stages and conditions, evolved or unevolved; in its typical sense it is always one. The highest degree of specialisation, in structure and function, which it attains in its adult condition, is its inmost degree from the beginning, and is also one; its general character being also true of it in its unevolved, equally as in its evolved condition, excepting the modifications due to external influences in its evolved condition. In the inward gradation of its original type and condition, each inner part contains the essential and refined substance of its outer. So, in its evolved condition, each higher contains the essential and refined substance of its lower. Natural selection is here as to substance of being; and, in its natural gradation, it extends to matters of maintenance, propagation, and all things; in religion it is the doctrine and work of election; both the natural selection and the spiritual election being each radically fixed in its respective type, universal, and eternal decree unerringly executed. Absorption of refined, or renewed, substance, so selected, is as a diet of food, or supply of recruit, to the onward movement and growth; the special points of such changes being those of one, four, seven, and ten. The nature of the original difference in kind and degree of structure and function, or organisation and specialisation, is in accordance with the difference in the nature of the life of the being, species or class, sub-kingdom or kingdom, of beings; and all is traceable and referable to the Divine Spirit as the original and universal cause and executor of all things. With Him is the all-being Om, which, according to ancient belief and doctrine, contains all the seeds of all things, in all gradation of being and types of beings; ever begetting beings, and ever pregnant with beings. In a secondary sense the creature acts as He acts; the creature is made to act in creating, the begotten in begetting, the produced in producing. The development of the individual being is the rapid and brief repetition or recapitulation of the development of the species under the law, or creative operation of the physiological functions of transmission and nutrition, or reproduction and adaptation. And God said, let the earth bring forth the living creature after his kind, cattle, and creeping thing, and beast of the earth after his kind; and it was so. And God made the beast of the earth after his kind, and cattle after their kind, and every thing that creepeth upon the earth after his kind; and God saw that it was good. In the primary and secondary sense it is God's work; God said, God made, and God saw—it is all of God, and therefore good.

And God said, let us make man in our image, after our likeness; and let them have dominion over the fish of the sea, and over the fowl of the air, and over the cattle, and over all the earth, and over every creeping thing that creepeth upon the earth. So God created man in His own image, in the image of God created He him; male and female created He them. And God blessed them, and God said unto them, be fruitful, and multiply, and replenish the earth, and subdue it; and have dominion over the fish of the sea, and over the fowl of the air, and over every living thing that moveth upon the earth. And God said, behold, I have given you every herb bearing seed, which is upon the face of all the earth, and every tree in the which is the fruit of a tree yielding seed; to you it shall be for meat. And to every beast of the earth, and to every fowl of the air, and to every thing that creepeth upon the earth, wherein there is life, I have given every green herb for meat; and it was so. And God saw everything that He had made, and, behold, it was very good. And the evening and the morning were the sixth day. All that is here spoken of is in man.

Man is the representative sum-substance and sum total of creation. In the beginning the sum of creation is spoken of in the terms the heaven and the earth, in relation to God and as His creation. Here the sum is in man in relation to God and in His image; the two are God and man, with the heaven and the earth implied, or all in one God-man, the Logos, though the embryo of each higher being, or order of beings, does not pass outwardly and formally through each of the series of changes corresponding respectively to the permanent typical forms of those lower in the scale of division, so that it could be said to be each of them at each respective level; yet it is internal to them all at each and all of their points or steps of being, and does pass with them, internally and invisibly, through those changes. Man is radically and internally contemporaneous with them all from the beginning, or in the eternal ending-beginning of all. At his appearance at the end of the six days of creation, he is six Omic days old. The classification of beings in this chapter is, as that of creation, in three parts, not descending to further particulars, though, as has been already abundantly shown, in exquisite agreement with nature's particulars everywhere. The three of the fifth day's creation are the inhabitants of the sea, those more commonly moving in the sky or open firmament, and those that are fowls, but are less frequently moving on the wing. Those of the sixth day are also three, the creeping creatures as lower part division, the beasts of the earth as outer and wilder animals, and the cattle as next to man in the inner and higher part or circle. Man's erect form and posture of body indicate his being the inmost mid line being of the whole Om circle of the beings of sea, earth, and sky. Hence the Chaldeans pictured him with the lower part of fish-like form, the middle part human-shaped, but having some leading animal to the right, and another to the left, as a bull or a lion, or composite figures on each side, as representing all terrestrial animals, one of outer circle, and another of inner circle; and the head human, but having the mouth and nose formed into a bird's beak, to denote the sum-substance of all, and one combination of substances, laws, and relations in one Omic round form as to heaven and earth, God, and the whole universe. Man, as all summary being, contains a representative sum of all substances and all laws, in all relations and gradations; also, all resemblances and all differences. So that, in all things, he is like and unlike all things. There is in him the inmost and highest form of sum-substance of everything, of all which he is the representative sum; and in his highest nature and character all things are brought to an Omic focus next to being God, and ending-beginning in and from God; being so at the beginning, at the end, and ever in the inmost mid line as hidden or revealed, closed or opened, evolved or unevolved. So it is true of him that, in the inmost and highest sense, and as the ancients would say, the spirit of the gods (the Divine Spirit) is in him, the sum-sense of Elohim is in him, and in all in natural gradation. In the God plural sense of Elohim is the pronoun us, in the words, Let us make; and in the secondary sense or method of creation, repeatedly expressed in the words, Let bring forth, is the same plural implied, Let us—the all things as they are to be represented by him— bring forth man in our image, after our likeness. In other words, let us, the God Elohim in the primary sense, and us, the all things in the secondary sense, make man in our image, after our likeness. But the Elohim form is the outer of Jehovah, which is always singular: the Lord our God is one. Elohim is the sum of all forms of the divine manifestations, while Jehovah is always the mid line inner living and life-giving one Being, the inmost and highest of Father-Son, being and having being. In these three respects man is made, or is brought into being, and having being among all, and representing all, beings.

The pronoun, us and our, being plural as applied to God, and man being made in God's image, and after His likeness, and, indeed, in the image and after the likeness of all, the pronoun is plural also as applied to man, in the third person, them, let them ; an additional form of reason being in man's double character and personality of male and female, man and woman. Image and likeness are not used as identical in meaning ; the one signifies what man is as summary reflection of God and all invisibly, or in all inner and higher respects, underlying, above, and beyond, the region of the senses ; the other signifies what is meant as the further, outer, and lower sense and form of that reflection in the accompanying outer world, or region of the senses ; both being in all natural gradation. The three parts gradation of the higher sense is given, in the New Testament, as knowledge, righteousness, and holiness. Dominion is in all natural order, relations, and gradation, from God to and in man and all nature. It is intended for being, in character and act, like God's character and in fulfilment of God's will expressed in the divine manifestations, laws, and method of government, or like God in Himself, in man, and in all nature and course of events ; not for the degeneration, degradation, and destruction of the world or the creature, but for salvation, for preservation, and propagation, for increase and improvement ; Christ came not and comes not to destroy the world, but to save the world, and destroy the works of the devil. Next to the highest nature in man, under God, is animal life, next to it again is plant life, and next to this last is inorganic matter ; all from the Divine Spirit, to Him, and in immediate contact with Him. Scientists find that one of the surest marks of distinction between plants and animals, is in the nature of the food taken respectively by each, and in the results of the conversion of that food. Taken generally, and apart from certain minute organisms, it may be said that the food of plants consists of inorganic matter, as compounds of water, ammonia, carbonic acid, and some quantities of certain mineral salts ; while all known animals require proteinaceous matter ready-made for maintenance of life, manufactured in the first instance by and from plants. So, again taken generally, plants are, in this chapter, given in natural gradation to animals and man. The levels, relations, and overlappings in this gradation need not here be examined ; but it is helpful for this, and for all purposes connected with it, to have some acquaintance with the lowest known orders of animal life, alongside of what has been already observed of the like orders of plant life. The primary division of the animal kingdom into the Aconic parts number of sub-kingdoms, has already been noticed ; the rest of the gradation downwards, and part into its next, is into classes, orders, families, genera, species, varieties, and races. A system of classification may be superficial and artificial in being founded on merely external and adaptive resemblance of groups to each other; natural, in being founded on essential and fundamental structure; or philosophical, in being founded on real points of resemblance and difference, as in the facts and laws of structure and function, or morphology and physiology. The Bible is not committed by an attempt to make systems and definitions.

The only kind of linear classification that is possible is that in which nature arranges the objects in their natural relations to the lines of transition and to each other. This arrangement implies natural relations inwards and outwards, backwards and forwards, upwards and downwards; and it is that of nature and the Bible. At the fourth point of plant life special light and heat are produced in the work of that day, implying the natural means of what is called heat-stiffening and ozone distinct existence and use, which are connected with the process of absorption and change of plant substance and life into new or renewed animal life. Animal life is contained in the Om line from the beginning, but is thus produced or evolved into external world existence, through the fourth point, and made to appear at the fifth point (the half-division number), which places the plants in the position outer to the animals; so that the fourth point passage of the plants is the first point passage of animal life into external world existence, the seventh of the plants is the fourth of the animals, and the first of man, and the tenth of the plants is the seventh of the animals, and the fourth of man. This shows the leading levels, overlappings, and co-existences of all things; and points to the causes and occurrences of composite beings, as also the nature and levels of the structures, functions, and kinds of food of the respective divisions.

Man is the culminating head-sum of the six Omic days of creation; two triads forming into one in him, as in the human body there are two parts, of a triad each into the third, or head triad of face, cerebrum and cerebellum; in which last there is the sum-substance of all. His first day of formal existence is the seventh from the beginning; and it is creation's mysterious passage in him with God. It is in this day's mysterious state that God blesses him and addresses him, as is stated in the three verses beginning with the twenty-eighth. In nature, in the Bible, and the religions of the world, this seventh point is that of the birth of the Aeonic Son, of seven points summary sacrifice, and of the weekly Sabbath, as also of peculiar blessing, formal engagements, and renewal into further life. It is in these mysterious passages of transition lines at one, four, seven, ten, that the leading creative or begetting, transforming or renewing, changes occur. In these secret and sacred passages there is always an ending-beginning, a re-creating and renewing contact with the Divine Spirit, as at the first or the beginning of creation, similar to, if not the same as, the contact of the relative with the absolute, a return to, or forming into, unity or oneness, and a re-opening and a re-division, a dying and a begetting, a generating act and a new birth. The Spirit is, in the highest sense, self-existing and self-acting; and in a secondary sense, every being is self-existing and self-acting. This is a first essential in the divine image in each created being. In the creature's act of Omic begetting there is a self-begetting, yet under and dependent on the Spirit in the act. The co-relation between these mysterious lines of passage is such that each lower order or level of beings is essentially and formally related to and dependent on the next higher in generative act and all else. As elsewhere said, all things are of God. In a secondary sense all things are also of themselves; of the earth ("let the earth bring forth"), of the water ("let the water bring forth"), and of themselves in process of reproduction. From the so-called beginning to the seventh point, and always, there is an underlying and comparatively hidden work of the Spirit, which is completed and finished in the formal production of man. The whole seven contain two triads into one, or ten points up to the garden. It is a whole underlying beginning work, clearly implying, in its one whole creation sense, a work of one Omic whole beginning day. So, in the fourth verse of the second chapter, it is referred to as the day in which the Lord God made the earth and the heavens, as meaning the same with the first words of the first chapter ("In the beginning God created the heaven and the earth"). Thus the beginning spoken of is the Spirit's creative work, in its primary and secondary sense from one to seven or ten, in the peculiarly and comparatively hidden sense, really so at all times: an ending-beginning Omic day's creation, ever beginning and being finished, and ever being carried on. Hydroid beings have their own marks, as in numbers and circlets of tentacles; the numbers being from one to ten or twelve, seldom more, and capable of extensile and contractile, or to and fro, action within the Omic number eight, or from seven to ten inches. Other marks of these tentacles are in their three circles of consistence in ectoderm, and endoderm, and body cavity enclosing a diverticulum, or side way, for reproduction by the side of the nutritive opening or passage, all as in the main body; and being also furnished with side thread-cells like side buds.

The hydra is peculiarly fitted for increase in numbers by artificial and mechanical means. Each of all the pieces into which it may be divided will gradually develope into a new and perfect polypite. This seems to arise partly from the original purity and strength of its protoplasm and ozone, partly from partaking so largely of the plant and animal double life, and partly from containing within it a transition line, and the implied peculiarly creative work of the Spirit in that line. Equally remarkable are its susceptibilities to the laws of seasons, and to the powers and influences of the sun and moon, as being for signs and seasons, days and years, and to rule over day and night, as stated in the first chapter. Its reproduction by germination, being more of plant nature, and appearing in order of creation before animals, is carried on in the summer season, when it produces one or more buds at a time, along its lower part from two to five, or from the second to the fifth day plant production time of the Bible. The stages of the growth of these buds are, first, the process of outcoming into full bud form ; then a tubular growth of it in its ectoderm, endoderm, and enclosed calcal (closed-end) diverticulum, or side way of the body cavity, which prolongation of growth brings it to the level of the fifth point or day. And now, at the level of animal production, it takes a composite form, as if a plant fruit, yet also a young animal Hydra with mouth and tentacles, showing the animal production point in relation to the Acoric inner line, and to the transverse transition line, as also a summary of the continued relations of plants and animals in their whole natural history. The young buds produce fresh ones before they become detached from the parent body, a process indicative, among other things, of plural growths and births, so common in nature.

The hydra mode of reproduction, in which the sexes are more perceptibly distinct and animal like, takes places at two points of the parent body, in the lower part and also in the higher part near the tentacles, the production in the lower part having sacks in which the ova are enclosed, and that near the other extremity being a conical process, showing an advance towards the cone and rod forms. Those below and above mature and fall off from the body-wall simultaneously ; when they come into sexual contact, and the ova are fecundated. It is probable that the contents of those produced at the base of the tentacles are of the nature of sperm for fecundating, and milky substances for nourishing the ova of the lower production ; and thus answering the requirements of the plant nature and the animal nature of the young creatures, as distinct natures, yet closely united in one whole body, and showing the order and advance in the relative growth and gradation, parts and processes, of the whole body and its divisions. Shortly, its lower part is fitted for adhering to some object, and it is furnished at the other end with mouth and tentacles. Its Greek name is Hudra, a water serpent ; and it is supposed to be the water form of the serpent, taken as figurative and illustrative means in the temptation of Adam and Eve, with her connection of eating the fruit and sum-absorption. Transition lines and forms of work are everywhere present, with an accompanying measure of life and sensitiveness. In the nervous system they gradually form a web-work and graduated convolutions, from the lowest point of rudimentary form to the highest in the human brain, the cerebellum, of which the weight is one-tenth of that of the whole brain. Transition lines and their effects are everywhere mathematically arranged. A species of this web-work is found at the base of the tentacles of these Hydra.

Another step of advance in these Hydroid Zoophytes is in Clytia, in which the zooids are for some time attached to the parent colony, then become detached, and pass some time in independent existence, after which they produce reproductive elements and perceptible social forms, when they appear as a species of jelly-fish, or Medusa. It is umbrella-shaped, or an upper counterpart of its parent Om ; coming to be open reversely by the Omic rod having reached the head point of its line of graduated number of advances, where and when the rod's head, which is always an Om, stands as upper, as the heaven is towards the earth as two sides of the open firmament, between which all works of creations, begettings, and renewals are carried on, in, to and fro, give and get, open and close, ending-beginning way. By its opening and closing action, it is enabled to swim and get its means of subsistence. From the centre of its concave side shoots down and back a nutritive form possessing a mouth and digestive cavity. It is penetrated throughout by transition lines in a mathematical complex system. A series of tentacles suspend or trail behind, from its circular margin, with small bend-like protuberances, as if indicating its natural history in steps and stages of growth, of manner of life and increase, its relations to other formations, and ancestral connections with its Omic source of being and having being. When come to full growth, its ova and spermatozoa and young are generated, and begin to repeat the course of its parent being.

Among the Lucernarida (of the Hydrogoa) there are instances of interesting phenomena worthy of notice, as in what is called the Hydra-tuba, resembling the fresh-water Hydra. Its gradation of changes are its out-coming from the parent Om as a locomotive ciliated being; after some time becoming fixed, trumpet-shaped, and having a mouth and tentacles ; then increasing in number by germination into colonies; next becoming enlarged, and passing through fourth-point changes; yet again dividing transversely by fusion into a number of segments ; when, lastly, each segment of the division becomes detached, with mouth, digestive cavity, and a swimming bell-head, or umbrella, by which it moves through the water, as at first. These six changes correspond to the six creation days through which the Omic one, rod, or radicle passes in its creative or begetting work from the first to the seventh point or day. It should be remembered that the three points from seven to ten are implied in the seven or as a summing up head to the seven, making a triad of triads ; a remarkable instance of which being in the eighth, ninth, and tenth ribs of the human body being united to the seventh, while the eleventh and twelfth are separate and free. Throughout this course of changes, up as it were to the Garden tenth point of plants, seventh of animals, and fourth of man, they are partly physical, partly plant, and partly animal ; but the sum of the whole is in their next and highest stage. Their size when divided into segments is not more than half an inch in height ; in their present advanced stage and state of feeding and active life they attain to a size sometimes of some feet in circumference; they mature, develop sexual forn s and essential elements of reproduction, and go through acts of fecundation; and on emitting ova they die, when the newly produced young begin again to repeat the same course from the minute and fixed state. Thus they are formed into one head-sum of all their natural history; as the seed or semen is the ending-beginning, root-sum, and the fruit, head, or representative offspring, is the ending-beginning head-sum of all; and as man is in and as to all, Christ in and as to man and all, and God in and as to Christ, man, and all.

4. The account of the Omic days is brought on and up into the accounts of the Omic ages. The former is the gradual fulfilment of tht fiat, fact, and fulness of let there be, let bring forth, and let us make, in one whole man, as the inmost being, full form, and head-sum, of the whole gradation of creations in one sum-creation of God-made man, in God's image and after His likeness, the Son of God. The latter is the gradual fulfilment of the fiat, fact, and fulness of be (fruitful, &c.), have (dominion and possession, &c.), as to this Son of God of Sons of God and man, having his inmost being and meaning, as also his highest level, form, and reality in Christ the Son of God and of man, and as to the graduated duration of the age of ages. This work of fiat and fulfilment is in gradation from the lowest to the highest, from the inmost to the outmost, and from the hindmost to the foremost, of every step and stage, particle and part, and whole, of every being and measure of time; and this gradation of all is the existing and continued fact from what is called the beginning to the end, or from the ending-beginning point, to that same again, in the ever ending-beginning Om. The gradation in the Omic days is the gradation in the beings, order, relations, and times, of the productions spoken of, distinctly and as one whole. It is the gradation in all after their kinds, and in each of all after its kind. And all is found now to be as here stated and described, as one whole creation of creations; man being the inmost and head-sum of all, having in him, given to him, put under him, brought to him, and named by him; and the correlations of him and them, and of all in him and them, are such that he and they and all in them are for each other in this gradation, under God, and towards God, in Christ, by the one Spirit. The whole Om, *i.e.*, and Aeonic being is in the Omic form and meaning of He and She, man and woman, Adam and Eve; she from him and she and he from God. All things are from man, as the inmost and head-sum of all, and are appropriately brought to him, and given to him and for him; and so are he and all in relation to God.

Man, as to his body, is said to have been formed of the dust of the ground; of the physical materials of particles and atoms and elements of wild nature, yet formed in a gradation of refinement in the inmost and highest kind of this world's creaturehood.

Much of what has been already stated, in way of showing the agreement between nature and the Bible, is from the regions of the too small and the too distant for the human senses without artificial aids, as the microscope and the telescope, to supply the general reader, for forming a clear and comprehensive view of the subject, through means additional to what lies within his ordinary reach. From many causes, among which is a false or assumed delicacy, the anatomy of the human body is less distinctly, intelligently, and systematically known than it ought to be. A few sentences may be here devoted to this part of the subject. The leading division is into the usual three in one parts of lower, middle, and higher; each forming into a head-sum of grove in Omic contents, shape, and meaning; and each a summary of distinct yet combined necessaries of preservation, propagation, and correlative existence and action. The lower and outer has more to do with the physical, the plant, and the animal, departments of nature, yet in necessary and essential relation and union with the middle and higher; its numerical and relative position being from one to four, and opening out with the middle in the fifth number; whence the number five is naturally somewhat peculiar to the Egyptians or Ham race, as the lower of three, Ham, Shem, and Japhet. The middle, as inner and higher from without and below, has more to do with manhood, family, and social life; its numerical and relative position being from four to seven, and is more of Shem race character. It is yet in necessary and essential relation to the other two; it implies the lower and much of the higher. The third, or inmost and highest, has more to do with the intellectual and the national character of things (peculiarly shown by the Greeks at the time of their sharing in the greatness of the Aconic seat of empire), and approaching to the level of Melchizedek character in the universal gradation of man and nature. It is also a summary of all, as of the lower form in highest character in the face, or frontal part of the head, as of the second or middle in highest character in the cerebrum or mid head part, and as of the third, or whole head summary form in highest character in the cerebellum or highest of all in the most holy place. The human frame, and above all the human head, is a miniature universe, one Om of all Oms, in all gradation of all combinations of all individual Oms; each Om a universe as one of all in one, with God in gradation in and with His creatures in each of all in one; proclaiming in unison and with one accord, "The Lord our God is One."

The skeleton is made up of two hundred distinct and separate bones, some of which become united in middle age. The lower part is made up of three in one parts, the pelvis and its two limbs, the legs. Each of the two limbs is in three in one parts, the foot, the two bones from it to the knee, and the one thence to the pelvis. The three parts of the foot are the toe bones, which are two in the great toe and three in each of the others; the instep part in five bones; and the ankle part in seven, twenty-six in all.

Between the foot and the knee are two, the splint-bone and the shin-bone; in the upper part of the leg are the thigh-bone and hip-bone; and the knee-cap is common to the lower and upper parts. The pelvis is formed of the two hip bones, the sacrum, and the coccyx. The thigh-bone is the longest and strongest bone in the whole body; its prominent ball-like head fitting into the deep cup-like hollow of the hip-bone, forming a ball and socket joint, all at the titan thigh and hip place (k own to Samson), and corresponding to the titan shoulder point of mid-part of the body. At the left and at the right of the body the hip-bone is in three distinct bones in early life, which are united in adult years; and each haunch bone is also composed of three, the ilium, ischium, and pubis; the pubis being the small bones forming the front part of the hip-bones. The upper limbs, or the hands, are attached to the trunk by the shoulder girdle consisting of shoulder blade and collar-bone; they have in each the upper arm of one bone, the fore arm of two, and the hand which consists of eight wrist bones, five palm ones, and fourteen finger ones, twenty-seven in all. It should be carefully observed that the pelvis and its limbs now stand as the whole lower part of the whole body; so that the vertebræ column stands related as one whole to the several of the frontal side of the body; having four small vertebræ in the coccyx, and five in the sacrum, both forming the back part of the pelvis, five vertebræ in the loin, twelve behind the thorax or chest, and seven in the neck—thirty-three in all. The whole body has much the form of a tree; the vertebræ column has its lower end to the back of the pelvis; the next, which is the loin part, is without ribs like the bare part of the trunk of a tree; then the dorsal part has two pairs of ribs of twelve each, seven true ribs of each being fixed in front to the breast-bone, and five false ribs of each not fixed in front; and the eighth, ninth, and tenth pairs being attached to the seventh and to the breast-bone, while the eleventh and twelfth pairs are quite free. Thus, there are twenty-four ribs, thirty-three vertebræ, and six hip-bones. The vertebræ of the neck have the peculiarity from all the others, in possessing in each of their short lateral processes an opening for the passage of a blood-vessel. The first two of the seven neck vertebræ are known by the names atlas and axis. The five bones of the sacrum are united into one ossified piece in adult life. There are many things which show that the ancients had somewhat full and exact, though not microscopic, knowledge of the anatomy of the human frame. The coccyx (Latin for cuckoo), which consists of four vertebræ, was so named because of its resemblance in shape to the beak of a cuckoo, and mainly because it stands behind the fourth point transition, begetting, and relieving passage, without taking much to do with the ingoings and outgoings of the natural course of things. The first or highest vertebra of the neck is a ring or Om-shaped bone in which there are two cup-like hollows, into which fit the two bony projections of the occipital bone of the skull (one on the front side and one on the back side of the spinal opening), by which the head can move or bend forwards and backwards, or the body so move under it. In the Aconic movement of the body the face is supposed to be somewhat cast and south and the back to the north and west, in natural imitation of the ecliptic motion of the sun, as between the shoulder points at the northern and southern tropics. In the north was the mountain Calypso, and in the south the mountain Atlas, as if supporting the heaven as the world's head; while the passage from east to west lay along towards the west between the two, corresponding to the spinal opening between these Omic hollows, in which the projections stand and move for support to the head, and for motion forwards and backwards and round from side to side. The south side one was, therefore, called Atlas, and the other Calypso; and both stand on the next and it on the next in Aconic backward succession of the Omic vertebræ of the backbone. The second bone, called the Axis, is formed into a modified projection, like a peg or pivot, on which the Atlas-Calypso is fixed; and on this peg-shaped vertebra it moves round to the right and left.

Each vertebra is an Om; so is each joint in the body; the leading Om in each part being in its head-sum grove, of which there is one in each part (lower, middle, and head), the head part being in three parts and three groves in one in a further gradation into one. The face is made up of fourteen bones, of which twelve are in six pairs and two single ones They are, one lower jaw-bone, one ploughshare bone of the nose, two scroll-bones of the nose, two tear or weeping bones, two nasal or nose bones, two cheek-bones, two palate bones, two upper jaw-bones. Thus they are six double ones and two single ones, or eight, otherwise six in each side of the face. Ishtar's descent for renewal, or new creation, of anything, was sometimes taken as consisting of fourteen steps, yet generally as seven steps; because both numbers are really the same as one same descent and one same face, one same course, number, or parts of creation, as in the first chapter. The idea and fact of creation, new creation, or renewal, is frequently expressed in Scripture by he fell on his face, or he fell on his face to the ground; which means that he changed and passed from the old, in whatever sense or character, to the new, or next. Of such expressions is, he bowed himself; the himself having the same meaning with the face, which is a summary of himself. When the six double ones are taken as six single whole ones, and the other two as one, the number is seven in all; and they correspond to the six days in creation, into the Seventh in which the eighth, ninth, and tenth are implied, as has been seen in the case of the ribs; while the two single ones are meant as free, in Joseph and Benjamin number. The skull is made up of separate bones, fixed firmly together, and forming a box-like oval case (cranium) containing the brain. There are three layers in this brain case; an outer layer of hard bone, showing the usual Om three in one form of three-fold circle or ring, with the one or radicle in brain substance or contents. Taken as distinct bones, they are eight in number and arranged thus, one ethmoid bone at the base of the front part and at the root of the nose, one splenoid bone at the base of the skull, one (occipital) farthest back at the base of the back, two at the sides, two at the sides and top, and one forming the forehead or crown All may be taken as six, seven, or eight, otherwise ten. In one sense the thirty-three vertebræ of the back-bone correspond to the Aeonic manhood number of thirty years, with three for the bodily parts and fulfilled work, as in the case of Christ. The whole is also sometimes taken as twenty-four in number, corresponding to the number of the tribes and Apostles, and the twenty-four Elders; these being (from below), phalanges, metatarsus, tarsus (of foot); fibula tilera, patella, femur (leg), ischium, symphysis, pulcis, ilium (pelvis), metacarpus, carpus, radius, ulna, humerus (hand), dorsal vertebræ cervical vertebræ, lower maxilla, occipital bone, lamboidal suture parietal suture, and frontal bone. Bones consist of three parts substance, one-third of organic or animal matter and two-thirds of inorganic or mineral matter; but the proportion varies with one's age, the animal matter being nearly the only apparent matter in infancy and the mineral nearly the only in old age, and the proportion of one third animal being in mid-life. Blood is carried to them by the arteries. A vertebra is of the usual Om shape with three parts from without to within, three projections without and three implied within, and a rib from each shoulder point turning round inwards; while the spinal foramen or canal, through which the spinal cord passes, is hexagonal. Thus out of the Om comes the one of everything in all gradations, laws, and relations, as to substances, numbers, forms, and all else. The lower part of the body is out from its head-grove point, having its first part from one to four in the pelvis, from four to seven in the usual form of opening and two sides in the legs, and its third part in the feet with their Aeonic numbers on the earth which has its all of the same character. The middle part has its first part from one to four comparatively hidden, then its opening with two hands from four to seven, and its third part in the outer hands parts. The brain is divided into two lateral parts, out from the Omic dark part to the face or front of the head, called hemispheres; which in turn are each divided into three parts, or lobes, the posterior, middle, and anterior.

Histology is concerned with the ultimate structures of the bodily parts, called tissues; the most important of which are seven in number, the rest being in Omic union with these, particularly with the seventh. They are, those forming bones (osseous), forming fat (adipose), fibre and ligament (fibrous), gristle (cartilaginous), muscle or flesh (muscular), nerve and brain (nervous), and connective. Tissues make up the organs, and organs make up the body. There are seven systems of organs, the food and digestive system, the motor or muscular system, the nervous system (directing), the nervous system (receptive or sensory, including the five senses), the respiratory system, the blood system, and the bony system, or skeleton. Bones serve for measures of extension between Oms, for protection to the more delicate organs of the body; and, with the attached muscles acting in the to and fro way of extension and attraction for bodily movements. In all things, at all times, and everywhere, the fiat let there be precedes in cause, fact, and effect, the fiat let bring forth. So the muscular tissue, though first and in itself one, divides into two, the involuntary and the voluntary. It cannot be too carefully remembered, or too oft repeated, that there can be no being or having being but as implied in the Divine Trinity. The Spirit is the original, self-existent, eternal, and universal Om. His outcoming necessarily implies Father one to the Son one, yet all the one Spirit. The Spirit, in coming forth as Son, comes forth from Himself in His self-character of Father to Himself as Son. In the eternally continued being and act, or in so being and having being, He is for ever (Neith-like) coming forth from Himself, from being His own son to being His own son; His so doing is also His coming forth from being His own Father to being His own Father; and a triad form of this coming forth is in father-son, grandfather-grandson, great-grandfather-great-grandson, through the fourth point into a son-triad of father-triad, and both triad of triads, into the usual tenth point. This was pictured by the Ancients in the form of a bifurcate or trifurcate instrument, like the three-pronged sceptre called trident, and the Hebrew letter shin. The three prongs, projections, or branches, are always implied, as in the outside of each vertebra, already noticed; the middle one being the onward midline, stem, trunk, and balancing three in one midbeing, in which the father-son begetting, creative, renewing, and all eternal and universal act of the Spirit takes place; whence it is the all in all being, position, and work of Christ the mediator. It is the origin and meaning of the term Druid (Gaelic, Tri-aodh or Tri-ath); and it is St Columba's profession and preaching motto, "'S e mo Thri-aod" (Thri-aon or tri-Adhamh Thriath) Mac Dhe (my Trinity is the Son of God). An apparent instance of two branches is in the merry-bone in the breast of a bird, and the arrangement of the ribs about the neck of man and many beasts: but the main midline of such instances is in the neck, in the bird's beak, and in the nose of man and beast as marking the whole forward part. It is the secret meaning of what is called (but seldom understood) the unicorn, the all one horn of eternally begetting being, the cornucopia (horn of plenty) the all one horn of eternally preserving being. It holds true of cycles as it does of individual single beings.

The forward measure of the step, stage, and cycle, is the backward measure of the same; the all and only begotten, or being begotten, Son, is all that is in the begetting Father, the all Divine Spirit. It is unnecessary to follow out this farther here. Both the involuntary and the voluntary muscular tissues throughout the body have one common source and cause in the Spirit's work, but coming forth in the let there be and let bring forth, or father-son, mode of action and movement, in backward and forward measure of what is to be brought forth or forward, in midline being and direction. Force moves in these measured steps, stages, and cycles, from closing-opening Oms to closing-opening Oms, all in contact with the Spirit. Instances of involuntary movements are in the beating of the heart and the circulation of the blood, in the work of digestion and muscular tissues in the whole alimentary canal, and in the receptive nerves; the field of the voluntary, or what is one's own, or secondary part, is more in the outer line, as in the limbs, the face, and the whole outer region of the body. Even in the mind there is an inner power and an inner activity of that power which precede, and are independent of, the voluntary and secondary (which goes far to explain hypnotism). Moreover, the involuntary stands as inner, and in causal connection to, the voluntary or secondary, in gradation from perfection down to zero or Om, and in a counterpart gradation from perfection at that end to zero or Om at the first end. Thus there is perfection with zero at both ends and from end to end. The Relative with its gradations of imperfections is thus incidentally necessary to the Absolute, and finds its perfection in its to and fro union and motion with the Absolute. Christ as Son is of, and from, the Father; He is also the Relative as well as the Absolute; and, apart from the Father-Son sense, and the Absolute sense, He can say, I can do nothing of myself, the Father is greater than I; but, as All in All, He does all in all.

Not to dwell here on the muscles and the substances for bodily food, something may be noticed about the blood. All parts of the body contain blood except some tissues with which the outside layer of the skin, nails, hair, and centre of the cornea or front of the eye are connected. Blood-vessels are of three kinds, arteries, veins, and capillaries; blood colour being more of a bright red in the arteries, but more of a dark red or blue in the veins. In reality the three parts of rainbow colour, and, therefore, the seven colours are in the blood. Blood consists of two parts, the liquid part and the corpuscles; the latter are again of two kinds, the more intensely red and the white or colourless; or rather in gradation of three, and then seven, or ten (as always in white). It contains all the fourteen elements found in the body; having seven by three, or twenty-one, of solids, and seven by twelve, or about eighty-four of water; and again the watery part consisting of water and dissolved albumen (white of egg). Its fluid part consists of two parts, serum (watery and yellowish), and fibrin; which latter is white, tough, and fibrous, and forms a kind of mathematically arranged network during coagulation or clothing.

This fibrin seems to enter largely into the matter forming the cell walls of the corpuscles and of the tissues and harder parts of the body, though not apart from the other matters.

What is of peculiar interest is what is known of the corpuscles of the blood. The red ones are so minute that about one-third of ten thousand of them placed side by side in a single line would go into the measure of one inch ; or one-third, or one triad, the one way, and three-thirds, or triad of triads, the other way. In certain circumstances, they arrange themselves in these ways. They form themselves in the piled arrangement at a certain time after the blood has been drawn from the body. It has been already seen that the sarcous elements of which the fibrillae, of which in turn the fibres forming tissue consist, are disc-like Om bodies, which are laid one upon the other, and which, by the colour at their junction being varied as at transition lines, give a striped appearance to the fibres. Transition lines, whether direct or transverse, do cause the formation to appear striped, Jacob's rods-like. All Oms have circular transition lines, there being a triad of Oms, an outer, middle, and inner, with the point of the one or rod in the centre, in one Om ; all which are distinctly found in all such corpuscles. These red ones carry oxygen from the lungs to the tissues, and carbonic acid gas from the tissues back to the lungs ; for all force acts by to and fro motion, in the primary sense. This carrying work is, as in all nature and all religions, a going down and up, a going out and in, a re-creating, renewing, and reviving, an Omic and Aeonic gradation process of putting off the old and putting on the new, of eternal life in eternal being and having being. Among the blood's chief functions in this work are to supply the glands with materials for producing gastric and pancreatic fluids as juices and bile, on the action of which the work of digestion greatly depends ; to receive, absorb, and convey to all parts of the body nutritive matter as in ordinary food, water, and oxygen, which last burns up hydrogen and carbon, by which chemical union heat is produced, and is equalised in temperature by the blood through the whole body ; to supply the tissues with matter for their renewal and growth, and at the same time to moisten every part and particle ; and to carry all refuse from all parts and tissues to the organs by which it is excreted from the body.

Those blood corpuscles, whose appearance is such that it is difficult to say whether they are colourless or white, have their distinctive characteristics mostly arising from their being of the summary nature and form of the first and tenth points. They are larger in size by one-third than the red ones ; and they are so comparatively few in number that they are only three, or a triad, to every thousand of the red ones. They are the chiliarchoi over the divisions of the community, or the king-queen Oms of the let bring forth, under the let there be, Aeonic line of perpetual reproduction and renewal, in the universal reign of Eternal Empire of the Eternal Father-Son by the Eternal Spirit. From the outmost circle to the centre of each there are six circles of dots, each inner of which is smaller than its outer, somewhat like the dotted disc of the sun ; yet moon-like, each, or some, of these wonderful corpuscles appear to be continually changing in form. Their contractile and extensile amoeba like modes of action have been called amoeboid movements ; but their movements are comparatively slow, and their situation is near the walls of the blood vessels or tubes, while the red ones are in the quick and·fast activities of the ever-circulating blood movement.

Thus it may be seen that these minute forms of being have their being and their having being in the nature and order of gradations and relations, source, substances, and laws, which nature, the Bible, and the religions of the world everywhere teach. Each of them has its sum-substance of all that obtains in nature in its miniature Om being and history. Each individual is a little world, and so is each combination of individuals, each community and each combination of communities. As a positive being, or at all a being, it cannot be unreal, informal, or unmeaning ; nor can it yet be without its incidental zero, shadow, or second self. Its comparative vacuity, or cavity, is essential to it, as such is to all being, within and without, and in gradation of transition lines, direct, transverse, circular, spiral, and all ways. So it has its network of fibrin, fluid, and comparatively open spaces within and in its walls, skin, garment. Its cell contracts and extends, bends and bulges, in all form and fashion, way and work, in self-action, yet under influences, according to condition and purpose ; all in all ways of to and fro directions of its life, by the All-Spirit of all life. Its net-work of form is present with it and in it, in all within and without, and corresponds to the causes and effects, laws and means, habits, customs, and necessities of its being and living; just as is true of all, from the most minute to the most mighty. Scripture does not, any more than nature, overlook its gradation of kinds ; but takes all things under the "after its kind" rule of wise classification, founded in essential nature and creation, both which are ever the same as faithfully taught in Scripture. Scripture speaks of the blood as the life of animal beings, as in the words, for the blood is the life ; words which, together with much more of its teaching and regulations about blood, sacrifices, and other things respecting life, show how carefully and successfully this and kindred subjects were studied and understood by the sacred writers. Life, in its different kinds in nature, is known in connection with light, liquids, solids, and gases ; all these, in some sense and form or other, have to do with all life of all kinds, in Him who is the Light of life and the Life of the world ; and all these have to do with the smallest corpuscle, and relative substances of the blood. Man is a representative being, in sum-substance, of all substances and laws, plants and animals, and all the processes within and without, of creation and providence.

The lowest known form of the Om is the lowest known form of the means of giving and getting, and of getting and giving life and al else; but it is the same in the highest and in all between, in nature, and in man, and not less in the Bible.

Man has the whole world, within and without, to subdue from the wildest and roughest to the tamest and the most refined; to reduce everything to its lowest and original sense and form, or to its first state, which is its highest and finest state; and yet to re-create and reproduce, renew and cause to grow again, everything after its kind, in and after the Spirit. He and his lowest blood beings and formations are correlated in mutual dependence, towards each other and towards the Spirit, for life, breath, and all things. His teeth are a representative and actual combination for representative and actual purposes. What is called Ptyalin, and has the property of changing the starchy matters of food into grape sugar, form, with water and a little salt, the so-called saliva or spittle used in insalivation. But this saliva is secreted and prepared from the blood by small bodies, which are significantly six in number, and are situated above and below, in the cheeks and under the tongue. Everything has its relations to heaven and earth; and there is an incidental titan meaning in the words, "the poison of asps is under their lips—their feet are swift to shed blood." The food has to pass over the mouth of the wind-pipe with its epiglottis and under the nasal opening. Its three stages of descent to the stomach are those of the oesophagus, which are, the pharynx, or upper part, the thorax, and through the diaphragm. The stomach itself has its three formative divisions or layers of outer coat of skin, middle or involuntary muscular fibres, and inner of skin of mucous membrane; which last is covered with small Oms, being the mouths of open tubes, called gastric glands, surrounded by a net-work of blood-vessels from the blood of which the glands secrete the fluid called gastric juice. The gastric juice consists of water and some salt, hydrochloric acid, and pepsin; and is the means of dissolving and changing the nitrogenous and albuminous matters of the food into peptones, which are mixed with the food by the constant churning motion kept on by the continually contracting muscular coat of the stomach. The fats are reduced into globules; and the mixture is now called chyme, the small blood-vessels of the mucous coat beginning at once to absorb the most liquid part. Continuous with the right-hand side of the stomach is the small intestine, also of three layers similar to those of the stomach; and in it the chyme is now mixed with three kinds of liquids, and gets the name, chyle. One of these three is the pancreatic juice, or the juice secreted by the gland called pancreas. It flows as needed into the mixture, and acts in further changing the starchy matters, and the albuminous compounds. A second is the bile, which, after being secreted by the liver, is stored in the gall-bladder; contains alkaline substances made up of compounds of soda; and acts in reducing the fatty matters into a state fit for entering the blood. In the third, the intestinal juices, there are three glands different in kind and situated in the lining membrane of the small intestine, called respectively, the glands of Brunner, the glands of Lieberkuhn, and Peyer's patches; and by the action of these the chyme is changed into what is called chyle, the food's last known stage before entering the blood. The number of steps in the process of changing matters of food into the state fit for entering the blood is six, namely, chewing by the teeth, or mastication; insalivation by saliva; swallowing, or deglutition, by the tongue, pharynx, and oesophagus; chymification, or digestive conversion of it into chyme by the juice secreted by the lining membrane of the stomach; further digestion, called chylification, in the small intestine by the intestinal juices, the pancreatic juices, and that called bile; and its absorption into the blood by the villi of the small intestine. Though these might be taken through the transition line of the seventh point with the three kinds of glands secreted and acting under the head of intestinal juices, and the natural connection of union with the seventh up to ten; yet the real changes are rather six in the sense of passing into a state of saliva, of chyme, of chyle, and of each of the three known as intestinal juices, the pancreatic juices, and the bile; while the three, which in connection with the seventh or with these through the seventh make the triad of triads into one whole ten, are the three intestinal juices, called the glands of Brunner, the glands of Lieberkuhn, and Peyer's patches. Among the difficulties in the way of a satisfactory knowledge of these last is that of making a distinct separation of their secretions, without which their real and respective functions cannot be clearly determined. Hitherto the process is a gradation of Ishtar descent, in putting off the raw unfitness of the matters being changed and reducing them into a state fitted for entering into the blood, by which, in the sense of Ishtar ascent, they are to be distributed to all parts of the body for renewed strength and growth. Each change is made at its natural level or transition line. The breaking down of the raw materials in mastication, and the chewing of them in insalivation, are in the level of the tenth point of plants, the seventh of animals, and the fourth of man, the physical being everywhere included. Chymification is on the next lower down level or line of the tenth point of the physical, the seventh of plants, the fourth of animals, and first of man. In natural order chylification is made in the line of the seventh point of the physical, the fourth of the plants, and the first of the animals. What now remains is the lower part of plants down from four to one; and the middle part of the physical from seven to four, that is as here implied in the human body. The remaining line of change is that at one of the materials in their plant nature, and at four of the physical. Perhaps anything of the mixture that may be peculiar of animal nature does not go down farther than the first point sense of animals, which is the lowest line of chylification, or, after the change at the first point of plants, it keeps farther in, and is distributed and mixed with the more fleshy part, while the more suited to the plant nature goes into the plant life in or connected with the blood. Thus the three last juices, so indistinct in nature and functions, may contain much peculiarly related to the lower part and outer region of the body.

The ascent of the blood is the means of the re-creative distribution of the food-matter to all parts of the body. A tripartite circulation of the blood is into the general, the pulmonary, and the portal; the first of which is carried on outwards through three sets of vessels, arteries, arterial capillaries, and venous capillaries, and inwards through the veins; the second is from the right side of the heart (as the former is from the left) out through the vessels of the lungs and back to the left side; and the third is from the heart to the stomach, spleen, pancreas, and intestines, where the blood is collected by the portal veins and conducted to the liver, in turn to be collected by the hepatic veins into the current which is on its way back from the lower parts of the body. In conformity to the gradual up and out growing and three in one form of the body and of other things, the heart is somewhat triangular or conical in shape, with the point of the cone downwards. As animal appears on the fifth day, so the heart is situated with its points beating between the fifth and sixth ribs. It is in the usual Om form of three parts inwards, two parts or covers of skin called pericardium, then its proper wall; the three being of tissue, and within all is the body cavity. Its one, four, seven, ten form is in two ways, from below and upwards, and then in summary chest or form. From below upwards the order is in the Aconic natural gradation. The outer of its two pericardial covers is loose, and therefore encloses a transition cavity all round between itself and the second cover, which latter lies so close to the heart that the second transition space all round is very thin or small; while the space, or already mentioned cavity, between the two covers is so open as to contain a plentiful watery fluid called the pericardial fluid. All this indicates, among other things, that there obtains here, as in nature, the gradation of lower and outer being more of water and plant kind in relation to the higher and inner or middle part, which is more of blood and animal kind. The lower part of pericardial double cover is attached to the diaphragm and to the blood-vessels by which the heart communicates with the rest of the body; which again shows the distinction of lower and outer plant in relation to higher and inner animal life, in orderly, natural, and essential relations, as represented here and elsewhere through the Bible. Be it observed that the lower part of all this, like the first three days of creation work, is in relative form and position from one to four; and that the rest of it is the all-round outer, like the other days of creation work, from four to ten, as all-round upper and outer in physical and plant sense. Now the heart proper must be more animal in nature, and must have two parts in upward and outward Aeonic succession to the already noticed first or lower part, making in all three parts in outward succession. It must also be in two parts broadwise, one on each side of the upward mid-line, and both below and above the transverse line that divides the middle part from the upper. This is found to be the actual division. It is the Omic and Aeonic form and meaning of the six days creation work, of man and nature, of Christ's Cross and Kingdom, of all things and the whole course of things. The upward mid-line, which is of curtain-like form of skin, is called the septem; the transverse curtain is in two parts, one on each side of the mid-line, each being valve-shaped and thence so-called; and the four parts or chambers are into upper two, or left and right auricles, and lower two, or left and right ventricles. The order of succession and advance in numerical, essential, and relative implication is here further seen in these valves and in the veins of the heart. The valve which divides the left ventricle from the left auricle is made up of a double fold of the same skin that doubly lines the heart, also of two joints or cusps like the points of the new moon, hence called the bicuspid valve; and, being further somewhat shaped like a bishop's mitre, it is sometimes called the mitral (Gaelic, currachd an righ, king's cap). That which divides the right ventricle from the right auricle is made up of the same skin, but in three flaps or cusps, and hence called the tricuspid valve. It is unnecessary here to speak of the relations of sun and moon, and the masculine and feminine principles in nature; they are relations that exist everywhere; and the indications of them here are evident and unmistakeable. Universal analogy seems to teach that the sun is supplied from behind, or somehow, with matter, or force, or both, for its ceaseless lightgiving. The largest blood-vessel or tube, the aorta, leads from the left ventricle down into smaller pipes, thence into capillaries which form a net-work in the tissues. These capillaries uniting form veins which open into larger veins, by which they pass into still larger veins; then, ascending on the right side into the one inferior vena cava, they terminate in the right auricle. By the contracting and distending of this auricle alternately with the right ventricle the blood passes through the tricuspid valve into this right ventricle, when the valve closes against its return, whereby a rebound forwards is given to it out of the ventricle into the pulmonary artery, by which it passes into the lungs, getting rebounding force from valve closing behind, to pass through the arteries, capillaries, and veins of the lungs into the pulmonary veins. From these veins it gathers into the left auricle and thence through the bicuspid valve into the left ventricle, and thence again into the aorta. Chordae tendinae are distensile cords, which are connected to the muscles of the skin of the ventricles, and are the means of keeping the bicuspid and the tricuspid from receding into the auricles when closing behind the onflowing blood.

Valves occur at Aeonic intervals, as transition points of passage, in the whole course of the blood, from its seat in the left ventricle through the whole body until it returns to the same seat, which it enters through the bicuspid valve. At this valve is, therefore, the ending-beginning point of its circulation as one whole ; in which order of connections the valve is the first point Om valve and the tenth point Om valve, as two, yet one, as the first and tenth always are. Thus it is the seat and centre point, the all summary Om, of prophet, priest, and king, or of the physical, the plant, the animal, and the human, in the sense of all being and having being. The measure of its gradation outwards is downwards to between the fourth and fifth creation days, where animal life formally and distinctly appears ; the under the fifth rib point of killing by the spear or sword, the side point of the body of Jesus pierced by one of the soldiers, whence forthwith came there blood and water. The tripartite gradation is summarily indicated in the tricuspid valve ; and the one, four, seven, ten, of parts and transition lines for the whole body is in the full central and fourfold summary of the heart's division into four chambers. Of all persons and things the bicuspid is the currachd and curusan, the cap and cup, the Father-Son begetting actor, as to outgoing and incoming, in endless round of ever ending ever-beginning course. The sun holds the mid-point in the mid-line and mountain of the mighty movement ; and the moon's course is round by the four parts, or chambers, marked by signs of the different forces and phases. Up from nature's lowest level, and in from its outmost horizon, to its bicuspid gates of life and sun's zenith of strength, are creation's ever proceeding works, Abraham's sojournings and wars of Kings, the wars of Troy and of Israel, all growths and advancements in all that is good, the universal struggle for existence, and all progression through antagonism.

The nervous system is directing and receptive. Its two parts are the cerebro spinal containing the brain, the spinal cord, and the spinal nerves ; and the sympathetic which extend to the thorax, the abdomen, muscles, and blood vessels. Nervous matter is the curd of milk, and is in three layers. The function of the nerves is to conduct nervous impulses to a nerve centre, and are called sensory or efferent nerves, or from a centre as the brain or spinal cord to muscles which they cause to contract, and are called motor or efferent nerves. Those in the head are called cranial nerves, those along the back of the chest the dorsal nerves, those along the small of the back the lumber nerves, those to the back of the abdomen the lumber plexus, and those reaching to the cauda equina the sacral plexes.

5. The brain consists of three double parts, the anterior or front, the middle, and the posterior, divided through the middle

from the front to the back into two lateral hemispheres, which are divided from side to side into three parts in each hemisphere; corresponding to the six parts of the face in two eyes, two ears, and two nostrils, and to the whole body in three parts of the left and three of the right. Two parts are each common to all, the mouth and the cerebellum; the former lying beneath the front part and the latter beneath the back part of the head. That which connects the spinal cord and the brain or head is what is called the medulla oblongata or oblong marrow, immediately below the cerebellum. The brain's average weight in man is about fifty ounces, and about six less in woman. The front part is a representative summary of the lower and outer part or region of the whole body; the middle is that of the middle and inner with the sum substance of the front part, as that of the head as the third summary part of the whole body with the second in sum-substance. The cerebellum is the sum-substance of the whole; and it is so fine in consistence and so highly complicated in structure as to be hitherto beyond all human means of analysis, as well as anatomy, and beyond all human power of distinct perception. It is the seat of the intellect, the oraculum of the most holy place in the Tabernacle and the Temple, as in man and all nature. It weighs about one-tenth of the entire brain; and it is the Ark of the Covenant with its decalogue, the ten words, in one-tenth point of all tens and all tens of all tens of nature and man. Entirely without it there is no intelligence, no will, no consciousness; but its gradation in distinct character downwards, and in whatever direction, is difficult for the writer, and perhaps equally for the reader, to follow far. From the under surface of it and oblongata twelve pairs of nerves pass out through the body, as the twenty-four elders of the body congregation and the commonwealth of Israel; some being sensory and some motor in inlet and outlet, and find pasture of the Good Shepherd's flock of creatures, subjects, and those whom He is not ashamed to call brethren; for He has prepared for them a city. These nerves, though in one way thus twelve in number, pass out and in through nine, otherwise ten, pairs of openings in the base of the skull, and are hence sometimes called the nine pairs. They have essential, Omic, and Aeonic, respect to the six days' creations, otherwise ten, into Joseph-Benjamin twelve summary of summaries of tribes and Apostles, in gradation of all numbers of beings, the mid-line Apollo's nine muses, in orderly gradations and relations through the world of worlds and age of ages In colour the grey matter in the brain is outer, and the white inner; the former serving as the body in which the latter dwells and acts in knowing and being known, giving and getting, to and fro, union, communion, and action with the inner and outer world. The double front, and the double middle, parts of the cerebrum are so large as to occupy the whole space from front to back, except the lower part of the back, where the sum-substance of them forms with the cerebellum the third double part, of all which the cerebellum proper and their ultimate substance are the highest, finest, and inmost sum-substance of the whole body.

In the medulla oblongata and the spinal cord the grey matter is inner and the white is outer; the grey being arranged in the former as a somewhat mixed and irregular mass, but in a more regular column in the latter. The white seems to be more of the nature of ozone, and the grey more of that of protoplasm. The grey is more cellular, and the white more of tissue and in the walls of all cells. Everywhere the white acts in to and fro gland work secreting and begetting new or renewed forms or additions from itself, and, in a lower and secondary sense, from the grey. The white has its head sum substance in the cerebellum. In the medulla oblongata and spinal cord it embraces and covers the grey, with the spinal canal through the entire centre. From the back to the front a middle line passes dividing the whole column into right and left lateral sides, corresponding to the mid-line of the whole body and each part therein. No Om, or cell, is an absolute circle, much less an absolute globe; otherwise there could be no intercommunicative, in and out, to and fro, dealing between the absolute and the relative. It is rather in the shape of the third letter of the alphabet, more or less closed with an inner and outer space and contents. The unclosed points are called cornua (pl. of cornu, a horn). It is so in most parts of the body; the opening being to the front, or downwards. The kidneys are an exception, having their open side to the back and themselves mostly concealed in fat to keep their excretion from the life matters of the body. The arms and hands, the ribs and many of the nerves, close inwards; and the whole body close in by bending forward its upper and lower parts. Most things in man and nature have this bending in but open form in measures of modification of nature's closing-opening, and ending-beginning, forms. Even the Om one, or rod, and all lines, however straight, are made up of additions of onward motion in Om rings of this shape. The Ancients represented the sun's path round the earth as thus open at the midnight turning point from west to east, as if crossing a transverse transition line of what they called ocean stream, a matter to be noticed farther on. The spinal cord is about eighteen inches long, which make a triad of six inches each, in respect to the three parts of the body. An upright formation with two branches at the upper end, one to the left and another to the right, like a cross, or the human body with outstretched arms, stands in the base of the cerebellum, and is called the ventricles. Here also the two halves of the cerebellum are connected by a band, or bridge, of nervous fibres, called Pons Varolii. There is no impassable gulf between God and any of His creatures. This bridge and the medulla oblongata are the seat of the nerves connected with breathing, swallowing, and other involuntary movements; and they are two parts most essential to life, its enjoyments, and its activities.

Perhaps the most remarkable of the many remarkable formations and figures in this wonderful part of the body, the cerebellum, is its tree of life (Arbor Vitæ). Its plate-like layers of white and grey matter so lie together and to each other, in such gradations and relations, that, when cut crosswise, they present the form of a tree of most exact and beautiful shape. This fact is personally of peculiar interest to the writer, from the wonderful circumstance of a birth-mark, of a like distinct tree form, being situated in the outward skin and flesh, extending from above his left shoulder to within a small distance from the base of the cerebellum. The connections of these facts with each other, and with their causes, purposes, and ends, may be not less difficult to know than delicate to comment upon. It is peculiarly striking how clear and strong is the resemblance between these things and the moon's representations of man and tree, of Omic hills and hollows, innumerable Omic, or cell-like forms, Omic convolutions, revolutions, and phases, the white and grey consistence, the course and nature of motion and influences, and all the rest, in relation to the sun, and to sea, and earth, and sky. At the same time the nature, position, and functions of the cerebellum point to a kind of being of less outward prominence but greater inward power than either or both of sun and moon. Though covered with darkness it yet dwells in self-light, which is inapproachable and full of glory; and is ever in communication with all other kinds of light and life. It is an inner being of sum-substance and form of every being, giving and getting, creating and renewing, all this, whether sun and moon, sea and earth and air and all else. It has its being and work from the beginning and the Spirit's moving on the face of the waters as really up to the fourth day, before the outward appearance and prominence of sun and moon, as in them and with them thereafter to the seventh, or the tenth. It is common to all, and, therefore, has here the sum representations of all. Its convolutions are equally fitted for the lowest and lowliest of creeping creatures as for the highest forms of beings of the greatest magnitude.

The term soul, when employed in the Bible as distinct from spirit, seems intended to apply to life as existing and being manifested in the cerebrum, and the region of the senses through the whole body, except the cerebellum; and to comprehend all that is implied in animal, social, and moral life. Personal experience is enough for any one to know that the heart, not the intellect, is the seat of all conscious pain and pleasure, approval and disapproval of conscience included. How much and how far intelligence exists in, and is predicative of, these kinds of life, in gradation down to their lowest level, if not to the lowest level of plant and physical existence, in co-existences and overlappings, is not here said; what is said is suited to truth and for ordinary powers of perception and practice. The cerebellum is, in some respects and forms, in all things; but it is also, in its distinct forms and implications, the sum-substance of all things in their inmost, highest, and most refined sense and character; while yet, in its inmost and highest distinctions, it does possess a nature, kind, and character or being, higher and inner than they all. It has peculiarly to do with the double idea of being from itself and they from it, of let there be and let produce; not apart from them, but with them, in them, and for them, and they all so in turn towards it. The breath of life is in gradation in them, and under man and God's breathing into his nostrils the breath of life, and he becoming a living soul; a soul human and higher than theirs, and his intellect human and higher in measure and kind than theirs. To become as God's, knowing good and evil, implies more than the perception of the fact of being subject to divine authority; it implies, moreover, personal and conscious enjoyment and reproduction of the good in the highest and nearest sense in which the creature is capable of knowing it, as God knows it. It implies the sum-substance of all things subjective and objective, matters of sense and all kinds of life, as well as of intellectual and divine nature. The very physical structure and connections of the cerebellum and of the whole body most clearly and evidently indicate this.

A representative summary of the nerves and the bodily senses is situated in the face, having their roots in the medulla oblongata; about the middle point of which the tree of life has its trunk fixed, as if rooted in the side of it opposite from that of the nerves, and from which it spreads through the outward length or measure of the cerebellum; while the cerebrum occupies the whole space above in four parts or lobes, the anterior lobe, corpus collosum, middle lobe, and posterior lobe. The cranial nerves are in twelve pairs, and the spinal nerves in thirty-one pairs; all being in special, though not exclusive connection and relation to the spinal cord, the face, the cerebrum, the medulla oblongata, and the cerebellum, in short the cerebro-spinal system. The sympathetic system is in two lines or chains, one on each side of the vertebral column on the back walls of the thorax and abdomen. Their connections are branched with the spinal nerves; from which it is seen that the two systems are naturally and formally connected, in some respects, distinct. Nerves of the sympathetic system accompany and are distributed to the walls of all arteries of the body and are in special connection with the heart, stomach, and intestines, which are also so far under the control and direction of the cerebro-spinal nerves. The influences and effects on and in the body are under the Omic laws of ending-beginning, closing-opening, and such like; causing contractions and distensions, and other effects, connections, and successions. Under the influence of fear these sympathetic nerves cause the muscular walls of the blood-vessels to contract, by which the quantity of blood contained is reduced and pallor ensues. This arises from the influence or message being expellant and destructive, as in the case of a marble struck against a stone wall. A pleasant and attractive influence has an opening effect on and in a blood-vessel, or gland, and a consequent filling and flushing of the vessel and gland by the blood, leading to animation and blushing, even when attached to shyness and shame.

The gradations and correlations of the various systems and parts, laws and influences, existing and at work in man, are such and so much resemble external nature, the world and all therein, in particular outward human society, that what is internal to him can be and often is spoken and written of in like words and modes of speech as in speaking and writing of what is external to him. The gradations and correlations among all the creatures of the world, from the most narrow to the widest sense, and in connection with him as their inmost and highest created being, or part of their comprehensive being, are such that the history of them and that of him, in creation and through the course of their and his common existence, is necessarily and actually much the same. It is, therefore, quite correct, proper, and convenient to give the world's history in the form of the history of man, in the father-son sense and form of parts, as ages and eras, periods, persons and things. In the highest sense it is the history of the absolute in the relative, of the Divine Spirit's self-manifestations, in Father-Son way and sense of all works in all beings.

Every new being in advance is by the outgrowth and creative evolution of the midline, and the absorption of the renewed sum-substance of the lower and outer. Thus, it may be said that the supreme and creative fiat of let there be, takes its secondary self of let bring forth into the sum-form of let us make ; as in the words, Let us make man in our image, after our likeness. Man is, therefore, the creature of God in the highest and most original and direct sense, and also of the combination into the highest sum substance in contents and kind of all the other creatures, while it still holds true that they all are out-branches from him, and of him, as he is the mid-line of them all. God Himself lives and acts in the mid-line sense of self-living and life-giving as Jehovah, and He is, and acts, in the more manifestative and outer sense of God Elohim, the last name being plural in the sense of His outer sum of all His distinctions in Himself and in all His ways and works. His inmost, most secret, and most sacred name is Jehovah—His name as to life and being, both which are unknown, and seemingly unknowable, alike in Him and in His creatures. All moving force has a head and body form, with an out-going of self-like yet varying forms, small at every beginning, as the grass and creeping things, and such like, at the outgoings of all the creative days. So mosses and convolvolus forms, hairs and parasites, attach to everything after its kind. To and fro force is in six principal and special directions of three pairs, downwards and upwards, backwards and forwards, to the left and to the right. At the head of each of the three parts of the body they make an Omic grove, as an ending-beginning, closing-opening seat and centre of life and all else, with hairs and other marks, all gathered into one sum-total of forces and forms, marks and meanings of third number in the face and beard, and of fourth number at the whole sum under the hairy scalp. These groves occur in front at the head of each part, because it is the closing-opening point of the Om, and they occur in front because it is the main closing-opening side of the Om, which is not an absolutely formed and closed circle. The same openings are also to the left and right in the out-goings of the limbs, of a breast, a nostril, an ear, and an eye to each side. In short, the mid-line divides all parts and openings into left and right, the cerebellum not excepted. The back and front forces and forms of each part of the vertebral column, join those of the sides round and inwards towards the front in the line of least resistance and greatest attraction towards food and family matters, as the ribs and nerves in connection or contiguity to the internals. A branch or limb cannot grow out of any formation except where an Om is present at the point of the to and fro force, which makes its way out thus through the Om. Such forces open out the bud in seed and stem, frequently with a new bud on each side, as at a shoulder point, leaving the false leaves behind, and growing into tree-form branches of temporary or permanent duration. The first arrangement of branches is in two sides, next in four perpendicular rows, then into spiral forms, as already noticed in plants. It should be observed that thus the one, four, seven ten form and sense are ever present in every shape and growth in persons and things. Every formation or being, whether in Om or cell, in seed or stem, in plant or animal, or whatever form, has its gradation in four principal directions and modifications of the universal one, four, seven, ten. Man, as the mid-line of all the creatures, which he gives out from the side in gradation of these transition points and lines, is, as distinct from them, naked, except the outer part of his head, they being to him his outer being and garment, somewhat as the relative is to the absolute, in all which God is the inmost, highest, eternal, and universal Being. In this inmost sense Jehovah stands to Elohim and other divine names ; and comes out at the appropriate Omic and Aeonic point in this part of Genesis, and at all such points at all times and in all things ; a special instance being in Joseph and in Israel under Moses, when the distinction is expressly and formally stated as thus between Jehovah and God Almighty. It is both essentially impossible to make an outward visible image of Him, and sinfully improper to attempt it. He is known and knowable as He makes Himself known ; and man and nature make Him known in the way and measure they are like Him and fulfil His will.

The Lord God planted a Garden eastward in Eden ; He did so as Jehovah and God. Eden is the representative sum-total of the all very good six days' creations; and stands for the place, condition, and circumstances in which the Garden is planted, as the central and summary Om, or grove, and seat of empire of the whole world. The gradation from without inwards is, outward nature, Eden, and the Garden-grove, making three in one, into the fourth or inmost form of being, namely, man, as the one, or highest and inmost sum-substance of all. Eden, in its literal form and meaning, and also as to what it thus represents, is the outer of Adam; being so, somewhat as El, or its plural Elohim, is to Jah or Jehovah. A, as sounded in awe, is the all ending-beginning sound, and is so taken in Abba, Father. Iah is the first modification of it from the lowest sound-point in the larynx outwards or onwards, as Son is in coming out from the Father in the self-living and life giving Jehovah Father-Son sense. El, or Elohim, is pronounced in the right side of the mouth; and, in that act, in the whole fact, in the whole Bible, in man, and in nature, it is the outer of Jehovah, the God manifested form and sense of the all self-living and all life-giving Jehovah. The Aeonic movement of the world's seat of empire is from the east westwards; so the God-planted Garden is said to have been eastward, or in the east, in Eden, in man's outer and God made all very good condition and circumstances of happy state. Eden is thus always eastward in its all-giving sun-rise situation of world seat of empire, relative to its situations of its further movement. So is it in the words connected with its coming into Chaldea or Babylonia, from the east, men were on their way from the east. East and south are taken in the world's northern hemisphere, in man, and in the Bible, as hinder and lower. Not only the chief seat of empire proper, but a gradation of seats, as in a number of centres, or towns, were and are taken as partaking in the nature of Eden, or the Garden of the Lord; as a principal or special place of Jehovah God, of man, and of nature; the inmost and highest being in it, as in everything, being God, Jehovah, the eternal all-creative and begetting and beautifying Spirit. The lowest form and means of creation are expressed in the words, the waters of life, having their outer forms in the primary, and then the compound, elements, of fire, air, earth, and water, and outmost in the visible forms of fire, gases, solids, and liquids.

In its comprehensive sense, the Garden is the all creations of the six, or ten, days, or the world as one under man as representative head summary; in its narrow, or inner sense, it is man as the human race; in its inmost sense, it is the individual personal man, body, soul, and spirit. His body is the representative sum-total of the physical, plant, and animal natures, in one human nature; and, in each of these, natural substances, forces, and laws obtain. Another form of gradation is in the water as in the lower part of physical and plant kinds in nature and man, the blood as in animals and man, and the breath of life and soul into spirit, also in animals or all, but in the highest creatural sense in man. The

Divine Spirit is one, yet also Father-Son two, and again three in one in Father, and Son, and Spirit common to both, one God. So is the Spirit in His work, in one, four, seven, ten, sense and form; its one course being like one outgoing, onflowing, father-son, and three in one, into fourth, or four directions movement. Taking running, and therefore living, water, in full mighty river of all life, substance, law, and virtue, as the sum-symbol of the spirit's presence and course of work, it thus as a river went out of Eden to water the Garden. It went out of Eden as all the waters of all Eden to water all Eden, but in an inner and special sense to water the Garden, as the inner of Eden; much in the same way as ground is the outer state as distinct from earth as the cultivated state of the soil and other things.

It has been already seen how the human body, and all and each of its systems, are divided into parts and purposes, forms and functions; and also how natural forces move in numbers of directions, all in one universal course, in the whole body, and all bodies and beings in nature. The course of the sun in diurnal and annual revolutions, including the four seasons, the course and changes of the moon and planets, and the precession of equinoxes, all in relation to earth, to the zodiac, and to the milkyway, have been seen to be under the same laws in the one universal course of movement, and in the exact manner represented in the Bible. Moving force has been found to have a head and body. So the river parted and became into four heads; one, Pison, towards the north; the second, Gihon, towards the south; the third, Hiddekel, towards the east; and the fourth, Euphrates, towards the west, a division corresponding to much of the symbolism in Ezekiel and other parts of the Bible. It means the Spirit's course of work in nature, man, and the government of the world. In this state of things the Lord God put man; things to be constantly and carefully, divinely and humanly, naturally and spiritually, kept and dressed, preserved and propagated; in the ever ending-beginning let there be, let bring forth, and let us make; and in the after its kind nature, forms, and laws of all, under the highest summary of in our image, and after our likeness. The Omic Garden is taken in its gradation upwards and inwards, the physical being taken with the plant formations in the name of trees of the Garden; the animals in their being all brought to Adam to name them, each name containing the representative sum-substance of the individual and of its class after its kind, in nature and man; and then man himself as inmost and highest and sum-substance of all. It is the all come to maturity in man and the world.

Particular care should be taken to understand as much as possible of the connection of all that is contained in these representations to the Divine Spirit, in His living and life-going, creative and controlling, renewing and regulating, absorbing and reforming, inbeing and Father-Son, Jehovah-Elohim or Lord God, meaning and mode of working. It is expressly said that the Lord

God planted the Garden; made to grow every tree that is pleasant to the sight, and good for food; the tree of life also in the Garden, and the tree of knowledge of good and evil; took the man and put him into the Garden of Eden to dress it, and to keep it; and commanded the man, saying, Of every tree of the Garden thou mayest freely eat; but of the tree of knowledge of good and evil, thou shalt not eat of it; for in the day that thou eatest thereof thou shalt surely die. Noah planted a vineyard, and Abraham planted a grove; but this Garden, this grove, this Om, is planted by the Lord God. Abraham and Noah are traced in Christ's genealogical table as each the son of a like patriarch, though having a special and pre-eminent position in that Aeonic line of eras and ancestors; but Luke says, what is naturally and historically given here in Genesis, that Adam is the Son of God; being so as the sum-substance man of creation, the first man, and the all man. The six days' creations at first, and at all continued first outcoming into being, are, in the first and highest sense, immediately from the Spirit in the Father-Son work of one, four, seven, ten, or great-grandfather, grandfather, father, son, sense; He being as God, or Jehovah God, in each relation, as faintly expressed in the term, God-father. All the creations have Him as their God-Father of all sum relations; out of which state of relations man, in his all-sense of God-made man, passes into being self-made in self-begetting a son, and therein into becoming father. Adam, in the proper sense, can have only one son, the son appointed by God instead of Abel, the son begotten by Adam in his own likeness, after his image, even Seth. In this transition change the sum-substance of the God-Father past is absorbed into man and woman becoming as Gods, knowing good and evil.

It is in this Father-Son sense and form that every seven or ten can have the eleventh and twelfth numbers, which occupy everywhere their summary place and meaning. Jesus Christ is the eternal and only begotten Son of the Father, the First-born of creation, the First-born of every creature, the First-begotten from the dead, and the First-born among many brethren, all in this Father-Son sense. He is Jehovah-God Son in the whole absolute and in the whole relative. What He is in the absolute He is in the relative as the one whole out-coming and second-self from the absolute; and He is so in gradation outwards and inwards, downwards and upwards, as well as backwards and forwards, or eternally onwards. Father-Son, in the absolute, implies no succession in the ordinary meaning; for the one Divine Spirit in being begotten as Son is being begotten of Himself as Father; according to Christ's saying, I and the Father are one. The Egyptian representation of this is in Neith, that of Greece in Athenè, and that of Scripture is in Melchizedek and Christ as Son of God. He comes as Son from Himself as Father. This neither implies, nor gives place or countenance to, selfishness. It wholly and absolutely excludes it; for, as He says, He came not from Himself but from the Father.

This excludes the self-destructive nature and meaning of selfishness, which is the sum-substance of sin. Self-sacrifice and selfishness are opposites, and are exclusive of each other; the latter is put away by the former in Christ. As the absolute, as such, has no Om, or help-meet, but its self-absolute, in gradation to its incidental non-absolute; so man in his highest sense has no help-meet distinct from himself. As the relative is from the absolute, and is the Om of the absolute, as real whole one and head sum-substance of the relative, so the woman is the Om of the man, as the real whole one and head sum-substance of the woman. The absolute, as such, is not the relative, as such, nor is the relative, as such, the absolute, as such. Hence they are each, as such, distinct from each other; but the absolute is common to both, and is the real one and sum-substance of, and in, both; all making three in one. The absolute, in self-living, self-moving, and self-having being, forms a self-relative, or second self, with which, and in which, it lives, moves, and has being, without losing its original distinct absolute sense. As the absolute, as such, is the whole and only one such; and as the relative, as such, is the whole and only one such; they are, as such, distinct two, and are eternally so. They also imply and suppose each other; and this means that the one is distinct from, yet in union with, the other; which means a to and fro distinction, yet a to and fro union and oneness. Again, they are living, moving, and having being, as such, as distinct, and as in union; which implies a to and fro living, moving, and having being, towards each other, as one whole and as two distinct, yet mutually implying each other in the living, the moving, and the having being, which are common to both, as the Spirit is common in Father-Son. The one whole is thus two, and is therein one. Taking the three in one as one triad, it becomes two triads, and therein three in one triad, in the same way as has been already found true of the one. Each triad is as one, consisting of ones; the two triads are one triad in what is common to both; and this mid-line triad sense, in which the two triads are one, is the summary of the two triads, contained in it, which makes the head sum-substance of the number three from seven to ten, as already found in the ribs from seven to ten, otherwise twelve, joined to the seventh, and as man is the head sum of the sixth into seventh days of creation. The first triad of the Omic days' creations is at the fourth day, where it comes, in sum-substance of physico-plant, into animal life on the fifth day; the second triad from four to seven. This contains the sum-substance of the first triad of plants, into one triad of both in sum-substance into man, as one triad of triads on the creative level of his distinct one, his animal four, and plant seven. The whole of this is into Ham-man creation, and this is ever the birth-point, or level, of Ham, as old world lower part of the Adam all-man, and of the Ishmael and Arabs, as Abrahamic world lower part. At his distinct fourth point, which is the seventh of the animals (Ham's fourth) and the tenth of the plants, is the Shem birth-point, at which the tenth point of plants and seventh of animals are to be absorbed into the ever onward line of first-borns of Israel. Hence is the offering of tenths or tithes, and the sacrifice of animals in passing through death into new and first-born life; all which belong also to the seventh day of creation, and, in short, to every transition line of one, four, seven, ten. All fruits, or sum-substance of plants, and all animals are, therefore, in him, and are given to him; one tree being forbidden to eat of, the tree of knowledge of good and evil. All this is creation work, a dawn to mid-day season of days, a spring and summer season of seasons, to man's nadir-zenith point and position, where there is no parallax in his being or having being towards his heaven and his God.

Man is here at the level of manhood self-action in self-preservation and self-propagation, in all relations. Hitherto the creative work has been that of production, in let there be, let bring forth, and let us make; in which work the outer at every point is absorbed, in sum-substance, into the new formation produced at that point; there being a triad sum-substance absorbed at every fourth point, and a triad of triads so absorbed at every seventh point, into one head sum triad into one tenth point, as in the head into the one point cerebellum; all under eleventh and twelfth Father-Son Spirit, into the produced one all-man, now arrived at maturity. Now and here, the same creative work is to be carried on as that of reproduction and continuous repetition, in one model of one all-man Adam, formed and ever being formed of the dust of the earth, or of all the elements of all things from the simplest to the most compound and complex; in natural gradations and relations of individuals and combinations of formations; each after its kind, and all in one in the image of God and after His likeness. Each being, from the most single and simple to the highest composition and combination, has a body and head of some three in one form of outer and lower, of inner and higher, and of inmost and highest, being, in creative contact with the universal Spirit. The whole is one body under man, as one head, in Christ Father-Son Spirit. In the most comprehensive sense, man is one all-man, through all duration; but this is, in to and fro nature of things, divided into Aeons, or ages and eras; and each of these has a head man Adam as part of the whole all-man line of patriarchal periods. The gradation of these Aeonic heads is into dynasties, as from Adam as Son of God to Noah and the Deluge, under Adam as lower part of himself as all-man; from Noah to Christ, under Abraham; and from Christ as Head, or three into one, to the making all things new. Under these are period-men as given in Christ's genealogical table; each being the only begotten such son of his predecessor. Under each such head the beings of nature are in gradation outwards and downwards as given in these days of creation; which gradation of creations in all relations, is ever being carried on in ending-beginning, Father-Son Spirit creative course of productions, as lower all-part; then in ever begetting reproduction course, as mid all-part; and both into one sum-substance heads in Aeonic onward course of age of ages.

Adam's sleep is the all passing out through the tenth point all sum, as the all-passing out through the first point; the one into begetting mode of production, as the other into the creative mode. Force forms an Om in all motion like itself. So man makes an Om, a woman, out of and like himself. The man and woman are the Spirit's sum-Om in the whole of the creations and creatures, and now they are His Om in begetting and reproductive work in all gradations in man and nature. Eve is the mother of all living. Thus she is taken out of the man, and is, therefore, called woman; thus she is the mother of all living, and is, therefore, called Eve; and thus, therefore, shall a man leave his father and mother, and shall cleave to his wife, and they shall be one flesh.

And they were both naked, the man and his wife, and they were not ashamed. It has been seen that the action of the muscular walls of the blood-vessels is mainly regulated by the branches of the sympathetic nerves, which are distributed to the walls of those vessels. Hence, when, as under fear, those nerves cause the muscular coat to contract, the quantity of blood flowing into the vessel is thus reduced, and the result is pallor. But when, as under the influence of anything causing shame, the sympathetic system is so affected that the blood vessels distend or dilate, the quantity of blood fills them, and the part to which they are distributed indicate the effect in blushing. Here the condition of the man and woman is prior to the knowledge of good and evil, which could, from without or from the brain, or from any single cause or concurrent causes, influence the nerves so as to actuate the blood vessels. The man and woman Om in coming up from the original creative point, as inmost of out-branching creations, and as so in each creation and creature, has those outer creations and creatures for covering and absorbed means of onward growth, somewhat like a child in the womb, till now come forth as nature's naked child in the sum-substance of the creatures and creations. Here also man is in his lower born part of three in one all-man form; as Ham is the lower of Ham, Shem, and Japhet. Ham in his congenial regions of the world is generally naked up to puberty, and partially thereafter, and is not ashamed. Born out of the womb of nature's place, position, and processes of creation, as an infant out of its mother's womb, man is naked until clothed in the articles of clothing furnished by, and suited to, the providence of his new condition and circumstances. The main point of implication is the transition condition of nature's creation and childhood, as to any creation, in passing from the comparatively passive and irresponsible period of existence to full development, formal maturity, and responsible manhood; all in peculiar relation to the reproduction and redistribution of created beings, or the external and open, as well as the internal and hidden, ways of preservation and propagation of them, after their kind, in time and space. The Garden into which they are put is an Omic grove, the outward, visible, and summary form of the original and typical Om of all forms and processes of creation with the Spirit, in the secret and sacred source of all being and all wellbeing. And out of the ground made Jehovah God to grow every tree that is pleasant to the sight, and good for food; the tree of life also, in the midst of the Garden, and the tree of knowledge of good and evil. The universal tree form of all creations and manifestations lies at the foundation of all forms of religion, and of all forms of existence. At the sea-river grove of Eridhu, in Chaldea, it was symbolically held that there had sprung up there, in a pure and sacred place, a black pine, with living roots of lustrous crystals, extending downwards into the deep unseen, and towards the centre of the Omic earth, having a creative connection with an all fountain-head grove, never penetrated and never seen by man, yet everywhere appearing in inward and outward representations formed in its image, and after its likeness. It is the sum-emblem of the Spirit's universal manner of work in Christ as the universal manifestation of the absolute and the relative, and of the absolute in the relative. The sea-river is the out-flowing of the Spirit in all gradations of beings. The crystal roots denote the Spirit in all elements and all kinds of life, in all ramifications and relations in all existences. The deep unseen and centre of the Omic earth symbolise the zero-shaped passage of the Spirit's issues. And the mysterious grove beyond all created ken is the eternal and all sum-source of the relative in the absolute, of all types and all potential and possible existence in the absolute manifested in the relative. The black pine represents the Omic and Aeonic midline in everything; black, because unseen, and because it is the all Omic one, the Spirit's all creative, productive and begetting rod, Christ the Father-Son creative and redemptive mid-line All in All. Hence pine wood was much used among the Ancients in charms and conjurations against all evil and untoward influences. Its very shadow was held sacred, wholesome, and effective in putting away all evil as the all shadow of all good. It is the Spirit's eternal and universal life-source and all-heal sanitation. In gradation inwards man's fruit trees symbolise his means and ways of food and seed for preservation and propagation. The same gradation obtains also in animals inwards from beasts and birds of prey, reaching to man's inmost soul and spirit, and ultimately to the Divine Spirit in the Father-Son.

CHAPTER III.

It is known that molecules, such as the bacteria, increase by a process of endogenous division, till they form short staff-shaped filaments; that by the same process they increase still farther into long filamentous bodies, when they get the name, vibrios; and that both forms, the bacteria and vibrios, exhibit a serpentine or vibratile movement in the fluid or infusion in which they live. The serpentine form of being and action of force, in both body and mind, has always been taken as the sum-emblem of the mid-line in preservation and propagation in all relations of all beings. Nothing can be made and nothing can exist without a mid-line; and no system, no vesicle, no passage, part, or particle of anything or in anything can be without a mid-line. The digestive canal has its mid-line passage, and everywhere in its circular and longitudinal wall; and so it is in the intestinal canal. It is so in all the blood vessels, as the heart, with its ventricles and auricles, the aorta, arteries, veins, and cells, and not less in the capillaries, out to the epidermis, and through each hair over the body. So it is in the nervous system, with its brain, spinal cord, and senses; and equally so in the respiratory system. And so is it in the seminal system, forming into its diverticulum of lateral tube, with caecal, or cupid-blind, one extremity, and springing from the side of the general digestive system, with which it forms into one common tubular outlet or passage, as representative of all systems, forming into one ending-beginning and dying-living process of preservation and propagation, as to the whole body and all bodies. At every point in and over the whole body the dead refuse is being separated from the living matter; so that every point, in form and action, is a dying-living point. Man's breath is in his nostrils, as the passage of life and death; and so it is in every pore and passage. The open passage of the urine, or dead sea water, is the passage of the semen, as water of life. There is no new creation or creature, no renewal of being, no recommencement of work or process, no real begetting, without or short of going down to the Leucadian rock and the waters of life of the secret Om and its summary transition passage. Through all summary or universal death is the only way to all summary or universal life, and the passage is ever as into new earth and heaven, through an ending-beginning of, in the beginning God created the heaven and the earth, through an ending-beginning of Eden Garden Om, in the image and after the likeness of the original all prototype, through which the absolute is being ever sacrificed into putting off the all old and putting on the all new relative. By the mysterious combinations and working of these zeros and ones, cells and radicles, testes and rods, or Omic mid-lines, every formation is produced in antitypal image and likeness of the one original prototype. There exists only one original and universal type of all things; and all beings are outgrowths in natural gradations of that all prototypal one. These outgrowths, all and each, enlarge and diminish in to and fro, dilating and contracting as cells and their walls do, open and close as buds do, branch out to an equatorial circle, and form into an Omic cap top as the earth, cones, and all else do. So does the human body grow in one tree form, diminutively summarised and represented in the tree of life in the cerebellum. The most original and universal idea is the to and fro form and motion, or action, of force in Omic one and zero being. This to and fro motion is upwards and downwards, as in a straight line, rod, staff, or stem; also in every direction outwards and inwards between the centre and the circumference at every point in the line, rod, staff, stem, trunk, and all else. This gives a tree to have branches in all directions, varying in ways already noticed. One variation in the human body is, that the forces are brought to converge and meet at certain points to form parts and appendages, as limbs and branches within and without, into one representative of things and all systems of things into one tree body of upright trunk and left and right limbs. It is the only possible form for satisfying the requisitions and conditions, the intentions and results, of crucifixion. Thus all are one tree of life, ever passing through death into life, ever dying but never dead, ever putting off and away its oldness in ever becoming new. All to and fro force has its ending-beginning extremities, its midline, and centre points, and its Omic circles and layers; implying all relations, gradations, and possibilities of variation; yet all in gradation of types and unities, from all one and its all nothing to all one and its all nothing. Force in motion is active and passing into acquiring, possessing, and occupying new space, new land, a God-promised land. The all-sum Garden is creation's ending-beginning point of ever passing into being fruitful, into multiplying, and into replenishing the earth, as also in subduing and occupying it. It means progression through antagonism, a wandering to and fro, a going down into, and an exodus out of Egypt; a war with the Kings, in Trojan war fashion; and a course of building cities along the world's midline seats of empire.

6. The midline is one, in all round and longwise extended form. It is two, with a sum of two and fro force to the left, and another to the right; hence is increase by fission. It is in waving motion into shoulder points; and hence increase is by gemmation. It is in layers; and so increase is by encystation. It is in Aeonic succession, and thus increase is by genealogical begettings. Be the form of increase whatever it may, it is founded on its previous mode and form of creation; and all have their root types and beings in the original Om. This original Om, through the deep sleep outbringing of it, is taken in its external world form in the field sum outer layer of things, then in the Eden sum mid layer,

and thereafter in the Garden sum inner layer. This gradation corresponds to that of physical formations as outer, the plants as mid beings, and the animals as inner. Both gradations are one; and man and woman are put therein, as to outward condition and circumstances, and in personal formation of personal sum of things. Eden is in respect to place as Eve is in respect to person. Abba, Abha, Ava, into Java, or Father-Son Jehovah, is the Father of all living. Under this the man name is taken from Abba or Abha into Adam or Adhamh (as sounded in Hebrew and Gaelic), as being, under Jehovah God, the Father of all living. The fifth letter sound in the English alphabet is in Hebrew the outer of the first (Aleph), as in El (God). So Eden is the outer of the man as to place; and the two make Adam-Eden, or man-place, father of all. Eve is Ebha, as feminine of Adhamh, Abha, or Jabha. With Eden, or Edhin, she makes Eve-Eden, the woman-place mother of all living; and with Adam, she makes Adam-Eve, the man-woman father-mother of all living.

Of all living beings the serpent of the to and fro force, motion, and desire is the most subtle, artful, original, and universal. With it, and in its action, one goes out to the outmost and down to the lowest level of begetting reproduction. All living beings, as one all-man, act as in one Garden-Eden-field world, as the original all Om of creation, brought forth into the external world for all living thus to act therein in this universal begetting reproduction. The organ and act of the begetting process are of the serpentine to and fro form and meaning. It is in the image, and after the likeness of the Jah, Adhamh, Ebh, and Edhen mid-line tree of life and tree of knowledge of good and evil. It is from the level of consciousness and to and fro subject and object, up to the highest light of intellect and highest flight of imagination. Brahmans and Buddhists, Hebrews and Greeks, and the Ancients everywhere have held that animal desire, soul-desire (in Socio-moral sense), and imagination, into selfishness, are the three in one serpent of the world, that they are naturally and necessarily good, but that, when unnatural and selfish, they are evil, and must be renewed. The work of the Garden is to keep it and dress it, renew it, improve it, and preserve it; all which can be done only by begetting, or reproducing and regenerating, and so preserving everything after its kind. The order of doing so is by beginning at the outmost and lowest points, the real change being from the lowest and inmost to the outmost and highest.

The work can be done only by the all-father one and the all-mother one, the Serpent and Eve—the Serpent here taking the place of God in all respects. It has been seen that, in the nature and order of action, the one is before the Om; and, therefore, the serpent is the leading actor in the process of action in and through which creation is passing into begetting, production into reproduction, involuntary and irresponsible, into voluntary and responsible action. It is put in to and fro question and answer, denial and affirmation, ignorance and knowledge, untruth and truth, wrong and right, darkness and light, death and life, nothing and all, no God and all being gods, and all possible implications of all-sum of all things, ever passing from what they are in, ever passing into what they are about to be. All the absolute and all the relative, all actuality and all possibility, all any way, every way, and otherwise, must be and are implied and included. It means the all-sum of all good and all evil; the passing of the all very good through all evil into all good, through all darkness and death into all light and life, through all Omic nothing into being as gods; all in Omic and Aconic summary of gradations and relations. It comprises three triads of sum-substance parts, each and all as one originating from, and terminating in God, the All in all.

First, let there be passes into, let bring forth; both in sum-substance pass into, let us make man in our image, and after our likeness, which in all sum-substance is being as gods; or, in the inmost and highest possible sense, the whole sum-substance is God, the beginning and the end, the first and the last, the ever ending-beginning All. Then, the involuntary, as in nature and the inferior animals and in man, passes into the spontaneous and voluntary in man, and it is difficult to say how far down in the scale of creation; and the voluntary further becomes comparatively supreme in man, under God and terminating in Him, as well as originating from Him. Again, all things are given to man in their natural gradation, the earth to dwell in, to cultivate it, and to live on its yield and increase; the trees, or all plant life, the animals, or all animal life—all these given to him, made subject to him, and in all sum-substance in him; and he, with the woman, in one corporate humanity, put into the world of three in one field, Eden Garden as sum-total under God, and terminating and originating in God. Thus each one, each summary, and all, form out of, and again form into, a three in one whole being of all-man Son of God. Motion implies change. Force and all things are constantly passing through change, from what takes place in the smallest particle to the greatest and highest transition change that ever takes place in the successions of the age of ages. There seems to be nothing in the creation, course, and government of the world more mysterious or more difficult of understanding than the lines of transition passage and change. They are, in a peculiar way, creative lines in the Spirit's work, in which the mode of His operation is unknown. He is ever creative at every point; but, at Aconic intervals, one, four, seven, ten, lines occur and serve as special ending beginning creative passages of changes as through death into renewed life. An instance of these changes is in the involuntary passing into the voluntary, in gradation up to man's free will in its mysterious relation to causation, human responsibility, and divine sovereignty. What can be understood respecting this matter may be more easily perceived in the light of the facts and correlations of things rather than from any formal statement that can be made regarding it. In the strictest, inmost, and highest sense, the Spirit is all sum being ; and the incidental all sum being, as to all created beings and peculiarly as to these transition changes, is summed up into the serpent representation. All incidental implications as to being and action, creatural free will and free yet responsible action, are here contained in this serpent sum total, and are treated clearly and concisely, formally and fully, in the Epistle to the Romans. The sum of creation's transition lines is implied in this all sum transition into the creative begetting process specially spoken of from the Garden to the Deluge. The righting, remedy, and renewal of things are in the omnipresent Father-Son mid-line and living-purifying water and blood, or the Spirit in Father-Son Jehovah God. The species of animal meant by the serpent as an emblem of the all-parts action is supposed to have been of the now extinct order of fish-bird-reptiles, the Ichthyopterygia (ichthus, a fish, and.pternx, a wing), also called Ichthyosauria (ichthus, and saura, a lizard). Some of this order were in shape of body and limbs, partly fish, partly reptile, and partly bat-like ; and were fitted for sea and air and earth modes of life. The Deinosaur, found in fossil remains in the oolitic and cretaceous rocks, is said to have been not less than sixty or seventy feet in length. This agrees with the Chaldean representations in tripartite emblem of the human body as a summary of creation and begetting production ; the lower part being fish-iike, the middle part human with a terrestrial animal to the left and to the right, and the head human with the face partly bird like. The Biblical representations of the same will be found farther on. Here the representation is in tripartite one sum of the Spirit's way of creation work passing through the all-sum of the incidental shadow of all (as to creation), as through one sum transition passage into the begetting or reproductive process. What is meant by the serpent being the most subtle is the lowest and nearest ending form and nature of the creation mode of production, as in the transition through which each and all pass, to the lowest and nearest beginning form and nature of the begetting mode. It is the most subtle in being the all-sum transition line of the ending-beginning of the one mode into the other, on all levels, and in all parts and points. In its lowest and outmost, inmost and highest, sense and form, it is the relative non-being of all being and all having being. It is the denying and opposing mimic and murderer of whatever is, the first, last, and all enemy. Everything has its sum-total personality ; and this gives it to have its personality, as father of lies, and all implied relations. Its assuming and presuming existence has the pride of being absolute, eternal, and universal, ever in heaven and falling from heaven, ever destroying, being destroyed, and self-destroyed, but ever in endless incidental existence, power, and rule, in heaven, earth, and sheol. It is the seven Maskim, the seven evil spirits, the foes of heaven, and earth, and great Ea. But there is one higher than the highest of them, the eternally begotten Son.

Whatever is done through the secondary sense of anything is originated through, and in creative and productive relation to the original presence, power, and action, of the Spirit, who is really the underlying and all-sum of both forms. These are much the same as the covenant of grace and the covenant of works; the one being the original, inmost, and underlying, and peculiarly related to let there be; the other being more in the actual working out of things, and more related to let produce. Again the one, that of grace, is more related to all things being freely given in and to man, as his being, his faculties and his freedom, his power, possessions, promises, and prospects, and all; the other being more related to his exercising and occupying all things in accordance with, and fulfilment of, the divine will. What is given to man is a matter both of work and trust, the preservation, propagation, and improvement of all things as they are already made. Whatever he is or can do is all of grace, even his very being. The sum of what God is in him, to him, and through him, and all things is charity; and the sum of what he and all are or can be in right being, and having being is charity; what Buddha would call universal charity. He is to hope in God and all good. Divine grace and true faith are specially related to his mid-line, inmost, and highest being. By both in mid-line Christ he is to do all; all as a work of faith, patience of hope, and labour of love. At every stage of force, form, and function, in all habits, laws, and customs, there is a thou shalt not eat thereof, thou shalt not do anything but agreeably to the powers that be. Against anyone acting otherwise, there is the Jewish ultimatum of, we have a law that he ought to die. In the higher part of the outer line in nature, in the Bible, and in human society, there is always found a self-deified order of titans in power, possession, and pretensions, whose sum-substance is laid up for absorption through transition changes into the ever new order of things. This sum-substance is always carried in from the titan shoulder point and on through the transition line into the new order and growth. The serpent does not use the double appellation, Lord God, in speaking of God, but simply God, the Elohim as the outer of the full form of Jehovah God, or Lord God. Elohim, as outer to Jehovah, is in the inmost, highest, and most essential sense, the tree of knowledge of good and evil, the tree of all divine manifestations in all gradations and formations of beings, in all laws and relations, order, and course of events, in the sense and way in which the invisible things of God are ever being made known in the things that are made, as elsewhere summed into His eternal power and Godhead. Jehovah, as in all respects inner to Elohim, is in all respects the tree of life to all this. At the end of each season the sap of plants descends, the shoots cease to grow, and the buds close to an Om shape. In the beginning of next season the sap ascends from the lowest level, forming as it were a new tree, along the trunk and branches and to the buds, which last re-open with new ones at the shoulder point in the side of each. The shoot point is thus made an Om (as the woman out of Adam's deep sleep), for the forward mid shoot and for the side ones, making three in one. In animals the ribs, both false and true, do not stretch out, but turn round from the vertebræ towards the front, the true and perfect ones meeting in the sternum, and each pair forming an Om. So Adam, in descending and ascending, as implied in the deep sleep at the Garden time, comes forth in an end-beginning newness with an accompanying Om, called rib, as it comes in rib-circle form, not at either side, but at the begetting grove situation below and in front, often called by the Ancients the south and the east. It is a sum-substance starting of all in a begetting process and renewal, from the beginning, and is, therefore, somewhat similar to what may be seen to obtain in the instance of the honey-bee. In the lower part it is much as in plants; then passes into animal changes and forms; and lastly, comes out in distinct man and woman. The child in the womb goes through all this; a kind of course which accounts for the appetites ordinary or otherwise of females during pregnancy, and obtaining with natural modifications in all beings. The masculine and feminine principles in nature are represented by the serpent and the woman; and these work up and in from the lowest and outmost to the inmost and highest in the all-life Jah; all having been created in God's image now become as gods. All thus move forward in creative and renewing process in every thing to the level of mature development; then in self-preserving and self-propagating condition and action under the highest all-summary in Jehovah-God. The gradation of parts in nature is the same in man and the government of the world. Special resemblances exist between the parts of all things on the same level. The outer and lower in kind is emblematic of its inner and higher, as that of physical nature as to plants, and that of plants as to animals. What is true in the nature and history of the one is emblematic of what is true in the nature and history of the other, as in a tree in respect of animal and man. This kind of emblems in relative and comparative gradations is found in dreams and in the writings of the ancients everywhere. Thus three kinds of trees were found naturally emblematic of the three parts of the one universal tree in nature and man. The apple tree symbolised the lower part of man; the pomegranate, or grain apple tree, symbolised the middle part, or the whole region of the senses summed into the face; the mandrake symbolised the cerebellum summary and Ishtar or Athenè nature of the whole; and the original, inmost, and highest in eternal nature of beings was symbolised by the black pine among the Chaldeans, and gopher wood among the Hebrews. It is possible that the black pine and the gopher wood tree were the same, at anyrate in meaning of symbol.

The eating of the fruit, and the effects of doing so, are in the usual gradation. The tree being good for food is in special relation to the preservation of life or of having being; its being pleasant to the eyes, or the Oms, is in special relation to propagation; and that it is desirable to make wise in the special relation to the inner being of all that goes to constitute the person or thing. The tree of life has more to do with being and let there be; but this tree of knowledge of good and evil has more to do with having being and let produce; and the fruit is the sum-substance of having being and let produce, in summary and highest relation to God Himself in all sense of having being and of let produce. The serpent is the sum-substance of to and fro force, in the character of masculine and feminine, as to substances and laws, in the form, from root to head, of the Om and rod, as full form organ or means of the propagation of being and let there be. Necessarily and essentially the gradation of this is from the lowest entity of being up to God Himself, as is indeed here formally represented; for the serpent is to eat, in this sense of fruit-eating, and through all the days of its life or of existence, dust or the elemental and essential sum-substance of all being in the Father-Son propagation of all being, from the lowest and outmost to the inmost and highest. The Hebrew term for eye is that also for a well of water, and for any closing-opening of any kind or measure; it being applicable to the smallest pore in the human skin, or anything else down the scale of being, as well as up to the open firmament, or the open universe. The true translation or rendering of the term is Oms, or any word of that import. The intercourse is first between the serpent and the Eve-Om, in the sense of the physical and the plant beings, as lower and outer; then it is between Adam-husband and her in the animal and human sense; and again it is in the highest sense summed up into dealing with the Lord God. That the eating thus is forbidden and yet necessary to do or to be done is essential and necessary to the very being, fact, and idea or meaning of the to and fro force and form, being and having being. Not to eat the fruit is stagnation and death, cessation and annihilation of being, and absolute and universal nonbeing, which is self-contradictory, senseless, and impossible. To eat is to do what is forbidden and is also to die; but both to do and to die must be; and through universal eating and dying can universal or any being continue to be and to have being. The to and the fro of being, of force, and of everything forbid each other, yet cannot continue to be without each other. They are in all relations, and imply all relations. They are both competitive and concurrent; they meet and become one in the mid-point and mid-line in everything; they originate with the Spirit as the universal and common cause, and in the same they have their ending-beginning. The Spirit is in essential inbeing and omnipresent contact in and with every person, part, and particle of all beings. He is being ever self-manifested in modes and forms of being, as in the spirit, soul, and substance of beings, in the modes and forms of force and motion in beings, and in the outward modes and forms of appearances, actions, and events in and among beings. The modes and measures of His self-manifestations are modes and measures of modifications of Him. These modifications imply identity and continuity in and through change in kinds, modes, and measures of relative forms and limitations, restrictions, progressions, and antagonisms, and all the known laws of beings. All these imply each its respective duration and manner of being in time and space. Thus there is constant and endless putting off and on of all these modes and measures of modifications of being; each of the two having a law of an eternal nay to the other, yet each mode and measure of modification having its mode and measure of duration, in time and space, alternating under these two eternal nays. The antagonism of these nays is essential and necessary to the being or possibility of any form of being, force, motion, and action, yet it is so as centred and rooted, or in having its Om and rod, in the mid-line and the Spirit. The two nays are, as all things are, in eternal unity and harmony in the Spirit and the mid-line, the Om and rod, and the Father-Son, all being and all having being in all relations and duration.

In manifestations of being there is an out-coming, a let there be, a let produce, and a let us make, in distinct forms, with a law of alternations, of spending and storing of force and energy, in progression through antagonism, in preservation and propagation through change. Let there be, or let there be all, has its nay of let there be nothing; let produce all, of let all be reduced to nothing; let us make all, and all-sum, of all, of let us unmake all to universal nothing. The all-sum nothing is the ultimate all-sum of the line of least resistance, through which all being, and modes and measures of manifestations and modifications of being, travel, or live, move, and have their being. The sum of the nay to being is non-being. But it is through this transition centre and line of non-being that the all-sum rod of being passes into all forms of being. Such centres, or comparative centres, are the Oms, the valves, the transition ending-beginning, or stopping-starting points of all beings; the all centre is the Om of the all-being.

The Elohim of things, as they are, forbids the change implied in eating the fruit; the all-change of the whole Elohim form of all things being put off in the whole Elohim-being passing through a begetting or new-birth process, from the lowest and outmost to the highest and inmost; the all change of death to the all-oldnesses and renewed life in and to the all-newnesses of things; yet the change of the Spirit's ever putting forth an ever-living and life-giving Jehovah-Elohim being in all things, ever new, and therefore ever naked, but ever being newly-clothed, blessed, and beautified. The change is a new creation, a re-creation, a reproduction, a making again all things new, exactly in the order of the works of the Omic and Aeonic days of creation. In and through the serpent and the woman the work of the one and Om is gone through, as from the beginning to man and Jehovah-God, and in the same order. The whole is being killed and caused to die, and passes through the process into new life ; and the sum-substance of the whole in laws, forms, and all else, passes in the same way into like newness. As being created it is, in whole and every part, naked, but not knowingly till it is known through experience. In the sense of the oldness of the letter, or old Elohim of laws and all else, to eat is sin ; but the Spirit ever putting forth all Jehovah-Elohim being in ever newness, the old Elohim of law and all else is changed into being also put forth in ever newness, and therewith the oldness of law, sin, and death, with all their old implications and accompaniments. The sum-substance of all pass on in the usual three relative layers. The curse is in gradation of consigning all to their respective spheres, positions, functions, doing, and suffering, in the preservative begetting and propagating, from the turning or transition point of manhood to the return of the dust to the dust as it was, and the return of the spirit to God who gave it. The absolute in coming forth into and in the relative, and going back or withdrawing, is the all sum of to and fro form of growth from elemental seed dust and spirit's forthcoming from God to the return to the same, or the eternal one sum ending-beginning of all. Here, from manhood to the complete return, the forthcoming fulness passes on by absorption in the being begotten into the begotten, till the old form or oldness of the fulness is put off; while in sum-substance both the fulness and its form are continued and nothing is lost. The absolute continues in all respects as the absolute, while passing into, and existing and acting in, its sum-Om, the relative. Each sum-stance, in passing on in the mid-line new life, puts off or aside an overlapping father, with the implied grandfather, and great grandfather. The lowest and outmost ending-beginning of the begotten productions are in form and substance nearest to lifeless and dried up, or outhardened, matter, as in the prickles of thorns and thistles, here taken for all such outmost and extreme points in all nature as to man and all formations. The turning here is the Ebal and Gerizzim of the all-man's entering into the actual possession, use, and enjoyment of the land which the Lord God gives, namely, the earth and all things ; this being man himself as the representative sum substance of all under the Lord God ; and, in the highest and inmost sense, man and woman with all as become as gods, and, therefore, the Lord God as all in all. The true and full possession and portion are Christ, Jehovah-Elohim in all sense and respects in Christ, the eternal and universal Spirit in the whole absolute and the whole relative.

In eating the fruit the serpent, as the Omic one, acts with the woman as the Omic feminine, in the involuntary region from the lowest and outmost points as in the physical and plant formations and up to voluntary action in animal life ; then the serpent and the woman in sum-stance and form of the action pass into the region of the voluntary, where the sum stance and form assume the voluntary nature and character, and the act is performed as by man and woman ; and at this point, and on this level, the whole Om, in sense and form, is brought to the utmost and barest nakedness, and of creation work as distinct from begetting work ; and thus must begin with the Spirit and Jehovah Elohim in the begetting sense, as it ever begins and ends, and ends and begins, in the creation work. Both the creation work and the begetting work begin and end, and end and begin, in and with the Spirit and Jehovah Elohim. In knowledge of their nakedness the man and woman, as representing all downwards from the level of not yet including the Lord God in the begetting sense, make and use aprons of fig tree leaves. The fig tree is emblematic of home, homestead, and home life. It is not said whether the leaves used were sear, decayed, and fallen off the tree, or green, fresh, and living. It is implied that the condition of things is at the maturity level of the leaf as outer to the blossom of plants, and the grove-growths on the animal part of the human frame. The plant condition is at the first tenth point fruit for food and leaf for covering, as in creation development, at which further growth, with further flowering and fruit-bearing, will follow in begetting co-existence. Everything is naked in coming out of its Om. There is implied the ever new setting up of house and home conveniences and comforts. Up to this level creation formations were the outer home-form of man in and under Jehovah Elohim ; that form of old home conditions is cast off, as the leaves of the fourth year back of even evergreen trees are cast off, while the new season growth are being produced. Thus two stages in the effect of eating are gone through, namely, the being good for food in the sense of sustaining and developing life, and of seed-forming into maturity for begetting mode of reproduction, all in the involuntary region and condition ; and next, in the opening of the eyes, all the senses, or in all respects of full development. These two are the lower and middle parts ; there being implied the physical, plant, animal, and socio-moral aspects of character, but not the highest sense of intellectual summary. Accordingly it is hearing with the ears, as specially related to the cerebrum, or body and head middle part, that is spoken of as means of coming to deal with the Lord God's voice and person.

There is a gradation of dependence of the lowest and outmost on the next inner and higher, and of each inner and higher on the next, up to God. As to being, life, and action, there is an implied reference in each lower and outer to its higher and inner, in all things physical, plant, animal, social, and moral, in relation to the cerebellum and its intellectual summary, and in it to the Divine Spirit. This is strongly expressed in conscience in referring all things to the Supreme Lawgiver in the intellectual summary and to the Spirit, a matter to be noticed farther on. Now the act is in dealing formally and Omically with Jehovah Elohim, in which the man and woman come into the intellectual summary development, and become as gods. At this point they are in bare nakedness of full Omic development and condition for all begetting mode of production. Here is the eternal fact of what is elsewhere expressly said, thy Maker is thy Husband, and of the truth and reality of becoming as gods. In truth and reality Jehovah Elohim is the inmost being in all beings. In a good sense the Serpent and the woman are the full-form Om with the Spirit in the Jehovah Elohim creative and begetting work ; and it is this which gives it to be, in the bad sense, the sum or personal evil in representative character. This appears farther in the statement concerning the relative being and begetting in the preservation, propagation, and relations of all persons and things.

Each being has its kind and form, place and function, assigned to it by the nature and necessity of the essential mode of existence and the all disposing will of Jehovah Elohim. The curse, or destiny, of the serpent is in being consigned to moving on its belly, on the universal Om, in all gradation of production, and in eating dust, or in forming, emitting, and issuing elemental seed of all being in creative and begetting action. The gradation in the serpent representation, taken outwards and downwards, is, first, the necessary mid-line of to and fro action ; then the second-self, or outer and lower nature and form of the one whole to and fro meaning and action; and, lastly, this incidental second or outer and lower side being in an incidental and necessary evasion of, and kind of opposition to, the Spirit's all gradation of inner and higher sense, and ultimately to itself into sum-total of ever suicidal working in reducing all beings into nothing. In doing all this, it serves in ever forming a gradation of a necessary line of least resistance, and so forming an all-suitable and all-easy Omic belly, or couch, and transition lines, for all being. In this it has its destiny under all cattle, and under every beast of the field, a destiny of lower and outer, behind and beyond all substance and mode and law of being ; and all that is true of it, is true of it all the days of its life of incidental killing and self-killing, yet indirectly and necessarily serving in all creative and begetting action among all being. It belongs to all being, and all beings belong to it. In its full personal form it ever and correctly says to Jesus, as in speaking of all the kingdoms of the world, all these are mine, and I will give them to whomsoever I will. Jesus does not deny it ; but He commands him to keep to his destiny of province, place, and position, relations and functions—of, behind Me Satan. In this behind sense Jesus never personally nor in His disciples so much as looks behind. Remember Lot's wife. In this sense the Jehovah Elohim, as supreme and inmost in all gradation and relations of being and having being, in all creative and preservative, begetting and propagating action, puts difference and opposition, antagonism and enmity, between the Serpent and the woman, between her seed and his seed. Thus the Om and rod in the good sense is upper and inner to the same in the bad sense; and this is true in all creative and begetting seed, in respect to all being from the highest to the lowest; the sum-seed, on the one hand, being Jesus, and, on the other hand, being Satan. And thus the woman's seed, as upper and inner, ever and in all gradation downwards and outwards, bruises the head of the serpent's seed; and the serpent's seed, as lower and outer, or in the behind sense, and in the same gradation, bruises the heel of the woman's seed. The tripartite gradation is, first, in the cattle as symbolic of the higher in man, and domestic and clean animals among the inferior creatures; then, beasts of the field as to the middle part in man, and all beasts between the domestic animal and the creeping things; and thirdly, the lower part of man, and the creeping things of the external world, down to the lowest being (Gen. 27).

The destiny of the woman is in the usual three parts, first, in greatly multiplying her sorrow and conception, sorrow all incidental to the turning-point and changes of passing from creation's full development into the sphere, condition, action, and declining life of the begetting side of every being's course of existence, and of her as the one whole feminine or mother of all living side; second, in the same side of bringing forth children; and thirdly, in her desire being to her husband, all into the three in one, or fourth point sum, of being ruled over by her husband, a ruling of being upper and inner in all respects, as the one is to the zero form. Man's destiny is the whole summary and is also in three parts, first, in relation to the ground, as the lower part of all in himself, as simple man and all-man, the forbidden eating being put into the form of expression of thou shalt eat it all the days of thy life. Then for the second or middle part, it is the cultivated ground or earth, tilled into bringing forth, and constantly in need of continued cultivation and improvement; which condition, at best, will have its incidental declining, wild, and bad side of running out to the outer condition symbolised by thorns and thistles. The third, or head, part is put in the words, sweat of thy face, which is the summary ending-beginning and, therefore, followed by, till thou return to the ground, for out of it thou wast taken; for dust thou art, and unto dust shalt thou return. In the highest sense of man's return it is that of the spirit to the Spirit, to God who gave it.

Adam gave names to the animals in their relations in himself and outwardly to himself. He now calls the name of his wife,

Eve, because she is the mother of all living, in her relations in him and to him. The inner meaning of creative power and work is from the same source and of the same nature as in the begetting mode of production. It is that of the Divine Spirit in the Jehovah Elohim Father-Son sense. But the change of passing from the creative proper to the begetting proper is such that the latter is, in a sense, the sum-brother and son of the other as sum-brother and father. Adam is first the sum-man of creation; but, by passing into the begetting sense, he becomes, in his begetting sense, the son of his creation sense. Eve, as a term and in meaning, is related to Abba or Abha, to Adam or adhamh, and to avah or ovah in the name Jehovah. As the feminine, in form and meaning, she is the original and virginal sister wife of these, and the mother of all living. All this is the ending-beginning transition line passage into the begetting mode of reproduction. What is said is true in some way and measure of everything after its kind.

Unto Adam also and to his wife did the Lord God make coats of skins, and clothed them. The gradation as to the nakedness and its covering is in the usual three parts, first, when it is said that they were both naked, the man and his wife, and were not ashamed; then on eating the fruit, when it is said that the eyes of them both were opened, and they knew that they were naked, and they sewed fig leaves together, and made themselves aprons; and thirdly, when the Lord God is spoken of as having made coats of skins, and clothed them. The first is under let there be, when they are as newly born out of the creative region into the begetting region, and they knew not the act or the fact of the change, or their consequent state. The second is under let produce, which has always the original, virginal, and essential let there be for its inner and father-brother and mother-sister; while itself is the outer son-brother growth and covering. This let produce outer growth and covering of the internal eternal and unchangeable let there be, has its creation gradations from the beginning up to the Garden summary, and is taken as sum-substance in the forbidden but to be eaten fruit. This sum-substance fruit is the Omic form of things like the all-Om with the Spirit at the beginning. It contains the sum of creation work up to the eating of it, including even the three in one sum of the eaters; so that the eating is the all self-eating and the all else eating. This is the universal sacrifice of eating all else and all one self, or the universal Om eating itself, and so ever reducing all to the original all-nothing-nothing-all, or ending-beginning, state with the spirit; out of which all are forever reappearing, through eternal and universal death into eternal and universal life.

The outer all of let produce is the fig tree home of the let there be; and the fig leaves are the representative clothing forms of the formations of the region of the let produce, such as the leaves of plants, the scales and skin-forms of fishes, and the feathers of birds, all included in the Chaldean representation of the all-man's lower part. This let produce covering is in modified and overlapping sense and form continued up, with the sum-substance of the all lower part, in and on the middle part, and thirdly summarised into the face and cerebrum, indicated in the Chaldean representation by the nose being formed like the beak of a bird. In all this let produce sense of gradation and modifications, the man and woman sewed fig leaves together, and made themselves aprons ; aprons because the gradation of modifications of all things is more distinct, open, and full, in the front than in the back, and contains all the summary Oms, groves, and openings, while the back is more of the erect one or rod form with its essential head in the cerebellum. Taking the whole body as one Omic form, it moves, in all action and change, in and through the means of all that it is, and has, in its front side ; this being the serpent destiny of walking, or moving in, all the (begetting) days of its life, and being also the absolute's all moving in all having being in and through the relative, as belly, front, or mode and means of manifestations. The sum-substance part of the body is the cerebellum and the back, under and in relation to which all the rest live and act ; and is the highest to cover the rest, and to represent the Lord God in all relations to the rest. Along it is the tree of life, the diverticulum to which is the tree of knowledge of good and evil. Through it lies the let there be in relation to the rest as the let produce, as a whole and each part and particles. Thus the Lord God gives being to, and makes coverings, or skins, to, the all man and woman, including all beings. As the whole relative is the means, or skins, in which the whole absolute dwells in having being, the Lord God in the things that are made ; so the man and woman are in their outer forms of sense region and means of appearing and having being. As the creation works culminate and are summed into man-woman as made in the image of God ; so the man-woman development for begetting mode of production is in skins, coverings, and manifestative means of having being, like those of the Lord God Himself, and made for them alike as for Himself.

Man as rational recognises the truth of a God, divine things, and moral actions. The gradation in his powers is the same as in the divine ways of work within and without. Empirical knowledge is much as to things in the mass. It partly involves instinct and sensation, and partly the beginnings of the scientific proper. Instinct and intuition lie nearest to consciousness. The distinguishing characteristics of science are truth and generality ; truths partly separated and partly integrated, and generalisations graduated. It passes into the philosophical in unified and highest generality. It rests on phenomena discovered by the senses. It postulates uniformity, and is excluded whenever it can be denied, but compels conviction within the range of its own postulate. All truths are united by ties and bonds, the number and intricacies of which man cannot fully trace.

7. The next part higher is the sphere of reason, corresponding to the sun light opening up of things at the fourth day of creation. The senses make known that particular or single things exist, but do not show them as distinct from the general. Reason, as the faculty of relations or the power of conceptual thought, sees the universal in the particular—particular because partaking in the general idea. The general issues in the particular. Philosophy may be said to be the science of concepts. Unity and diversity combined give the concept. The binding force, or Logos, is the main attribute of reason; or reason and speech are the Logos in this form of things. Sensation and science co-operate, subserve, and are included in reason. Reason finds formations and combinations among the objects presented to it, sees them in their relations to each other as particular and general, parts and wholes; and makes new formations in certain relations after the manner of those in nature, both the formations of it and of nature being alike and confirmatory of each other. Within its sphere are analysis and synthesis, forms of deduction, proportion, equation, and redistributions. It finds three in one, or into a fourth, everywhere, and it makes use and application of the same in such ways as in the Syllogism and analogy. It finds in the whole gradation of things and of the knowledge of things the fact that the lower or preceding is substantially carried forward into and continued in the higher and succeeding, and also that the analogy of things and of its own formations exhibit the same. A higher form of knowledge is thus foreshadowed, indicated, predicted, and reasonably to be expected; a kind of knowledge consistent with reason and with all forms of knowledge, though in some respects higher than and different from those forms prior and antecedent to it. It, and indeed all things and all knowledge, say that it is the one God, the Three in One, that is manifested in all; at whatever time and in whatever manner and measure within the range of creatural ken. But what kind of knowledge that higher one is, reason cannot define; no logical definition can be given of it, either before or after man attains to it, only reason naturally agrees with it, and cannot in the nature of things really contradict it. The comparative value of general propositions relates to the exercise of reason. Generalisation is the product of abstraction; abstraction consists in dropping out of sight a certain number of particular facts and constructing a formula which will embrace the remainder; and the comparative value of general propositions turns on the relative importance of the particular facts selected and on those rejected. Man finds not only the creatures around him on earth by the law and order of their creation distinguished into orders, groups, classes, and so on, but the heavenly bodies also in mighty systems, groups, and clusters, existing and moving in orderly relations and arrangements, making up one boundless, wisely regulated, controlled, and conducted whole; and, endowed with reason, he is fitted and led within a limited sphere to imitate the action and rule of the infinitely wise Creator and Ruler of All.

Within the same sphere is the exercise of conscience, a subject surrounded with many difficulties and diversity of opinions. It should be borne in mind that there is not, and that seemingly there cannot be, any creature or capacity that is only or wholly passive, at any time or in any condition or circumstances. Active and passive are predicable of everything. From the very beginning there seems to be nothing that is absolutely or wholly new. The substance, qualities, and laws of everything are traceable through the past to the beginning and its relations to the absolute. The law of continuity in these respects is unbroken and unchanged, even through the special points of creative energy, as in one, four, seven, ten. Conscience, in the first view and form of it, is original and simple; but within the sphere opened up for the exercise of it, of reason, and of free will, it is actively and passively associated with reason, free will, and social feelings, affections, and emotions. It has its relations, interactions, and influences with all that is within and without; so much so that it, like every other capacity, is in a sense itself opened up into an apparently complex form and character. Under the law of cause and effect, and of the active and passive, it influences and is influenced, acts and is acted upon, just like any other power or faculty. It presupposes and is dependent on intellectual light and relations, as these are presupposed by justice, and moral and physical freedom. In social life and action the truth of the greatest generality is to conscience as it is in physical and intellectual relations to reason. Intellect perceives the truth; conscience acts it out in the social relations and activities of the living agent. It has its intuition and instinct and exercise as to what is and what ought to be; what man's duty is to himself, to others, and to God, or to nature, to man, and to God, all according to the universal rule of justice and true freedom. Its rule of utility and pleasure is in truth and justice. Intellect, light, truth are, to the first element in God's image, knowledge; as conscience, life, and practical knowledge, are to the second, righteousness. These before being opened up and in being again combined form and manifest the third element, holiness: and the three are what the will, or the person, ought to be. The term image seems to mean the divine archetypal idea, and first form and measure of all things, in a higher, more inward, and more essential sense than the term likeness; the former seems to mean the more spiritual and invisible, and the latter the visible and corporeal. This is man as created, re-created, renewed, or re-made. To be so is man's duty to God, to himself, and to all others. This has the sanction of the rule, or law, or necessities of man's being, of man as an individual, and as a part or whole of human existence, and, above all, of God in whom he lives, moves, and has his being. Without it there can be no proper ground for self-respect, for the respect of others, or for that of God; nor can there be any approvable action or conduct. The essential meaning and order of the three Christian graces, faith, hope, and love, correspond with this.

Man is meant to be in sympathy with God in all the moving power and character of His creative and governing purpose, with a believing, righteous, and loving soul. In truth, none can discern the relations of things without entering into the forces and qualities which really constitute these relations; and none can enter into these forces without sharing the divine impulse which has constituted the universe, without entering into the principles of the tie that bind them together. To discern human life implies entering into the ties which bind men together. No man can make progress in the possession of truth without making progress in the love and righteous practice of it; and he cannot make the latter progress without also making progress in the possession of truth. The sense and action of conscience are founded on that which constitutes its underlying and unchanging element of natural and eternal justice and freedom. The straight line in which man is absolutely bound to be just, is also the line in which he is absolutely free to be just; the being bound and the being free are both together essential to responsibility. To this in its essential and personal form and meaning the voice and verdict of conscience refer in all things. The law in the moral government within and without is the same; it is the law of the Divine Creator, Ruler, and Judge. To be in favourable relations to this line or level is to be in peace with God and virtually with all; to be in righteous conformity of character and conduct to it is to be in conscious peace; the opposite of that state and conformity implies moral bondage and remorse or dispeace, to be in conflict, or to be out of harmony, with God, with one self, and with all others. Like all things in the relative it is limited, dependent, and incomplete, not supreme or final; and so is the government itself while yet conducted in the relative. In itself it is nothing, but it is all in what God is in it and to it. It is on its way to a greater perfection on a higher level of knowledge, union, action, and enjoyment in this life, that is, in the third stage of seven to ten, and to a complete perfection in a stage and state still higher, towards which the whole work of knowledge, righteousness, and holiness, otherwise of faith, hope, and love, is being omnipotently conducted.

Conscience and moral principles have been from the beginning what they are now. In the Chaldean penitential hymns forgiveness is prayed for as to sins seven times seven in evil or heinousness. One prayer is put in the form of five double lines and two summary lines, meaning the significant twelve; and all have much resemblance in spirit, sense, and form to the psalms of David. Conscience has to do with all social relations and intercourse in all beings, in a rudimentary sense even in the lowest atom, and growing in form, power, and exercise as being grows through all its ascending stages; this is a law common to all things. It implies freedom or justice among all beings in all states and stages, conditions and circumstances, interrelations and interactions; a freedom founded on equality in the sense of the fact of being and of being as such, in the sense of distinct existence, and in the sense of distinct personality; and that equality founded on that which is the one common source, one common underlying element, one common sphere of existence and activity, and one common end; all having one common sanction and binding will in the character and power of the eternal yea of truth and the eternal ought, must, and shall be of the law of right and righteousness, from, under, with, and to the one common absolute as Father of the whole relative and all that is in it, our Father and the Father of our Lord Jesus Christ, who combines in Himself, as God-man, the whole absolute and the whole relative. The prototype of all this is in the relation between the Father-Son and the Spirit. Let no one defraud men of the liberty and rights they have in Christ Jesus. The equality of rights is founded on three things; on being from the same common source or Father; on being of the same nature and class of being; and standing on the same level in the scale of being. All of the same race, class, or species, and on the same level, or from the same parent or predecessor, and existing in the same universal relation to the absolute source or Father, the Creator, have absolute equality of original and natural rights. From the first form of created being throughout the whole created universe each one being has in it the substance of its created parent, both and all having an essential, necessary, and causal continuity of existence and dependence on the absolute. It is thus a substantial continuation of its parent or predecessor, of which it is itself the continuation, the identical substance, with the same laws, nature, conditions, and relations, as there is need of such provision. Again, the parent, or predecessor, has also counterpart claims on the descendants, as they owe their existence and their all to the parent in an immediate sense, as the first and original parent stands immediately related to the absolute, and as the whole relative stands in whole and part to the whole absolute. Having the same nature and being of the same class or species imply the same relations and the same general necessities, and therefore the same rights in the whole or each part or individual; also a sameness of rights and duties in relation to all other orders and classes of beings, and as a whole and each to the one absolute. And lastly, as standing on the same level in the same scale of being, the same species has the same field of existence, activities, and advantages, means and opportunities, the same common motives, rules, and ends; as also the same common relations in all that is within and to all that is without. All this holds true throughout the whole sum of being in all relations from the smallest atoms and entities to the highest order of things with the Lamb in the midst of the Throne in Heaven.

Law, morality, conscience, are everywhere. Light and righ are eternal, essential, and universal. Without them there can b no life and no living; with them will, force, motion, act omnipotently with infinite wisdom and infinite righteousness, forming everywhere in part and infinite in whole into the sum of all virtue and all influences, Love, the ending-beginning of all things, God is Love. The eternal yea has its eternal incidental nay, no-yea. The yea has the right to be all and is the positive all in all gradation, but is denied by its incidental nay. To this original point is traceable the struggle between right and wrong and the universal struggle for existence. The fact of the incidental nay is not evil in the sense of being the necessary incidental shadow of the yea or of being; and its apparent struggle for existence is for good in so far as it is the original means of manifestation of the original yea. The couch of yea as all being is nay of non-being; and the gradation from nay or nothing is up to the yea of all being. The nay is of the same import in relation to any part of the gradation as in relation to the one whole gradation of being. It is evil in the sense of want of perfect conformity or any opposition to the yea, whether in part or whole of the gradation of being. The full form of the nay is in being the zero of the whole one absolute. At this point of full absolute and its full zero is the beginning and end of the whole relative. It is the full Om-point of the Spirit's work, out of which and into which is the Father-Son work of creating and begetting all things. There can be no change without the nay, the nothing, or the Om one and zero. Without it there must be absolute stagnation, cessation, and annihilation to non-existence; and even all that is into an absolute and universal nay, which is absurd and impossible. There can be no existence without a measure of the yea and the nay correlated and also related to one common mid-point and mid-line. But the nay or zero cannot stand as outer or lower of any position and substantial being, because it is nothing. The gradation must be in varied forms and measures of being, with the implied and attached nay, zero, or Om. The absolute is self-causing and all-causing. The absolute in self-causing passes itself into the nay, nothing, zero, or non-self. It does so as Father to itself, through that nothing or zero, in becoming its own Son-self. The zero of what it was is mother to the zero of what it is now. The zero is thus caused to change from the former zero as mother, into being the present zero as daughter, with the change-causing absolute as Father, and the former zero as mother. As self-causing the Father passes into being Son in the sense of the Son being from Himself in being from the Father; and in this sense the Son is the true Melchizedek without father and without mother. In the all-causing sense the Son is from the Father or from Himself, but not from the nay or zero; in which sense there is with or in Him no yea and nay, but all yea, as observed in the New Testament. He is the Truth without any nay. And Sarah is thus daughter of the same Father as Abraham, but not of the same mother. It is the Father that implies all relations; and, therefore, gives to be brother and sister. The zero is thus, in relation to the whole absolute, the sum of the whole point or line of least resistance, with and through which it is possible to act in Father-Son creative and begetting sense. The whole and every part of the relative thus comes out and down from the whole absolute, all in the Father-Son and Om of and by the Spirit ; out and down through the gradation of beings to the outmost and lowest, otherwise the inmost and highest, point and level at the all zero, which is at the all absolute, both for ever together making the full Om of one and zero.

As the zero, or Om, is attached to the one, or rod, of all being, the side of least resistance will first be in the direction of the onward force, motion, and action, the absoluteness or closed valve being behind. This is the to and fro, or backwards and forwards, creative and begetting mode of action. It is the one, or rod, coming directly from itself and father-self, implying two and the common underlying spirit, or three in one. The process being eternal implies that the Father and Son are eternally co-existent, while eternally passing on in eternally begetting and being begotten. So in a sense all the ancestors in the eternal genealogical line are co-existent, while eternally passing on in eternally begetting and being begotten. They, as Christ says, are all alive to Him. In this no one dies; nothing is lost. The absolute coming forth on the zero least resistance or Om side, it is implied, as Christ says, that the Father is greater than in this sense than the Son ; the Father is greater than I, or he is greater than Himself ; while the mid-point, or mid-line, or rod of mid-points, holds the real and formal absolute as the balancing point, or line of points, or line of rods. Every three in one form has thus a right, a left, a back, and a front, or one, four, seven, ten, round the mid-line, or round each rod measure, or intervals between every two cells, or valves, or walls, or transition lines. In nature and in the Bible, as well as in the religions of the Ancients, the left is taken as the weaker side, and the front as the begetting side. There must be equality and inequality everywhere, a gradation of inequality regulated by an equalising power according to an equalising standard. So it is in all nature, in all man. in all beings. Otherwise there can be no force or motion, being or having being, creation or begetting. There must be everywhere a to and fro, a going out and coming in, a going down and coming up, a backwards and forwards, an Ishtar being, action, experience, and effect, in all onward course, in all Om and rod sense and form of all being. Throughout there is the zero and serpent, Cain and Judas, side of incidental inequality and imperfection, darkness and death, and nothing; yet all things move on in the eternal Jehovah Elohim Jesus of all being and having being. There is thus a sense in which the universal struggle for existence is right, another in which it becomes wrong. It is absolutely right that the absolute should have all possible claims, because of being the absolute, and because the whole possible relative, incidental or otherwise, owes its existence and its all, even to being so much as an image or incidental shadow of the absolute, to the absolute. From Him, and through Him, and to Him, are all things; all things belong unto Him. Every being has right to the only means essential and suitable to, and provided by nature for, its life and existence; it is its right to itself as well as to God, and its God's provision for it. Every being contains its sum-substance of its parent or predecessor in the same line of the scale of being, and of the beings or substances that have constituted its predecessor and itself; and is dependent on such or the same for its subsistence. There can be no integration of matter without matter to integrate; there can be no living without the means of life. Even self-causation, or self-creation, implies, first, the necessity of being; then the self, or ego, making itself, of itself, for itself, and necessarily existing in eternal continuity of eternal identity. To know anything thoroughly is to know it to its nothing, to its Om of non-being; and this is essential to absolute omniscience, as God knows Himself. To cause anything wholly and thoroughly is to cause it from its non-being; and this is essential to omnipotence, as God is self-cause and all cause.

Unmaking and re-making are necessary to all preservation and propagation; it is a going down to the original Omic nothing and growing up again a new being and having being, as in eating the fruit and in Adam knowing his wife. There is in the nature of every thing a growing up to full development or manhood; then a bearing fruit as in plants, and begetting reproduction as in animals and man. In the fruit there is the sum-substance of the past growth to the full development; then a going down in seed-sowing to the Omic nothing, a dying in the soil, to new life and re-growth to full development. So at manhood there is the begetting by seed going down to the Omic nothing, and there a passing into a new life and being and re-growth to manhood. All this is the Jehovah Elohim, as implied in the nature of things, and in the fruit-bearing and having children, is always represented in Scripture as being from and by God. It also implies being as gods, and doing as God does. In every Omic change there is going to God, and a beginning again out from Him and with Him. At the seventh creative and begetting day or level there is a bringing up and in God's image and likeness, as in Adam and Enoch; and at the tenth point there is a becoming as gods, to begin again as gods or as God Elohim. What is not fit for passing into being with God is passed on in sum-substance, or scapegoat, into a repetition of the creative and begetting course or cycle; this is the true doctrine of transmigration of being.

Every atom of matter, and every entity of force, and every form and measure of motion, are under a species of law and conscience. Every atom has a freedom common to all others; no two a'oms are in absolute touch, they must be equally free. Whether the creatures are fixed and comparatively stationary, as in the case of plants, or have the power of locomotion, the law and conscience of equality of freedom and rights must be kept. Man has all things under him for his use and needs, but he is bound to conform to law and conscience. Conscience is the con, or co, or Om, of every thing and of all things. Its utterances and axioms are may be, should or ought to be, must be, and shall be; they are such in nature, in man, and in God. The gradation of being is its gradation. It is original and co-existent with all things; it is co-eternal and co-extensive with all being; but, as opened out, active, and passive, it has an acquired experience. The Father, or the absolute, may beget the Son; it is an admissible permission, with a background of possibility of existence and action. This passes into ought, must, and shall beget. The Son must be in perfect conformity to the Father and the fulfilment of Him; and must be the same in nature and express image of His person, and be so for ever. The whole is one necessity of existence. Something, God, must exist. Being is a physical, moral, and intellectual necessity in necessary freedom. God must be; and must be all in all. The all good eats up the all evil, in eating up its all self eternally into and in eternal newness of being and of all. There may not, ought not, must not, and shall not, be any change in God as such, or as that which is common to Father-Son, the Spirit. This is the prototype and the sum of conscience in the all being of the absolute and relative. The intellect is first and forever one; but, like Father-Son, subject and object, and other things, it appears and acts in the varied forms of reason, while it retains its unchangeable oneness. It has to do with the fact, the truth, the what is in, into, or within any and every being: it penetrates into thing and brings out the fact, the what is in it. Conscience is the sheath, the manner, the how of all existence, all life, and all activity, the self-consistence of being and of the shadow or image of being, the standard law of the how of all being and having being, and reaching to all that is incidental to being. Sin must be what it is, and must be dealt with as such.

The will is the heart and soul of the forward force in living instinctive and intuitive consciousness. It is enlightened, controlled, and directed by intellect and conscience. It is under the influence of causation and motive both within and without, always in reference to the unchanging and omnipresent Spirit, that constitutes the original, supreme, and universal standard, rule, and causal energy; the exemplification being in the Son, who says, not my will but Thine be done. To say that there must be an external cause apart from the self-cause, the free-will, to begin the change or act, is not true. That which supplies the power is already there, and it can, at least, bestir itself, and begin to move, however imperfect its initial efforts, without any external cause to set it in motion. The will is a very limited force in human nature;

but within narrow limits, it is free to commence a struggle without any external action upon it, and constantly does so. If not, then the whole language which ascribes righteousness and sin, merit and demerit, to human action, is erroneous from beginning to end, and the very essence of the Christian Gospel is false. Man lives, moves, and has his being in God. He and all creatures are for ever under let there be. But he and they have a kind of a derived let there be, a self-causing, and an all-causing within a limited sphere. Still there is a necessary causation, or causal necessity, of the conditions of being and of having being, which must be conformed to, a necessity which is not inconsistent with, antagonistic to, or contradictory of real freedom and responsibility. Form is necessary to thought; but the mind is free to think in form, as in distinct thought, word, and act. It has been already seen that gradation is necessary to being and to having been, as in to and fro, out and in, and other directions of motion and action; and so is it true of the will and its character, conditions, and motives, neither necessity nor freedom being excluded. Necessity and freedom are true of all beings; despite all incapacity and circumstances, culpable or otherwise, of any possible kind or amount. Work to be noble, or acceptable, must be work for good; it is a duty to God, to one self, and to others; and an essential of its fulfilment is that the doer should be left a free agent. In the gradation in which the will is to act it is implied that the moral is above the physical, yet that the physical and the moral are in one harmony; and that the moral agent is to act in that harmony in all imitable and divinely aided respects, as God Himself does.

The ideal of the ethical man requires him to limit his freedom of action to a sphere in which he does not interfere with the freedom of action of others. He is to seek the common weal as much as his own, and, indeed, as an essential part of his own welfare. Peace is both means and end with him; and he founds his life on a more or less complete self-restraint, which is the negation of a selfish and sinful struggle for existence, and self-aggrandisement. Society not only has a moral end; but, in its perfection, social life is embodied morality. The limitation of the mistaken and wrong struggle for existence is one of the highest objects and ends of Society. History teaches that no race multiplies until it does of its own development; no race has had to kill itself down in order to get bread. The will is the one whole mid-line of the three departments of forces, lower, middle, and upper. In Christ it is the fulfilment of all things; the Apollo conformity to the will of Zeus; the I have performed the work the Father gave me to do. It is the mid-line of all right and righteousness, all light and love, all good and glory.

Imagination is image making, the creative faculty, the Omic capacity in creation, preservation, and begetting reproduction. Its full-form is in the original Om, in man's creation in the divine image, in the woman's distinct formation, and in eating the fruit and begetting action. An act of it is necessary in perception; and an act of generalisation is necessary to convert perceptions of the same sort into conceptions. It is necessary to every new formation, in generalisation as well as in perception, in formations of simplicity and complexity, of uniformity and multiformity. It has always its centre point, which is the point of knowledge of good and evil, of going to the Omic nothing and constructing a new formation. Love between the sexes has to do with the connection of the organs of generation to the spinal cord and by it to the brain; and the mental and moral feelings are influenced. There follow animal desire, admiration, and esteem, leading to the selection of the object and convenience of place and means of company and intercourse. The outward bodily changes, corresponding to Omic changes within, at the age of puberty, such as hairs on the chin and cheeks, change of voice with enlargement of the larynx and fall of the voice, and the manly look and action, in man; the growth of hairs on the pubes, the full formed parts, with fatness on the mamma and over the female's whole body, giving it an attractive look, have also to do with it. The motion of the nerve, in man and woman, is mostly by thought, sight, and touch, in all which the imagination holds an essential part and place. In the lower animals the nerve is affected by touch, sight, and the olfactory nerves; and a lower species of imagination holds a place corresponding to that in man's higher one. In truth the nerve and imagination act so in every thing, as both having to do with the beginning and new forming of things. A going back to the absolute and a kind of intercourse with it, as the creative cause, is necessary to the origin of species, and, indeed, to the production of any new formation. In the Spirit's whole work there is something inner and higher than creatural means and action. The highest form of the Spirit's begetting work is in the eternal Father-Son; and in the conception of Jesus there is no man-intervention. It is the bringing in the first begotten into the world, accompanied with, And let all the angels of God worship Him. It is the head sum of what is peculiar in all the patriarchs of Christ's line of genealogy, as may be seen further on.

The full form of the imagination is to be used in the introduction of an age of the highest form of inspiration. In the past it has been that influence in intercourse with the Holy Spirit which rendered the person so influenced infallible in the communication of truth, prophetic or truth as being revealed thus by the Spirit. Scripture gives no logical definition of it; and in the nature of things such cannot be given. It is a work spoken of as of the Divine Spirit in peculiar contact and action with the human spirit, in knowledge as communicated on or at the meeting line of the absolute and the relative, by which the recipient mind is given to see what is made known as with a glance, or without the ordinary mental process of thinking by ordinary efforts and means, and has to do with the light of things as they are at the time, or are to be, or both. The mind is caused to see them as from the stand-point of the Spirit, in the oneness of the light in which they are seen, and in the oneness of the aspect or aspects in which they are made to appear. This knowledge is not communicated through sensation, nor through a process of reasoning or exercise of the ordinary faculties. The mind receives it as standing behind all these. It is the nearest approach, short of the beatific vision, to seeing them as the Spirit sees them. But it is in the natural gradation of parts of sense and form that the mind can retain it and communicate it to others. It must, therefore, take the form natural to the mental faculties for apprehending, retaining, and communicating it. At first the mind is passive, but not without being also active in being receptive. All passivity has its concomitant activity. Some minds and some states of mind are more fitted for being subjects of inspiration than others; an important matter but not to be dwelt on here. The inspiration may come as if by a whisper or word, as a flash of light in meditation or study, in he exercise and experience of a deep reverie, in a dream, a trance, or a vision. In the inmost and immediate sense inspiration, like all divine activ'ty, is in let there be as without any ordinary means, then in let produce as in the exercise of the mental powers and representations specially selected and formed. Instances of such representations are numerous through the Bible, and in the experiences of men. Objects already known, and whose qualities, connections, and relations having to do with or bearing resemblance to the matter being made known, are taken into a fitted construction or formation to represent that matter. The point of the Spirit's operation herein is like that in photography, the point of being made bare and naked of all else to receive the impression of the object or knowledge to be retained and made known. It is a special Omic operation for special purposes; being yet much of the same nature with all Omic operations in nature. The exercise of the natural powers of the mind in what is called imagination is much of the same kind, or is much in the likeness of this operation, and so is every Omic operation in nature, in man, and in all things.

Those persons who are peculiarly susceptible and capable of inspiration might be said to be prophets, whatever the amount of their prophetic experience may be. The knowledge communicated as related to things which take place on earth is susceptible of being formed into distinct thoughts and clusters of thoughts, and of being expressed in signs, words, and discourse in common language. The secret things of God, as those which do not belong to the manifested mind of God in the course of things on earth or in the relative, are not revealed; they belong, as Moses says, to the Lord God, and cannot be uttered, or it is unlawful to utter them, as Paul says of his own experience in his approach to them in the third heaven. So says Jesus to Nicodemus, If I told you of heavenly things. The mode of the Spirit's operation here, as in all works, is inscrutable and indescribable. There may be some resemblance between this operation of the Spirit on the consciousness of the subject and the mode of communicating sound by the medium of the air, light by that of the ether, and other sensations by that of touch. Impressions by external objects are thus made on the nerves, and through the nerves on the brain, and through it on or in the mind. The mind from within makes impressions on the brain, the brain on the nerves, and the nerves outwards. The action of the Spirit may come in at the outer or any Omic point in these connections; but it is most likely to come in at the inmost point of contact with the mind as in the original Om and in moving on the face of the waters, from which point the thought formation is constructed in the usual gradation as the matter made known is to exist or occur.

During the human spirit's time of abode in the body its means of communication with the outward world is through the senses, as outlets and inlets, by which the mind, in the ordinary exercise of its faculties, holds intercourse with its objects. The ether seems to be the ultimate means of intercourse between the mind and the external world; and the motion of it seems to be modified by the material formations of created things, as outward matter in its infinite variety forms, that of the body, and the nebulous, gaseous, and liquid elements.

Discerning the signs of the times may in certain respects be often without inspiration. The works of nature have fixed laws, and are conducted with connections and certainties which are arithmetical and geometrical; the ability to discern the times may be through study, attention, observation, comparison, and computation. But there are aspects of things, in which they are always to be viewed as under a complicated, mysterious, and sovereign control, and therefore to be understood by some special light, as in inspiration, dreams, and other ways. The knowledge given is always absolutely certain, though frequently not understood. As to Scripture, the inspiration is plenary or common to all the writings; but the way to get to see this fact is to get to the standpoint of the Spirit or the sacred writer in seeing the truth as so inspired. This is what was meant by the sacred writers; and one guiding rule of interpretation is not only to get into the standpoint of the writer and the Spirit, but also to take each particular passage or statement in the combined light of the whole.

Common dreams are from various common causes; but prophetic dreams have a cause underlying the conditions and relations of life and common natural phenomena. It may be impossible and unnecessary to know whether angels and departed spirits have any thing and how much to do with these dreams, or whether they are wholly and exclusively caused by the Spirit. The ethereal element may have something to do with them as means, it cannot be the real agent. The language or imagery in dreams are often natural objects and ways of action, relations and connections, representative of what is thereby made known concerning the objects or events predicted. Physical means are made use of to represent what is to be prominently physical in the event; social means are added to the physical to represent what is to occur in the social; in matters prominently intellectual, public, and national, the highest means of representations in nature are made use of. All that is according to the normal and healthful course of nature is indicative of good; all that is otherwise is so of evil. The low, mean, and dangerous among brute animals are symbolic of the same among men. Physical difficulties and dangers represent the same in social life. Relations are interchangeably used, the official very commonly for the social and the social for the official; so also as to trades and occupations. Distinct sounds, words, sentences, even lines of poetry in language or languages known to the person (seldom in an unknown one), are frequently made use of. The sentences and lines of poetry may be such as were known to the person before, or may be quite new. In short, all natural objects are in some respects representative of each other, and they are so employed in dreams up to reason. In the sphere of reason the lower representations are continued and made use of with the addition of rational groups of conceptions, social relations and conditions, and forms of speech, and so forth. Prophetic dreams hold equally true with inspiration; they are infallible, though they are in the use of means of knowledge mostly conducted by representations. Of the beatific vision little can be said. It is inscrutable and indescribable. It takes the form, gradations, and like relations of known things, into the sphere, state, and objects proper to it.

The creation of the woman out of or from the side of the man at the fourth point of embryonic or personal development may be seen to be quite consistent with what obtains elsewhere in nature. There is nothing more difficult of understanding or belief in it than in many other modes of increasing and multiplying in nature; nothing more so than in the absolute becoming an opened out form of two in the relative; an opening and closing which is constantly taking place in everything in the relative, as subject and object in consciousness, and all else. Man bears God's image in what he is and does, or in himself and in his history. In his first he is one, in his second he is one one, in his third he is three ones, in his fourth is a transition point. This answers to God's name, El-El-oh-im, that is El, two Els, three Els, and the oh standing for the fourth point, and im for an indefinite plural; the God personally is Jah and El as one on to the fourth point God, then Gods, or Jehovah Gods in one inner line of Jehovah and all outer lines and forms of Elohim or Elohistic manifestations. It is Lord of Lords, God of Gods, King of Kings, All in All. All things are manifestations and repeated forms of the one El. Every person and thing is a god in so far as he or it is a true manifestation of the deity ; in this sense all persons and things are im of El. When the woman is spoken of as being taken out of or from the side of man, in his deep sleep of summarising the sexual divisions of all creations, one form of the leading idea is that man is the distinct personal summary of all creations, from the very first, lowest, and outmost, to himself as the inmost and highest ; and that, in this deep sleep of taking all the creations into two sides, the woman is taken as the whole female, or Omic rib, side of the whole sum man, and that he is distinct from her is, and continues to be, the male side of the whole sum, and indeed of every individual, creature, or form of being.

8. The taking the woman out of man's side answers somewhat to the opening out of the absolute into the relative twofold form of heaven and earth, firmament above and earth below. It answers to God and His image, His necessary shadow, or one and zero, God the Absolute, and man His summary image of all manifestations. Somewhat in the same way is man towards the woman. So elsewhere it is said that the head of the woman is man, as the first whole formal and typical existence or created being ; that the head of every man is Christ, the first and full formal existence and type in all things, God-man. In this original and fundamental relation of things is to be found the nature, foundation, and standard of the equality and inequality, the resemblances and differences, between man and woman, their correlative states and status, rights and duties. All manifestation, in its inmost and highest import and ideal, is a manifestation of God in Christ by the Spirit ; its highest creatural form on earth is in man and is taken as the main or head and trunk line in the world's whole history ; and its gradations are chiefly in outer and under directions. The history of any person or thing must contain the facts and implications of these outer and under directions regarding him or it ; then those related to the actual time of being and action ; lastly, how he or it passes into the future.

The rule of subduing the earth is the divine command and example ; the whole rule is implied in the image of God, or in what there is of God in man as the sum of what God is in the whole inferior creation. The image in the order of its three parts is the sum of the learning and training, the social experience, and the accomplishments, of a young man through the three stages of his young and private life, as a preparation of what he is to be in person and practice when he appears in public and enters into public and conjugal life. So fitted and equipped, man is placed in the Garden ; and the second test and proof of his fitness for the life on earth, on which he is entering, is the naming of the creatures of earth among and over which he is to live out that life. The naming is as to what is also within him ; for he contains in himself the substance of the physical and animal, together with the divine image in the sense of knowledge, righteousness, and holiness. The naming also implies that all things within him, as also without him, are to be kept, to be enjoyed, and to be made use of in the graduated relations, kinds, and positions founded in creation and divine appointment. While the second test is naming the animals, and correspond to the animal life from the fourth or fifth point to the distinct creation of man, the first is as to all plants that have been given him ; and it is of importance to notice that the fruit was forbidden before the naming of the animals, as there was also made known the work of keeping and dressing the Garden. So that the order is, first, the physical and plant life in express relation to the water in rivers, the keeping and dressing of the Garden, and the forbidding of the fruit ; then the naming of the animals, in relation to all animal life to the double summary of things in man and woman or wife ; thirdly, the summary trial in the Garden, all ending in becoming as gods ; it is all the fourth point, sum, maturity.

The naming of the animals implies the power of speech. To know external objects an image of them on the retina is necessary; in order to perception by the mind an act of the imagination, or an act of forming an image of the object by converting the mere sensation into perception, is necessary ; an act of generalisation is necessary to convert perceptions of the same kind into conceptions; the representation of the conception by a sound is naming ; and names are language. This is the gradation of creation, and a matter worthy of careful study ; though it cannot be dwelt on here. The outward and audible or visible sign of reason is language. Speech and reason are an expression of the Logos, or summary manifestation of the All-Being. The underlying element or being has no form ; it is as the Spirit, formless and unchanging, yet all-causing as to form, change, and all else. The first distinct form or manifestation of it is in the Father-Son, universal Logos, with interactions of subject and object, all relations, and all else, and the Spirit in common. In creation a distinct form is given to every thing, which, in relation and interaction with other distinct objects, implies subject and object; and the third underlying being is common to both in all. The means of the distinctive form is the skin, crust, shell, or body given it and assumed by it in coming forth into distinct being. If this body or formative means be taken off or cast off, the creature becomes unknowable by sensation, and therefore by imagination and perception ; hence no conception can be formed of it and no name given to it, except from what was previously known of it, or what may be known of it from inference, or other sources. In dreams, trance, and visions the distinctive crust or form may be given and made use of only for the time being. Even then, if the form be different from all that is known in nature, the object represented will be impossible to utter, except vaguely and faintly through its nearest comparative resemblance to objects already known in nature. It is so with language. The mind must begin first with sound in the form of a vowel, as *a*; then the parts of the sound must come out, as in creation, and in order to creatural and word distinction, in father-son forms cut and crusted by consonants, as *b* or *bh*, sounded as in Gaelic as *v*. Abababa expresses three in one, *a* being the one vowel. This applies to persons and things. So is it in nature, as in the crowing of the domestic fowl. It is the first word representative form of creation, a repetition of which is being forever made in all continued creation, preservation, reproduction, and activity personal and otherwise. Every act, step, and stage is an opening and closing, an ever recurring repetition of Abba, or Abababa, as full form of three in one doing all. Among the inferior animals, the three in one is distinctly sounded and oft repeated, as by the domestic fowl, pigeons, and numberless others, as may be noticed by proper attention. Syllables, words, and sentences, are further redistributions of these vowel-consonant forms. These crusted or clothed forms are necessary to distinct thoughts, as bodily forms are necessary to distinct outward creations. The deaf and dumb can form and make crusted signs, but cannot form and utter words. The automatic action of the nerves and muscles may be defective in such cases. This opinion seems to be supported by the fact, that what effectually cures the nerves and muscles of stammering, cures also and simultaneously of deafness. These defects may be due to a peculiar relation to a transition line, or to a peculiarity of the line on which they are conceived and born.

Each step in the gradation of plant and animal life closes and opens on or in the creative line which distinguishes it, as such lines distinguish and separate the orders, classes, genera, and species, from each other, though in a larger and more permanent manner. The capacity of speech or sound has the same gradation as in other things. Words are names of concepts, not of things; the mind in thinking forms crusted thoughts which it utters in crusted sounds. Form, in some distinct and separate manner, is essential to every thing, except the universal and underlying Spirit, of whom no image is to be made; the attempt being a violation of the second commandment, and a successful attempt being an impossibility. In order to make an image, form, or manifestation, it is necessary to imitate nature, or go back to the underlying all creative Being, as the source of all things, in physical formations, plant and animal generation, conscious action, and imagination. To go back on ourselves is personal selfishness and self-deification. To go back on another person or thing is going back on our fellow creature, person or thing, which is a species of selfishness and deification of such beings. To cause or lead others to do so to us, or to themselves, or to other created persons or things, or to use persons or things, short of God, as such, is a gradation in selfishness or a species of deification; and in every case it is sin, darkness, and death. The spirit in all things is the background Being of all possibilities. The interactions in the laws of force, light, life, subject and object, sex, and all action, are givings of self and selves to Him, and gettings from, or out of Him, in all living, moving, and having being. One is active and passive in self-giving and all-giving to Him ; and is so also in self-getting and all getting from Him. This implies that all things are, in some respects, in Him as they are known in all their time and modes of being, and that he is the prototype of them all in His outcoming in all Father-Son, creative, and begetting modes. Both masculine and feminine, or brother and sister, son and daughter, are from Him ; but the feminine comes forth as sum of the less resistance in a second and secondary place and relation, out from the Omic side of the masculine as the sum of the greater force ; and hence the woman is spoken of as from or out of the side of man. The to and fro force as masculine is with and in man, as a force reflection of the Spirit ; and the complement of that force is in the feminine. There is a reflection of force in the power of resistance ; in this sense man is alternately positive and negative, active and passive in himself, and towards the Spirit ; and so, in a less sense, is the woman towards man and the Spirit. To resist the Holy Ghost in a sinful sense implies the assumption of equality, independence, and opposition towards Him. This sex form of less resistance is original and essential to force, motion, life, creatural sex, and all else ; and has a representation of a self-acting common being, as in the absolute, in the common gender embryo, flowerless plants from those at the bottom of the sea upwards, and such forms.

The idea that man was first, or up to his fourth point, which is seventh of the animals and the tenth of the physico-plant life and formations, of both genders, implies that the whole from the beginning to that level is taken and regarded as the lower part ; then from it to the begetting of Seth and the mentioned sons and daughters, as the middle part, and from it to Adam's death as the overlapping and completing third part. This stage of development corresponds to the age of puberty, or about thirteen as containing three parts of four years each, otherwise thirty, or three tens, of full manhood. At the beginning of their conjugal life Adam and Eve were placed in Paradise or the Garden of Eden. Men have never been able to agree about the locality of Eden. There is far more than a particular locality meant. It is a state of holiness and happiness, of innocence and bliss. The pleasures are physical and animal ; animal, social, and moral ; and also a summary of these with what is spiritual and religious in the highest sense ; or they are chiefly in knowledge, righteousness, and holiness. The garden, in the most real and fullest sense, is man himself, or man and wife, and the world. They, the place, the sum of things, and the state of things, are from the same source, the Creator Himself. Man as the all-sum represents God as the All-sum ; and the one all-sum is made, and is to be kept and continued like the other All-sum. They, Adam and Eve, are an epitome of earthly or created things. As to their bodies they are of earth and identical in nature with earth. The right to earth, or the place and state in which they are placed, is the same right they have to their being and to have a continued being on earth.

In the onward course of things the head sum of the substance of the past is ever being eaten up. The Jehovah Elohim, head sum of all beings, is absorbed in the gradation of all beings upwards and inwards, under the all-man and all-woman representation, in the serpent to and fro force and process of action and influence gradation, from the lowest and outmost to the highest and inmost in the Jehovah Elohim sum. The nectar and ambrosia, or the divine nature and sum, of things are eaten up by the gods, or gathered up and in as things of the gods, the divine perfections, principles, powers, and forces. Chronos is said to have swallowed and absorbed each of his sons to the Deluge, when Rhea gave him an emetic of a stone in swaddling clothes, which led to his giving forth himself and all in Zeus, or Abraham. All in all gradations are included or caused to follow in the same absorption of all and each, to the very lowest, into, and through, the Paradisaic line of transition, to reappear in naked newness of being and having being. It is the all-fruit, eaten, and ever being eaten, by all; and all become as gods, or are, as to being and having being, as one Jehovah Elohim. Every new man, and thing, is made of a seed and nourishing substance brought forward from the preceding one; also in the same manner and likeness or image (Adam begat a son in his own likeness, after his own image), and way of renewal and repetition of the old or past. Transition in these respects is not by buying and selling of land and slaves. Land cannot, in the nature of things and the nature of common justice, be subjected to buying and selling. The only forfeiture or alienation of it is by and through sin; and even the sinner has his continued right to it so long as he is continued in life on earth, and so long as he possesses and enjoys that right with comparative propriety. Man's capacity of improvement, which of itself distinguishes him from the inferior animals, has always and every where, even in Eden, a sufficient scope and sphere of exercise, of work, and enjoyment. He is to dress and keep the Garden, to work it, improve it, and keep it from a state of deterioration. His physical endowment is so inferior to that of all the other creatures of earth, that, without this capacity for supplementing what nature has done him in the physical sense, he could scarcely maintain an existence in any part of earth. His improvement is implied, in an active and passive sense, in his original endowments and the corresponding nature of his surroundings. It has also its essential and necessary connection with social development, with learning to co-operate in society, with civilisation. Whatever time elapsed between his original personal creation and his being placed in the Edenic state, he is represented as being introduced into that state as endowed, matured equipped, and every way fitted for that state in its public, conjugal, social, and universal character.

The Garden is the transition line, state, place, and passage from the creative into the begetting character of all things from the lowest and most minute being up to man and God; the fruit is the puberty or maturity for so doing; and the act of eating the fruit is the act of passing from the creative into the begetting being and having being. According to a Chaldean tradition, the Garden, or grove, and its sacred tree were sometimes separated from the holy Æonic mountain and transferred to a near and accessible neighbourhood. The head or tenth point of the outer line is the head or tenth point also of the transition line lying across from left to right; and is, therefore, at the distance of from seven in the midline to this tenth point of outer position. But the whole absorption, as of all, and as of each of beings, must pass through the midline of all as such, and of each as such. The appellation, Tintirki, the place of life, was given to Babylon, to the mid district in Accad or Upper Chaldea, and to a place at Eridhu in the deepest plain of the lowlands at the mouth of the Euphrates, or its meeting point with the sea, a spot consecrated to Ea and Oannes. These places of life were the representative groves of that country for the time being, or for all time. Saviour Meridug was said to be the son of Eridhu, because that place was regarded as the sum or ten-one grove, or begetting place of Ea-Oannes, in their combined work of all creative and begetting new and renewed life and all formations. The Saviour of the world, under the name Meridug, appears through the begetting by the Spirit, in the combined meanings of Ea and Oannes, as the visible appearing out of the invisible, and of being the medium or mediator in which and in whom all things and all persons pass through all transition lines and points.

The law of impelling and resisting force, like that of subject and object, underlie and is essential to all movement. The impelling form and the resisting form are mutually and alternately present. The force which is really one becomes alternately the one and the other; its form and action are essential to all activities, in all relations, and in all causal connections and combinations. Every entity of force has its crust or vesture, and its opening and closing valve, a nerve action, a heart beating, and an absorption or ingathering from its surroundings, in a single or original form or in a superstructure and superorganic environment. It has its essentials of its original being, which it never loses, its vowel spirit which never perishes. It is forever active and passive, passive in being active and active in being passive; in being so it forever forms, and forms into, a new vesture or crust; it has its measure in time and space; and it has an experience and a history. Its acquisitions are subject to growth and decay, to enlargement and diminution ; the substance of which consists of shell or vesture formations and of what they contain of the unchanging element ; and this substance, in a fit state for its digestion or use, it absorbs, eats, or carries along with it for future need. What of this substance is of shell essentials goes into its shell formation ; and what of it is of unchanging inner element goes into its inner element. It has its youth, its mid-time existence and decline, or its closing and opening. In its redistributive formation it has its gradation of steps and stages, it carries the essential substance of its former acquisitions and surroundings, in the name and meaning of jewels or precious things, with it into the next and new stage ; but the new nature of the new stage requires a new means of life. These means are partly new, and partly refined from the past to suit the new and higher level and life, and so on upwards and onwards. The ascending line corresponds with the forward creative movement in the creation of all things, the nebulous and gaseous, the gaseous and liquid, the water and milk, the milk and honey, the honey and nectar, the nectar and manna, six in all ; the seventh being in the supernatural as the hidden manna and the tree of life, as the sum and substance of the past relative. Signs or essential marks of all past steps are preserved and retained forever ; nothing is lost ; the great fossil strata remain in their natural order and relations, already completed as six in number. Earth's crust contains six layers of them, said to be each a mile in thickness The form and distinct beneficial result of past civilisations may be difficult for man, as now living, to recognise ; but their substance and beneficial effects are never lost, nor do they ever pass away ; they have eternal life. In this way the new superstructure and superenvironment contain the substance of its predecessor. It passes through the creative one, four, seven, ten passage line. In doing so it undergoes a change by the creative energy and softening, moulding, renewing, and reforming touch of the unchanging element the Spirit ; and resumes its ingathering or absorbing of materials from its surroundings, in the original manner of absorption by the cell. While there is thus a continuity, as of Father-Son genealogy, kept on, it has its resemblance also to grafting. Briefly put, there is the original being ; then there is the formation of its acquisitions, or learning, in its native light and power, through intercourse and experience with itself, with its surroundings, and with the underlying and omnipresent Spirit ; there is the ingathering and carrying along with it of the substance and results of that experience ; in going into another new step, there is its passing through the creative or re-creative passage, resembling sleep, trance, vision, death ; in the reappearance of it in a risen and renewed life there is the beginning of a step or era of another scale of six steps, formations, or children ; terminating again in a seventh, or tenth, according to its position in its scale of redistribution.

From the Spirit outwards the natural gradation obtains in the whole scale of being. The Spirit's seven summary parts work, called in Revelation the seven spirits, had, in the Chaldean conception, corresponding seven evil spirits, called Maskim. They had their birthplace and proper sphere in the Abyss, the incidental dark zero or Omic shadow of the fountain head grove of the Deity, or the Spirit; the land that no creature has ever seen or ever penetrated. Thence is all life; so the Psalmist says, with Thee is the fountain of life; in Thy light shall we see light. They correspond as incidental dark reflections of the Spirit's work in seven or ten steps and stages of all gradations, to the Spirit's creative or causative steps and stages in all work and all being and having being, as in the sun and planets, the signs of the Zodiac, the division of eras, times and seasons, and all else, and pre-eminently in transition lines, as in passing through death into life, in the war of the Kings, the Trojan war, and all such. Their substantial and positive original forms are in the good angels and all created spirits as distinct forms in distinct likeness of the Spirit. Hence they were represented as reflective messengers of the gods or of the manifestative Elohim. The lower of every being is, in a sense, its female, or couch-bearing part. So, at the lowest point or level of every gradation, is this zero counterpart, as negative to positive, darkness to light, death to life, evil to good. These evil spirits were, therefore, called throne bearers to the gods in all gradation of motion, movement, and action, as moving with the lightning, on the wind, on the clouds, and all else. Scripture speaks of God as making darkness His secret place, His pavillion dark waters and thick clouds of the sky, as riding on a cherub, as making the clouds His chariot, His spirits His angels, and the flame of fire His ministers. Like Thetis, they had for special abodes the hollows of the sea, and the bowels of mountains, the mysterious transition lines and stages of the Spirit's relations and actions. Like the holy angels they are of a higher nature than material earthly creatures; and are, therefore, so in sex or intersexual relations, angels, and they as incidentals, being from the Spirit otherwise than by ordinary generation. They are foes of great Ea; and in transition changes, they have a conspiracy against Ana like that of the gods of the Greek Olympia against Zeus; like that against Christ, as described in the Second Psalm and recorded in the Gospels, and all such downwards. In these transition plots and ways of action all nature is included, as in eclipses, darkness, earthquakes, and so forth, such as attended Christ's death: the Aeonic meaning of this nature inclusion being that spiritual powers are to outward things as water and mind are to such commotions of earth or nature. Their work is mischief and misery; and prayer and praise they heed not. Their favourite spheres of abode and action are in all meeting-places, as the lower heavens where sky and earth meet, then of water and earth, and other such. Symbolic representations of them are everywhere, as in cloud formations, devouring denizens of the deep, the more destructive birds of air and beasts of earth, men oppressors and tyrants, and whoever or whatever tends to reduce things to confusion or chaos or any form of evil. An eclipse of the sun or the moon was taken as symbolic of a transition change in a community, or nation, or Church, or the passing on of the seat of empire from a place or country. Such changes are summary works of the Spirit, and His ways of work, and so incidentally of their works and ways. This explains why an eclipse was spoken of as the work of monsters or wild devouring beasts; the eclipsed or suffering object's associates and titulary gods, as the true God, or in gradation the Sungod, Ishtar, and other planets, the Zodiac, and others of the all Elohim, apparently forsaking it or him, the object; till Nebo was sent to Ea, who sent Meridug to go and overthrow or drive away the evil spirits. These spirits have their full growth as attached to outward formations in Aconic titan points, and answer to the Greek opposites of the Spirit in the lower world of transition lines, as Minos, &c., and in the distinctive characters of nature powers and forces. The minor spirits of the same nature, but lower in gradation, were the Anunnaki, answering to the evil genii of Greece, and to ghosts generally.

Fear of ghosts is connected with feelings of exposure, nakedness, weakness, and guilt; in such circumstances as in darkness, in the distance from society and shelter, being comparatively bare or naked as to the common means of nature, as in sickness, conscious nearness to death, and all such, as in which one feels possibly or presumably exposed to righteous judgment and suffering, or to evil genii or spirits of evil. For a covering, because of the angels, long hair has been given to woman. Every being has a form of covering; the absolute has the relative in its infinite variety of forms, and all other beings after its kinds. Shell, crust, or garment is formed in and by nature through the weaving interaction of natural forces according to natural laws, as impelling and resisting forces. Permanently effective force works out changes of relative position of two kinds, the invisible and the visible. In the former of these two the transposition among the units of particles are those constituting molecular changes, including chemical composition and decomposition, or molecular modification. In the latter the sensible transpositions result from certain of the units, instead of being put into different relations with their immediate neighbours, are carried away from them, and deposited elsewhere, which is called sensible re-arrangements. These sensible re-arrangements are the means of form and structure, and the action implied in them is also implied in the formation of crust through the interaction of impelling and resisting forces meeting in the internal or external skin or crust formation in the surface of the body.

Paradise is from the Greek, meaning garden. It was described by the Chaldeans as a great mountain, with a garden, watered by springs becoming great rivers, having two trees of sacred character and wonderful properties, and as being the principal abode of divine, human, and all creatural life. It was located in the first great transition point in the eternal and universal tree. In relation to the beginning of the world the locality was supposed to be in the far east ; and in relation to the side of the westwards lying midline, along which the special abode or seat of empire moved through such transitions, it lay to the north, or in the tenth point of the outer line and of the transition line. It lay along all the transition line, through which the mountain midline forever passes. This transition line was the Arabi through which was the change of renewal as through death into life. Through this mysterious line the spirits of the departed passed to dwell in the place of everlasting bliss. Prolonged life on earth passed through it as renewed in the main (mountain) line. The outer formations of things also passed through it renewed as such, and the oldnesses of all things disappeared. The mountain was often spoken of as that of Bel, in the Apollo-Briereus sense, or Christ's two-fold nature, the divine and the human. The north and south were symbolised by the two horns of a buffalo at rest, for the Greek mounts Calypso and Atlas, touching the heavens as if supporting the northern and southern skies. The hills in the countries along the main line marked its orderly parts ; and, therefore, had palaces and temples built on them, often with hanging gardens, sometimes watered by machinery ; the leading idea of such gardens being, as in nature, that of groves for begetting, nursing, and advancing all kinds of life. The course of existence of all beings or of any one being is a tree. The nearer that course is to the spirit the purer, better, and happier it is. The Nirvana, or true heaven, is in being in the highest and nearest state and character to the spirit in Christ of which one is capable.

To overcome all troubles and trials, pass safely through difficulties and dangers, obtain deliverance from all evil, and attain to Nirvana, are all by the spirit in the midline Mediator. The battle of Bel-marduk and the dragon held an important place in the cycle of Chaldean tradition and Assyrian sculptures. Bel-marduk may be taken as the Greek Apollo-Briereus, or God manifested and working in divine and human form of mediator and Saviour in all things. Mummu-tiamat was the impersonation of chaos or of all darkness and disorder, as the sum of the dark shadows of universal being. The fickle and flickering, subtle and supple, delusive, deceitful, and dangerous meeting line of light and darkness, life and death, good and evil, was represented by the serpent or dragon as the animal bearing the nearest resemblance to this line, which in reality is the transition line, and, therefore, the nearest in false resemblance to the shadow of the spirit and mode of working of the spirit. The personality or personification of evil is the full shadow form of the outer line or of the transition line, and so far of the spirit. Eternal warfare is waged on this line between all being and all shadow of being ; a warfare incidental to the eternal laws, relations, and interactions of all being, as positive and negative, attraction and repulsion, subject and object, and all else. Tiamat is the Egyptian Typhon, and the Bible Satan, the personal or personified evil. Anu as Father and His heavy bent armour, the sickle, shepherd sword and bent bow were supposed to be, like Saul and his armour, too old and unfit for the purpose of gaining ever anew in a war that is ever new. As David, or the natural sun ever moving in light and life, strength and splendour, it was Belmarduk's work to go eternally forth in the Aeonic war chariot, armed with ever new sword, bow, and thunderbolt, sending lightning and arrows of light and life before and all around. Arrow shooting and all means and acts of warfare and hunting have to do with putting away the old or what is, and begetting and bringing in and on the young and new and what is about to be. The sum of this is in sonship or the eternally being begotten ; and it is, therefore, in Belmarduk, as moving forward from Anu. So do Adam and Eve, as the all-man and all-woman, and all created beings, now move forward from God, or the Spirit, in the Father Son sense, in all begetting production and modes of action.

Jehovah Elohim sent the man forth from the Garden of Eden, to till the ground from whence he was taken. So He drove out the man ; and He placed at the east of the Garden of Eden Cherubims, and a flaming sword which turned every way, to keep the way of the tree of life. Jesus Christ is the whole tree of persons and things : the three-fold sense and form of knowledge, righteousness, and holiness, into the one or fourth sense of personal life in glory. He, or the spirit manifested in Him, is the real and inmost being and meaning of the whole tree of life and of knowledge of good and evil in all gradations, in all sum of Jehovah Elohim. The symbolic tree parts of hemlock, apple tree, pomegranate, and mandrake, and all that they symbolise, have their whole meaning in Him, as the whole absolute and the whole relative ; and in Him is the highest and inmost approximation by man and nature to being as gods, or as God. In Him is the only way of conformity to the divine will, the only way of being like God in conduct as well as in character, the only way of doing as God does. From the dust of elemental being man and all things are taken, formed, created, or made : so man is sent forth to till the ground, or to act in forming or making all things from the same elemental dust, in begetting and all manner of acting like the Lord God. In this there is not and there must not be any going back, no turned faces. The ground and the promised land are before, not behind ; and the way is straight through the mysterious line of the one, four, seven, ten points. To try to live in the reverse way and on the dead matter of the past or outmost is to try, as a prophet speaks farther on, to live on dead dust in its worst form of one's own excrement, or as the dog returning to its vomit, the former of which no creature ever does. It is selfishness of the most corrupt kind and to the most awful death ; a death to all absolute and to all relative, yet a sin and a death becoming nothing in that very separation, and therefore disappearing with the reappearing and resurrection of all good. That nature and man may be, perhaps must be, raised higher and nearer to being as God than is yet made known is most likely ; but that advanced state and level of exaltation must be in the line of the one, four, seven, ten of the Spirit in Christ. The restoration to Paradise, or to a higher Paradise, is by looking, acting, and going forward in the Spirit's line and way of all work in Christ. The sending forth is from one point, step, and stage to another, as from the past and the old ever into the ever onward and the ever new. The new birth is never in and by the return to the same Om or mother's womb form of things. A fairy ring never grows but once in the same exact spot. The begetting Om is brought forth in the likeness of the Spirit's original creative Om ; still they are not essentially or literally identical.

In plants the bud gives out only one forward shoot in the one season ; the bud at the end of that shoot giving out the next, and so on. This forward or stem shoot is the genealogical son-shoot of each season ; the other side-bud shoots are its, "and he begat sons and daughters." At the end of the season the sap and the growing power return to the roots and lowest and utmost points in the soil, or ground, leaving the stem bud and all the other buds feminine, and distinct in form, each a virgin because at the end of its respective young shoot ; each shoot top one and each side one being thus made a distinct outward Om, as Eve from Adam when in deep sleep. The very descent of the sap and growing power is a wife-knowing in the sense of getting in, and from, the original Omic soil and roots, as in original and ever original creation, the new seed to ascend in all gradation to each Omic bud through which the respective shoots grow forth and out in season. It is a return and reflow of the blood, an ebb and flow of the sea, a closing and opening of valves, an inspiration, an expiration, an all Ishtar descent and ascent, the changes of the moon and of sun and seasons, and night and day, the march of eras and seats of empire, the all work of Jesus through all death into all life, and through the relative into the absolute. In all sexual intercourse there is this going down and out to all parts and particles of the body of each for the seed which contains a quota of sum-substance from every part, point, and particle ; and this is gathered up and in to the Omic organs and laid in womb's place and relations for a new growth after its kind, whether of plant, of animal, or of man, or all in one. In the Garden transition state, the fruit eating represents the Serpent to and fro action or intercourse of thus getting up and in of creative sum-substance from the original Om of the spirit's creative work to the begetting Om and womb place and relations in each being in gradation up and in to the Jehovah Elohim all sum and beings.

The reason given for sending the man forth from the Garden is, lest he put forth his hand, and take also of the tree of life, and eat, and live for ever. In the nature of things the fountain of life, the tree of life, eternal life in itself, and the nature and essential virtues of that life are above and beyond the hand, the will, the power, the influence, of man. Our life is hid in God with Christ; the gift of God is eternal life through Jesus Christ our Lord. The tree of knowledge of good and evil stands to the tree of life much as Elohim stands to Jehovah, as the region of the senses stands to the Ishtar, or inmost and highest region, in all beings. The reception, possession, and enjoyment of the gift of eternal life are not by natural means and the natural senses, or all that is implied in the sense region summarised in the hand representation, although all these have their connection to it, as they have to all persons and things, but by faith. It is not meant that eternal life is denied, or withheld from man, but that the region of being and work implied in eating the fruit is distinct from that of the inmost and highest region of eternal life, in respect to which man walks not by sense but by faith. More must be said of this farther on.

God placed at the east of the Garden of Eden cherubims, and a flaming sword, which turned every way, to keep the way of the tree of life. The cherubims were a compound image. Their number is always from one to four, never more than four; and they are the middle representation in every formation and being. The Chaldean form of Christ's ancestral line finds a prominent place and revelation in the legend of Eahan, written Oannes in Greek. It is described as having the lower part of the body of fish with feet coming out below similar to those of a man: a head partly fowl partly human; and having the power and use of human reason and speech. This being came out of the Erythean Sea, an ancient name of the Persian Gulf, but also meaning the waters of chaos or the nebulous, gaseous, and liquid elements in one, and denoting further the Spirit's work as necessary at every point through all time as at the first. Its complex form denotes the gradation of the first seven or ten days, fish including plants together with fowls in one lower part, with appropriate place in the face summary; then animal life, and lastly human life, with human reason and speech.

9. This compound figure represents man in his whole world summary, as the all-man, containing the whole works of creation in the tripartite division of lower, middle, and higher sub-summaries. It is difficult to know what terms the Chaldeans applied to the different parts of this division. One term, Kirubim, is known, and is supposed to be the same with the Hebrew, Cherubim. The Hebrews applied a distinct name to each part, and one for them all as one, Teraphim for the lower, Cherubim for the middle,

and Seraphim for the higher, while Elohim is the one for the whole, as outer of the whole inner Jehovah. The inner form of im is am, as in Adam, Abraham, and others. The man Micah, spoken of in Judges chapters 17 and 18, had a teraphim in his house of gods, or of Elohim. It suited the Danites, as lower part people and for lower purposes of new land, new beginning and begetting in life. The Cherubims have to do with more of public, social, and moral life, in addition to Teraphic implications of life. The two together are contained in the four form image of the Chaldean representation, more distinctly appearing in the Hebrew Cherubim, with the head of a bull, that of a lion, that of an eagle, and that of a man, as summary higher forms of the creations of the world. In these, as the things that are made, there are made known the invisible things of God, as His eternal power and Godhead, His perfections and powers, principles and laws. The third or higher part is symbolised by the Seraphim, containing the sum-substance of the others, together with more of the higher nature of things, as in fire, light, and spirit. The Chaldeans and the Hebrews, and the other ancient nations, maintained that these compound images represented all known manifestations of God through time, all the world's works and ways, arts and sciences, service and suffering, all the sum-substance and result of the past, all the indications and meaning of the present, and all the prospects of the future on earth and in heaven. They are panphibious, in the sense of all life-living and all life-giving, the source, the sphere, and the giver all things. In the eternal, fullest, and highest sense they are Elohistic, as summary representations of all divine manifestations in the Father-Son, God-man, all-man and each Aeonic man in Christ's genealogy, all men and all nature. Their sum-manifestation, as in all creative and begetting work, forever disappears and reappears. So the Chaldean Eahan was spoken of as disappearing and reappearing more perceptibly in distinct and well-known changes, as at night, at death, and all the more marked and impressive changes, but really in all things and at all times; plunging back to its first liquid element or ante-creation state of things, to reappear in the morning or renewal of everything. The Being so represented (really the Divine Spirit) is said to have set down His revelations in Books, or inspired writings, which He consigned to the keeping of men. He also continues to appear and reappear constantly and forever; and does so in most special and affecting ways, at long intervals. In Chaldean tradition or revelation, it is stated that between the first appearance and the first king there was an interval of two hundred and sixty thousand years, or periods of time. This interval seems to have been that from the beginning to the first man Adam, and may mean the lower part in physico-plant sense of a hundred and thirty thousand and the middle part of the same rate and meaning, corresponding to the Bible manhood age of Adam, multiplied by one thousand of creatural kinds represented. Each whole part is one consisting of three parts, which can be taken and written as one with three, as in thirteen ; an Om, or zero, added for a female counterpart, makes one hundred and thirty : and this is exactly the sum for the plant, again for the animal, and lastly for Adam. The one thousand by which this sum is multiplied stands for the unnumbered or numberless beings thus conveniently and proportionately counted, or taken in a summary form. So is it in such expressions as the thousands of Israel, in the Israelite number of one hundred and forty-four thousand, and such like. So the Biblical and Chaldean numbers are really the same, and are literally intelligible and true.

Ter of the term teraphim, is much the same as the Egyptain Tau, and the Hebrew tera, or tora, for the full literal sum of all divine manifestations, as in man and the ten commandments ; and aph or eph is the hard and outer of abh of abba. The er is the repeated form of d in Adam, as in the Egyptian Ra and in Abraham. Tora is more of an inner nature than tera, and both symbolise respectively the inner and outer of things, as of the law. The term teraphim, the Persian telephim, thus represents the lower, outer, or inferior tripartite nature of all persons and things. The representation is much the same as in the creative ancestral gods of the Chinese and the household gods of the Romans. The middle, or more social, moral, and public, part is taken in sum representation under cherubim, as from four to seven of all things. And the seraphim have more to do with the cerebellum and the intellect. The three terms apply to all beings, from the lowest to the Lord God Himself, but do so in the gradation of lower, middle, and higher. The term teraphim has more properly to do with all the creations up to the social opening up of things after the naming of the animals by Adam, and by every Adam or being, in coming out of his deep sleep as distinct man and wife, and in passing through the fruit-eating into becoming as gods, or as teraphim form and sense of Elohim. The term applies properly to the head-sum substance of all beings in all that lies between the beginning and the puberty stage, and opening out and forth into the middle or socio-moral part of beings, as all and each. At this level each being comes to be a first-born of creation, and all in one sum become the all-man first-born of creation in Adam, and, in the inmost and highest and fullest sense in Christ, the First-born of creation.

Accordingly, the Ancients made an image intended to represent a first-born son child, split open the top of its head, and sprinkled it with salt and oil, in token of the creations up from the watery elements, of the oil of plant sap, of animal oil and moist or fatty substances, of circumcision, and of the whole of the Spirit's work in regard to all things. To denote the to and fro action in nature, in creation, propagation, preservation, speech, and all motion, the name of the sum-substance of all inferior or lower Elohim, as in the to and fro serpent representation, was written in a golden plate, which was then placed under the child image's tongue; and it was asked to converse and tell of what it knew. Two lamps, one on each side, were added, to serve as eyes and as all-sum of things of left and right sides. Of course, in its cupid sense, it was blind. It was regarded as a representation of the source and means of prophecy in relation to all the past, the present, and the future creations, and the full head sum breaking forth of the all knowledge in eating the fruit of the tree of knowledge of good and evil. In sum-substance all this passes on in tora law and light, or all mode and meaning of things, into the higher or middle part and the cherubim, and thirdly into the highest form in seraphim; the whole being in Elohim. Thus the teraphim, cherubim, and seraphim, are a gradation of all that God makes Himself known as being and as doing in all His ways and works, bearing the distinct characters of prophet, priest, and king. A formal summary of the whole is in the most holy place of the Tabernacle, as in the head, and in it the cerebellum. This explains Rachel's conduct in taking with her the teraphim all sum-substance of Laban and Padanaram; that of the Danites in taking with them the teraphim and accompaniments from Micah; and that of Michal in placing a teraphim image for David. The aspirated first part forms of these names are ther, cher, and sher, and are pronounced in Hebrew, as in Gaelic, far down the throat; but without the aspiration they are ter, ker, ser. Their articulation is in tripartite gradation. They are pronounced in the same spot when down the throat, and again nearly the same spot with the tongue and palate. T is the hard form of d, c of g or of ch, and s of sh.

The number of the seraphim is never beyond six. The misery and suffering sustained in and by parting with and passing from the happiness connected with a lower sphere is compensated for by the deliverance from the incidental evils of that lower and the greater happiness connected with the higher; and there are many premonitions and anticipations, predispositions and presumptions, not to say promises and proofs, of this greater happiness in prolonged existence and into the actual enjoyment of it. The first letter of teraphim is a form figurative of the human body, or an erect form of three parts in one, which is the same really in every formation, even in that form assumed by the serpent, and also of the cross. The first part of it, tera or tora, means the original and essential form of three in one, throughout all nature and man, after the image of the triune God. Tora, in the first sense, represents every thing as coming forth into its form of being; every thing as coming out of the original cell, out of the nothing zero form. It is two in representing the opening of the passage as in the firmament above and the earth beneath, and the second step in advance; so also is it in plant and animal life. It has the number of the three layers form. As that within grows on, it leaves behind the first, and so on; succession of parts being left.

8

behind till it is out in three into a fourth or head form all, when it passes into the cherubim part. The normal orifice form is in actual conception and birth, or actual reproduction. The two-fold form is the two sides of it in persons and things, as man and wife, father and mother, brother and sister, organs of reproduction in form and sex. There is something in the substance and laws of things that is essential and eternal; and in this sense the essentials of all things are co-existent and coeval. For the knowledge and use of these all men consult what is meant by these figures, in whatever form, the highest being the intellect consulted in all wisdom. So do the farmer and the man of business, the scientist and the philosopher, the naturalist and the theologian, the artist and the theorist, every one in every power and capacity. God ought to be consulted as He makes Himself known in all gradation in nature and man, in all His works, ways, and word; and man cannot act in anything without consciously or unconsciously doing so. Tera, Tora, or Tara is the same as in Tera, the father of Abraham; and has its reverse form in arah of Mount Ararat.

The word cherub means animation, soul, and wind, as in, He breathed into his nostrils and he became a living soul. The position of the cherubim is specially in the middle part, or sphere of the social, the moral, and the public. A cherub may mean a gust of wind or motion of the divine Spirit; a thought or purpose in action, or any measure of knowledge, righteousness, and holiness. So God is spoken of as riding on a cherub, to denote His sovereign, speedy, and majestic action, in His public manner of the moral government of the world. In the full compound image, the head of the eagle stands for the sea and the air as to things without and within, that of the lion for the head-sum of the outward wildnesses of animals and all nature and man, and that of the bull for the pure, tamed, and man-service animals and all such in nature and man. The head-sum or lord of all is that of man, as the all-one become as gods or as the one whole Elohim representation. The number of the teraphim is meant to be not more than two or three images, generally one; that of the cherubim, four; and that of the seraphim, six, making at most twelve, as in Jacob's family. They are representations of God as manifested in nature and in man, materially and mentally; in thought creations, word creations, and all combinations of formations.

Each individual of all things, however minute, is a creature or Son with an internal Spirit; and this part and spirit form has its work of force preservation and propagation. The summary good reflection of every thing is its good angel; the summary dark reflection is its evil angel. This is true of things and persons, of properties and perfections, of faculties and capacities, of feelings and emotions, of thoughts and words; and thus angels were and are attached each to the appropriate soul, if not created with or included in the creation of that soul, formation, or being. The same is true of all light, truth, principle, rule, law; it is true of every thing in the sense of model, standard, and example. The angel is the ideal of everything; it is the being, formation, or creature as first formed in the mind of the Spirit; it is the distinctive, identical, and specific nature, character, or form of it in its most original and highest sense, as conceived in the creative mind, as faculty or imagination of the Spirit. It is the Spirit's first mental image of it, the Spirit's thought-image and creation of it. It is the first ideal form of the relative and every being and formation in it, as coming out of the absolute; and hence all the sum-angels, or legions of angels, attended and ministered to Jesus, and do so to the whole relative and all beings and each being in it. It is in the usual threefold gradation of lower, second, and third orders of angels. The distinction between the angel and the spirit in man is somewhat as that between the spirit in man and that in the inferior creatures or animals. Every representation has its angel; so a legion is said to have been in one representative character in the New Testament. It is always of a higher nature than that of what it represents on or under its own level; but it also serves in representing and ministering to all things and persons higher than that level. So in Hebrews the angels are all spoken of as worshipping the Son; and in Revelation the angel is spoken of as the fellow-servant of John and of all the prophets. As being the first ideal form, they are also the last ideal form in all being and all change; and have, therefore, peculiar relations and work in connection with conception, birth, and other changes through life, and death. This angelic form of things is the beginning of special changes, internal and external, so often spoken of in Scripture, as the three men appearing to and forming in Abraham and Lot, the armed man appearing to and forming in Joshua, and many such-like in the Bible, as in some form or other in all things in nature, man, and the Bible. Dreams of a lower nature are through the angelic teraphim regarding things in the region of the cherubim, and through the angelic cherubim regarding things in the region of the seraphim. The teraphim are often implied in the cherubim and both in the seraphim, if not so always, when the distinction is not expressed, or somehow indicated. The other two are implied in the Cherubim when taken as one whole compound image, as here at the Garden. Hence fire, though it has its tripartite gradation, is in the highest sense seraphic, and is here in that sense in the flaming sword, indicative of the highest and most powerful means of executing the divine will on earth. At the same time the condition of things here being mainly in the sense of entering into the socio-moral, public, and family life part, the cherubic form and sense are formally most prominent; and it is only of the cherubim anything is distinctly said. The substance or meaning of such representations as of dreams and prophecies is the new being or beings implied and forthcoming.

The sword is the sum-symbol of all force and action, and therefore of death into and unto life. All force goes out from and in to the cerebellum, though through the nerves and muscles, in all parts of the body. The cherubic image and expression belong principally to the sides and the front, and are most marked in the face. The tree of life underlies, and is inmost to, the tree of knowledge of good and evil. Both have their inmost and highest seat in the cerebellum, and forming out in its tripartite gradation in the connections of the lower part grove, of the midpart breast and shoulder grove, and of the head part facial grove. The nebulous, gaseous, and fluid forms of substances have like gradation in their more watery form in the lower part, in their more bloody form in the mid part, and in their more ethereal form in the third part. What is called a sea of water is more expressive of the lower part, a sea of blood is so of the mid part, and a sea of glass is so of the head part. Still all kinds of substances, fluid and solid of whatever kind, do in some sense and form belong to all parts of the body, and so of nature. All force, in all substances and all laws, has thus its all to and fro motion and action in all directions, in relation to the tree of life as inmost and highest sum-substance of all, to guard it, or to preserve and propagate it, as the tree of life, through all the processes of motion, action, and change, conditions, and relations. A smokeless and pure flame of fire is supposed to be a fit symbol, like the intellect, of all sum-substance of all force, substances, qualities, and laws of all being and having being.

The principal representation of this in all nature is the natural sun; rising forever in the east and setting forever in the west, forever in motion relative to north and south, and causing and controlling the seasons and seasonable changes everywhere; so guarding, or preserving and propagating in all trees or formations and gradations of life, and so turning every way to keep the way of the tree of life. In the body the face answers to the sun in nature; each sense is a living or flaming sword, and the tongue is the sum-sense sword, as the all of the sun comes by force and motion through the ether, the air, and all reflective and communicative means of nature. Force, in the sense of strength, power, and might, is in all gradation in nature and man, physical, moral, and intellectual, or natural and spiritual. The highest and inmost place is that of the intellectual and spiritual. So all force and all means and ways of force go out and down, Ishtar-like, from and in to the cerebellum, the highest and inmost court of causation and control, of might and right, of heaven and earth, in nature, in man, and God. The special centre of existence and influence, in the meaning and form of the Cherubim and flaming sword, on earth is always the world seat of empire in its gradations of seats of empire, which each nation ever strives to possess. Its Cherubim and flaming sword are always placed to the east, as here said to be the east of the Garden; just as they are in the sides, front, and face of the body, while the tree of life has its situation principally in the back, inmost and highest portion of the body, with the inmost and highest head sum in the cerebellum. All things thus rise and grow, as in nature, in and from the east, but move sun-wise for ever westwards. This motion westwards, or onwards and upwards, is essential and necessary to all life, all trees of life, the all tree of all life. Life is hid in God with Christ; but it is with and in Christ as the Son, the eternally being begotten Son who is in the bosom of the Father, in the Father-Son (east yet west) creative begetting force and motion.

Begetting in the proper, inmost, and highest sense is inclusive of all works of creation in respect of all beings up to the level of the Garden. To stretch the hand, as done in eating the fruit of the tree of knowledge of good and evil, is not to eat of the tree of life and live for ever. This latter is inner and higher than the tree of knowledge of good and evil, than the region of sense, than all the Elohim of things, belongs more to the Father-Son begetting proper, and is next to that Father-Son sense as in God. In the inmost and highest sense substances and laws, all formations, and beings, are rather begotten than created. This is the record, that God hath given to us eternal life, and this life is in His Son. He that hath the Son hath life. There can be no inner or higher or fuller act done in or by any being than the Father-Son begetting act, or that of the Son coming from the Father and returning to the Father. The sum-substance meaning of the act of faith in Christ the Son, and the Father in Him, and thus having the All-Spirit as well as thus acting by the All-Spirit, is the sum-substance saving act. This faith which is the substance of things hoped for, the evidence of things not seen, is that by which the elders obtained a good report, by which is understood and enjoyed in substance that the worlds were framed by the word of God, that whereby whatsoever is born of God overcometh the world, and that he who overcometh the world is he that believeth that Jesus is the Son of God. The restoration of man and of nature is implied in all returning motion, force, and action; and the all returning is in that of the Son to the Father that sent Him.

CHAPTER IV.

THE things of nature and of man are the same, and are so conducted and governed by Him whose are all things. The physical configuration of the seat of empire portion of earth, is taken as resembling the human body, with the east and south for the left and front, the north for the right shoulder, and the body turning from looking towards the east in the morning, to the south at mid-day, and the west at sunset. There is thus a line of shoulder points from east to west along the line of the northern tropics, a mid-line along the equator or at the proportionate distance from the northern tropics, and the lower part of the body lies to the south of that distance, three in one city of head-sum of it being on its appropriate line as at Egypt. This agrees with the relations of the sun's diurnal and seasons' motion, as to the earth, the zodiac, and the planets. All motion is taken as being in some accordance to this. Water in motion is always an emblem of the Spirit. The river in its main and undivided body is the Spirit in the creative and recreative, renewing and refreshing sense, of the whole course of work and blessing in nature and in man. In cellular or globular formations the gradation is from the centre outwards and onwards; in annular ones it is in repeated forms, measures, and numbers outwards and onwards; in man there is an epitome of all, but the whole is summed up into the full form of the parts in one upright frame. The to and fro work is carried on in all directions. The creature that, in the incidental otherwise of things, as it were mimics all that is and ought to be, is the Serpent representation. Hence the Serpent is taken as a fit emblem and symbol of an embodied falsity, an all-formed and all-forming mimic body of the lower and outer incidental modes and forms in which all realities seem to become a mere empty mocking shadow, a falsity, a lie. At the parts and points at which it asserts itself as the substance, reality and truth, it parts with the substance of which it is the shadow and passes into its full unreality and untruth; and there becomes the incidental means and occasion of the real and true to appear in full form omnipotence. It is in its apparent nakedness and semitransparent appearance, though really thick skinned crust, limbless and harmless form yet poisoning liquid, like matter, that it most nearly resembles the underlying element of the poison curing, truly spiritual, pure, living, and life-giving spirit. It is in this respect that it symbolises the highest or deepest forms of subtle nature and action in the three departments of natural desire or lust, self-righteousness, and self-deification; and it finds expression in what men call deceit, hypocrisy, and sin against the Holy Ghost. Sin in itself and in its whole history is incidental and occasion taking. Its curse is that the course of things will keep it in the place, relations, and manner of the shady existence belonging to it in the nature of things, that, Simei-like, it must not go outside that place, and that the day thou dost go, or the day thou eatest of the forbidden fruit thou shalt surely die. The oldnesses of things are ever being left below and behind and without in a gradation passing into a dark shadow and disappearing. The very shade of the shadow or reflection of existence depends on existence or that of which the shadow or shade is or to which it belongs; in eating up that existence it becomes, as it were, existence and necessarily disappears in its shadow and shade sense, while the existence forever remains in eternal continuity. This is the curse on man and woman, on all nature, and on the Serpent and sin in all that sin is or can be. It is the incidental shadow of nature's blessing, or, in its highest nature and form, the Spirit's blessing, the blessing in necessary disguise, and hence appearing, and being bestowed and enjoyed, in its true character and garment of grace, a reward of grace in spite of dark and deadly demerit, yet a reward of graceful congruity in being according to the nature of things and according to the recipient's trained conformity of action and conduct.

The eating of the forbidden fruit goes on throughout the whole of nature in all time and man's whole existence on earth. A summary act and form of it take place at every point of transition small and great. Man becomes conscious of it in his own case as he grows in consciousness of volition and free action. The great leading transition points are most easily seen in the three leading stages of the highest and most distinct formations in plant, animal, and human kinds of life; but it is equally real and true in the life and history of nations taken as single or combined, in those of man's whole time on earth, and in those of all creation. Such absorptive transitions have their prototypal summaries in the three personalities in the Divine Being. The present seems to be one of these great transition times. There is a special sense in which the flaming sword is love, as the sum of all virtue, and all kinds of love in plant and animal; in the animal, social, and moral sense, and in the moral, intellectual, and spiritual sense. Then all these kinds of love, summed into the love of the Spirit, is love to God; and it is that to God and man and all beings in the one God-man; it being all clothed and crowned in knowledge, righteousness, and holiness. As the seraphim of a lower three they are in one point the teraphim in lower relation to the next higher. So man driven out, or sent forth, cannot get back into the Garden, or Eden, or get forward into it but through what is symbolised by these three images and the flaming sword. Of the three pairs of sensation forms in the face or head of animals and of man, and indeed in some sense of all beings, the first is the mouth and nostrils, to which the highest substances of matters of life from below gives exercise. This substance is incense as the combination or substance of matters of life from below and in connection with the stomach and the heart. The second is that of the nostrils and the organs of hearing, in sum as connected with the heart and the lungs. And the third or highest is the hearing and seeing, being in sum connected with all the three. The substance of matters of life in connection with the second is voice in sound and singing, metre and music, prayer and praise, as of all beings, or all the sons of God together. That of matters connected with the third is the reflection of the divine character in the divine image and in becoming in the true sense to be as gods. In the first there is the sum-substance return of all substance and all law and force to God, who is the all-sum Giver and all sum Getter. In the second it is the response of all good, and all good will in all beings to God and His glad tidings in Christ, the all absolute and all relative Father Son One Spirit. In the third it is the being all glorious and the all glory giving, like Him and to Him of whom, through whom, and to whom, are all things   So is it in the Song of Songs, chapter two, verses eleven to the fifteenth, and the whole book and all books.

As man eats of the tree of knowledge of good and evil, he is restored to the tree of life, as passing through the creative points which are forever in contact with all possible action. The tree of life is the inmost being of the tree of knowledge of good and evil, but its enjoyment is in righteousness. Knowledge and righteousness must be together in enjoying any kind of life. A living agent and his living, moving, and having being must be in light and freedom, or knowledge and righteousness; whether he is conscious of the same or not. Jesus Christ is both trees as the sum of all trees ; and man has both in passing through sin and death into righteousness and life. Christ is said to have died to sin once, and that in living He forever liveth to God. The birth of Cain and Abel is spoken of as having taken place after the expulsion. The phrase to know, implies an intercourse with the object as uncovered ; it is a knowledge of what the object really is in its inmost nature to its underlying being. Sexual intercourse has a special connection with the brain through all bodily connections by the muscles, the nerves, and the spinal cord ; and so with the social and moral feelings in to the intellect. An act of naked receptive power or element is necessary in receiving or giving a sensation or impression ; and a formative act of generalisation is necessary to convert that impression or perception into a formal concept or conception. This holds equally true of physical, animal, moral, and intellectual acts and processes. Difference of sex is implied in all things ; it is as real in mind as in body. The faculties in both sexes are identical ; but they have respectively their peculiar qualities. The average brain weight of woman is about five ounces less than that of man. There is a comparative absence of originality in woman. It is man's to know, the woman's to be known. The female intellect is peculiarly receptive, prompt, and subtle to take in all outward impressions. In no one department of creative thought can woman be said to have approached man ; their success in fiction is no real exception. The outcome, or effect, of any thing, as opened up, is often called birth, as the whole relative is the whole manifesting birth, outcome, or production of the absolute. In its first sense it is necessarily one ; in its second it is into two sides.

Adam's knowing Eve is here the summarising of the whole past from the beginning into two sum-sons, Cain and Abel. As all-man and all-woman, Adam and Eve act in passing out of the old creative past into the new beginning present, this all sense being inclusively true of all beings. All things thus become relatively two, one old sum son and one new sum-son, of that passing act or change, Cain and Abel, and make, with their previous oneness in the Adam-Eve, three in one, or into the fourth or Seth-son in the great Aeonic line. Of only two sons, the first, as elder, stands for the older and outer, and the second, as younger, for the newer and inner, of all persons and things, or all beings, represented by them. So are Cain and Abel, so are Esau and Jacob, and all such, into the all sum of the Jews and Jesus Christ. Chain is implied in the term Christ, as the old and outer of all beings. Ye are not of the world, as I am not of the world. This is equivalent to saying, and to the fact, that of four sons the fourth is the Aeonic son; so is Judah, and so is David taken as the fourth, and so is all such, into Christ the All-son. The word Cain, like its aspirated sound, indicates the hard, harsh, and rough old and outer of all things from the beginning. This outer is older, because appearing and being formed first, but is from the inner, and is the outer and older of the inner Abel, as Elohim is in relation to Jehovah. So Eve says that she has gotten a man from the Lord, the Elohim Cain man of the Jehovah Abel man. The literal etymology of Abel is Abba-El, Father-God. It is the inner Jehovah-El as from the beginning in all beings and each being, here implied as the all sum son of the all-man and the all-sum son of the Father-Son begetting in the whole onward course of being; the inmost and the highest being the Divine Spirit as such. The Divine Being is in it as Jehovah-El inner and as the spirit inmost sense; all here moving out of the creative into the begetting sense, and so in the sense of Jehovah-El Father-Son sense, and the outer of all this being in the Cain Jehovah-El Father-Son sense, and passing in the outer form of the line of genealogical begetting. Moreover, that Adam and Eve are become as gods has this same implication. The Abel of things is younger, and born or produced as second sum-son, because appearing later and coming forth as the inner. It should be remembered that the inner is always, by nature, necessity, and relations of thing, the real being and that which puts out the outer before it for being the couch, the cover, and the means of subsistence for itself in its onward movement in time and space. The inner is thus the Abel, the Father-God, in all gradations of beings from the Spirit outwards and downwards.

Abel is a keeper of sheep, but Cain is a tiller of the ground. The ground is the raw, rough, lower, and outer of all things, needing cultivation, improvement, and preparation for inner, higher, finer, and more refined being and having being, in all gradations. This is true as to the physical, plant, animal, human, and heavenly. Glass, brass, silver, and gold, and the precious stones represent somewhat of the gradation in kind and improvement by nature and man in the physical; and to the

Cainites belong much of the work and Judas bag-keeping of such, up to certain transition changes, of which the present seems to be one. The most refined in the physical is the living nature of its forces, substances, and laws; which are in contact with the self-living and all life-giving Spirit, and pass in improved condition through the gradation of plant, animal, and human, to the Elohistic level and divine contact of being as gods, and having eternal life in God with Christ. Cain represents the outer and lower of all this as essentially good and being ever improved out of incidental deterioration; and, in a second sense, as having an incidental evil attached, yet being ever put away, positively by the positive good, and negatively by self-destruction, as the opposite of the Spirit's self-living and all life giving. What is said of the Serpent as evil, of sin, and of Satan, has its peculiar implication in the Cain representation. In this character the Baptist addresses the Pharisees and Sadducees, O generation of vipers; and Jesus says, ye are of your father the devil. In an evil sense the seed of the serpent is sin, and personally the Cainites. When fully and formally taken, the evil father-son personality is Satan, as in the words, ye are of your father the devil, and Paul's words, thou son of the devil; and the last and utmost sense of the representation is the opposite of the Holy Spirit, as in saying that Christ had an unclean spirit, and in the sin against the Holy Ghost.

The true inner of all beings is the Abel, the Father-God, the creative and begetting, giving and receiving, the truly converted, improved, and refined. Cain's work is to till, or cultivate, the ground, and so convert it to what is called earth, in its universal sense. Cain himself means here mostly the outer as ground and plants. It is to do so, as incidental and necessary evil, indirectly to righteousness and life, and directly to self-destruction, self-extinction, and self-disappearance. It is to do so, as essentially good, though having evil attached, and though being comparatively outer and lower than Abel. And it is to pass, as converted and renewed sum-substance into Abel, and itself to pass on as outer to Abel in scapegoat being and work. The world as comparative and congenial to the Cainites is thus the ground in its raw, rough, and rugged wildness in gradation of all outer physical, plant, and animal being and having being; while the inner and higher in all is comparative and congenial to Abel, as in the arrangement of things at the meeting and parting of Esau and Jacob. Plant life in its crab or wild state is so to Cain; in its grafted or converted and improved state it is so to Abel. The trenching and harrowing, the cutting and killing, belong to Cain; the sowing and growing, the improved life and living, belong to Abel. The gradation of all wildness of animal life, as symbolised by so many instances from the worm to the lion and the leviathan, is Cain's; that of the clean, tame, and more homely, as symbolised by sheep, is Abel's. The giving and sacrificing of others to suffering and death are Cain's by character and office; the character being the comparatively wild and incidentally evil, though indirectly to good, and the office being comparatively and by position and relations Elohistic though indirectly to Jehovah-El. Cain is thus all as being forever changed and converted into being Abel; Elohim is all in the eternal outgoing and incoming of Jehovah, the all creative and begetting Spirit.

It has been seen that the work of all creations is in orderly gradation from the original and virginal Om of the Spirit to the distinct formation of the woman; that the deep sleep of Adam is from the original Om to that distinct formation of the woman; that Adam's knowing Eve, his wife, is from the original Om as one, and each Om in each being, up to the distinct Eve's one sum-Om birth of Cain and Abel; and here is seen that the all-sum working through time is, in whole and in each sum part and stage from the original Om to its Omic ending-beginning recommencement, by the older and outer Cain, and the younger and inner Abel, or the outer Elohim and the inner Jehovah, with the eternal spirit as inmost and highest. Every thing is being forever changed, converted, and renewed, but is conveniently spoken of as to the sum-substance in passing through the transition lines of passage. Hence are the words, in the process of time it came to pass, that Cain brought of the fruit of the ground an offering unto the Lord. The fruit is the head-sum of the yield of the ground; the offering of the sum-substance which is to pass in and as scapegoat, while the incidental evil is to pass away and disappear. The offering has thus to pass to the Lord through Abel, Apollo Briereus, Jesus Christ, through the sacrificial and all fulfilling seventh point, or one, four, seven, ten, into the divine conformity, divine image, and eternal life. This means the shedding of blood, without which there is no remission and no real transition; and of which the mere fruit offering, and that of the ground, not the earth, comes intrinsically short, like the Jewish offerings of Christ's time.

10. Abel's offering is of the firstlings of his flock and of the fat thereof. It is the head sum-substance of the whole of what he possesses in all gradation, and the fat or best thereof, the first, best, and highest of all, including also the same out of Cain's all, as the sum-substance of the physical and plant is in the animals and man. The fat so far represents the ending beginning protoplasm and ozone in every creative and begetting work. In self sacrifice the inner being, life, soul, and spirit of that being sacrificed, die to what they are and have been into being what they are becoming in themselves and to God, leaving off and behind the oldnesses of things of whatever kind. Change of being and of all is incidental to being and to all; yet being and all continue essentially and identically the same, as it were unchanging in all changes. So is it in all force, all life, and all being. So the offerer gives himself and all his in all gradation though in head sum-substance,

as in fruit, or firstling of flock and the fat thereof. He does so formally and at certain times of special transition, or always, as in service and suffering, and in changing and parting with what is being sacrificed or offered; while he really continues to be, to carry with him and in him the sum-substance of all things, and holds communion with God in whom he lives, moves, and has his being. The offering thus implies imitation of God's example in all things, a giving of the being and his all to God, and a festive communion with God in faith's sense of soul exercise of all powers, faculties, and capacities. What is offered by Cain is thus himself, in himself, and belonging to him in all gradations; and what is offered by Abel is likewise thus himself, in himself, and belonging to him in all gradations.

The Lord's disregarding the offering of Cain, or rather himself and his offering, is the beginning and following out of casting off and away of the old and unacceptable of things. It implies the head sum-substance of the unacceptable, then the heart and soul being of him as indicated in his wrath, and thirdly the whole sense region of him, as indicated by the falling of his countenance, which is the facial accumulation of all the senses. Taken as head-sum, that the Lord has not respect unto Cain and his offering corresponds to the cerebrum and cerebellum; that Cain is very wroth answers to the midpart and head-part of the whole body, and that his countenance fell is as to the sense region, and summed into the frontal and facial part of the head. Cain is thus the all of Adam, as the all-man, that is forever being put off; and Abel, or Father-God inner of all from the beginning, is thus the all of Adam to be continued as inner forever onwards through death into life. In reasoning respecting his wrath, it is shown that it is without all proper cause or ground. If he does well, he will be accepted; and in doing well, whether in the sense of being Abel, or being in or with Abel in doing well, or as distinct from Abel, there can be no good cause, ground, or room for envious and jealous wrath or unpleasant feeling. If he does not well, sin lies at the door, or Om of all inlet and outlet, of all to and fro action. Sin lies at the door of Cain as guilty of it, as seeking more evil to do and to bear, as crying for judgment and punishment according to law and justice, and as standing in outer and special relation to Cain. As it is through and in connection with the inner Abel that the outer Cain gets being and well-being, so it is also through him and in connection with him that he can have favourable relations to Jehovah and have deliverance from sin and all evil. The connections, co-relations, and relative positions and actions of both, as distinct and as one in the one all-man, imply all this; and the outward official position, standing, and relations of Cain imply the same. It thus belongs to Cain to give Abel as the world or all sacrifice, as it belonged to the Jews and Romans to give Jesus Christ as the world or all sacrifice. That Jesus says, that the judge in dealing with Him would, or could, not have any power over Him were it not given him from above, implies that the judge had that power; and Scripture expressly speaks of him that had the power of death, that is, Satan. Death is because of sin. The form, meaning, and relations, of all beings to the necessary zero and the line of least resistance imply the possibility of incidental evil or sin. The fact of that evil or sin is known in nature, in man, in the government of the world, and in the Bible. The necessity and the fact of sacrifice are known in the same connections and ways. Rule goes with Omic getting.

The power of the judge over Jesus, as given from above, is the rule here spoken of, and thou shalt have rule over him, that is over Abel, as the judge had power over Christ. As the power spoken of by Jesus was from above, so the rule here is spoken of by Jehovah Himself. In all things the to and fro force from within outwards is the same from without inwards, that backwards is the same forwards, and that downwards is the same upwards. There can be no force, motion, action, or being independent of, or apart from, the eternal, universal, and all-sum One Being. In the gradation of account of eating the fruit the excuse is followed in and up to the Lord God Himself, the woman whom Thou gavest to be with me, she gave me of the tree, and I did eat. All sin has a necessarily incidental connection with all voluntary and involuntary action, with all character, condition, and conduct, with all being and having being. The nature, sense, and action of conscience are such that it refers every good and evil in and up to Jehovah the inmost and highest being, with whom there is forgiveness that He may be feared, that every evil may be remitted and righted, rectified and remedied, and all things made new.

From man's distinct creation to the Garden is his distinct first part, from one to four; in the Garden is the entrance into marriage and family life, or the transition passage into that life; and here, from the beginning of this the fourth chapter to the death of Abel is the sum-substance of the middle part of life from four to seven, the family, socio-moral, and public life. Here Cain is man in general, man from the Lord as Elohim is outer from Jehovah; and Abel is Father-God man, or the Father-Son Aeonic God man, is inner of and to Cain. The sum of all relations and all else is in Adam and Eve, coming out in full distinctness as man and woman, brother and sister, man and wife; and now coming out in the full distinctness of acting as man and wife in family life, and social and public life, with the full distinctness of all the relations of parents and children, brothers and sisters, conditions and dealings in family, social, and public life, all given in a brief summary of what obtains in all time.

As tiller of the ground and in the process, or whole course, of time, in all particulars as well as in all sum, Cain brings of the fruit of the ground, as the yield of all his being and having being, in all relations and gradations of all things, an offering to the Lord, as the result of occupy till I come, in all occupying and all coming. In like manner ever does Abel, as keeper of sheep, or the inner of all things throughout all time. The sum-substance of the All-man, as Cain, is the outer; that, as Abel, is the second, or mid-part; and that, as Jehovah in and of all is the third or inmost and highest. The change is in the Lord's respect to all as coming to Him through Abel, but not as immediately and without the God-man mediator, from Cain, also in Cain's wrath, and in the falling of Cain's countenance; or, which is the same, it is in the passing on out of and from the oldnesses of all things in new Jehovah sense, in new sum-substance, and in new scapegoat, while the incidental evil is put away. All well-being and all well-doing have always all acceptance, from the lowest and outmost to the inmost and highest. Formal evil does not enter, does not find acceptance, and does not avail or prevail with Jehovah. Sin may lie and lurk at the door; but it cannot enter; and the sinner, as such, cannot. The inhabitants of Siddim could not enter with or after Lot and his visitors, the foolish virgins could not, even Israel as Egyptian and faithless could not. Sin, as incidental to force, has its summary representation in personal evil as a roaring lion seeking whom to devour; as incidental to all laws, it has the same in what is conveyed and expressed in such words as, we are not ignorant of his (Satan's) devices. Sin is all-betraying and all-destroying as to itself, and as to the sinner himself, and all else.

In the Cain side of the representation the Om is the ground; in that of Abel it is the flock; and in that of dealing by all, as to all things, with Jehovah, it is the door, in the all-sum Om of all outlet and inlet in all being and having being. The words, unto thee shall be his desire, and thou shalt rule over him, are much the same in form and meaning as those addressed to the woman, thy desire shall be to thy husband, and he shall rule over thee. The desire of the inner is always to the outer; which latter has itself and its all from within, but is being made, or is ever growing up, into all forms of substances, forces, and laws, possessions and powers, rule and dominion. The desire of Jehovah is to His outer self in the Elohim, that of the Father to the Son, that of the Spirit to the Father-Son all in all. Wisdom says, the Lord possessed me in the beginning of His way, before His works of old. I was set up from everlasting, from the beginning, or ever the earth was. So in all time, manner, and process of works, then I was by Him as one brought up with Him; and I was daily His delight, rejoicing always before Him; rejoicing in the habitable part of His earth; and my delights were with the sons of men. The desire of the woman and of the man with her, is to the fruit, and the desire of the Lord God, in the same gradation, is to them, and to all from within outwards; while sin gets not farther inwards than the door, but is being put away by the personal door, Christ, who says, I am the Door. The desire of the woman, as last appearing, and as mother of all living, is to Adam, as her all-man husband. The desire of Jesus Christ as all-sum of the inner is to the sons of men, or to Himself the all-son of man, as all outer. He, as all inner, gives Himself to all outer, or to Himself as all outer, and receives, gets, and takes all sum-substance of the outer to Himself, to the Father, in one eternal Spirit.

Christ's desire is to the Jewish nation and all the nations of the earth; but they have laws, rule, and power to arrest Him, judge Him, and put Him to death. The desire of the sap from the earth, and the light, the air, and the rain of heaven, are to the plant formations; so that the desire of physical and plant substances, and all that go to animal life, is to animal creatures; and so the desire of all is to man, the all-man, the sons of men or the all-son of God and of man, or that of Jehovah to the Elohim. Still it is essentially and necessarily implied in the universal law of to and fro being, and having being, that the desire of the outer is to the inner, and that it universally and always gives itself and its all to the inner, from which it ever gets it. He gives Himself in all, to all, and for all; and, in doing so, He gets all, takes all, and possesses all. They truly and well say, He saved others; Himself He cannot save. Universal loss in universal death must be; but it is all to everlasting life and everlasting gain. He that loses his life shall save it to everlasting life. In not saving Himself, but giving Himself. His life, and His all, He and they in Him give themselves, their life, and their all, to death; but in doing so, He and they save themselves, their life, and their all. This is the call of the universal and eternal to and fro being and having being. The middle point, or the middle of all mid-points, between the to and the fro, is the Son of God Son Man, of Apollo, of Abel, of Jesus Christ. This is essential to the nature of the constitution of all things, it is the organic law of Messiah's kingdom. He says that He is the Son of God, making Himself equal with God.

They of the outer line are gods; but they shall die as men. When He comes up to the stage of from seven to ten, and has decisive dealings with them, all things are summed into this midpoint of Son of God and being equal with God. Their oldness, outness, and wildness, their self-indulgence, self-righteousness, and self-deification, are summed into one perversion of Cain we, in Cain envy, jealousy, wrath, rivalry, denial, and opposition unto death, towards the Abel He, the I am He. This decisive dealing takes place where they are; the talking between Cain and Abel is when they are in the field. There Cain rises up against Abel his brother, and slays him. When they were come to the place, which is called Calvary, there they crucified Him. The Cain conduct is a summary of the slaying of the Lamb of God from the beginning of the world; that upon you may come all the righteous blood shed upon the earth, from the blood of righteous Abel unto the blood of Zacharias, son of Barachias, whom ye slew between the temple and the altar. Verily I say unto you, All these things shall come upon this generation.

Incidental evil and its manifold aggravations are not sinless because the to and fro law of force and motion is necessary to, and causative of, concurrent and competing motion and action, co-operation and competition, all comparisons and contrasts, affirmation and denial. The remedy, or that which is fitted and all-sufficient to put away sin is not in excuses, not in the power of Rome and of the world, not in the perversions and the seeking of signs as by the Jews and all nations, not in Greek gradation of intellect as in Socrates, Aristotle, and Plato, and the world with its wisdom, but in the All-one mid-line meditator Son of God, the All in All. This includes all possible particulars and instances of all possible good; and nothing can be lost or safely despised. Each mission has its opposition through death into life. On the return of Tiberius Gracchus from Sardinia he drew forcible attention to the fact that eighty thousand of the inhabitants had been killed or sold as slaves. So incensed were the classes at his advocacy of the cause of the suffering toilers of the world that a mob of them murdered him in the streets of Rome. They subsequently murdered his equally noble brother Caius for treading in his footsteps. Distinctions as of Socrates being the son of the marble cutter, and of Jesus being the son of the carpenter, are not to be overlooked in literal or symbolic representations.

All relieving and remedial means and movement have always been rightly viewed by suffering humanity as a reviving and redeeming visitation of Jehovah; and the leader of each such movement was appropriately crowned with an emblem of the character of that in which he excelled. The three colours taken for the Aeonic parts were green for the lower part, red for the middle, and white for the third. Jesus is the King of Kings and Lord of Lords, and is crowned Lord of All. A president of finance strict in faithfulness and perfect in good will and work is accounted a stranger because so much of a remarkable rarity; and he is rightly and readily naturalised by a people maltreated by caste and class, thieves and robbers, and crowned with a chaplet of foliage, in token of a thing so new as if the world was passing into a resurrection of new life, light, and goodness. And they rejoice to glorify him as Alemeon, son of Theon. The cross is an all-balancing emblem, with its upright mid-line of onwards to and fro Aeonic movement, its cross beam of to and fro side and round directions of force, its right and left hands and shoulder points of titan thieves and robbers, and the sum-substance of all passing upwards and onwards into the new and universal kingdom, the kingdom of truth and justice, mercy and peace, purity and love, and joy in the Holy Ghost.

Plato and the dialecticians may speak of principles and qualities, and of such as the three moral impulses of irascibility, concupiscence, and sympathy; but Jesus makes them three in one, by coaxing concupiscence from its ancient realm and bringing it down to want, and marrying them together by the tie of sympathy into placability and peace, not Cain irascibility and envy, jealousy and wrath, murder and rapine. Cain outer gods usurp and assume the place, position, and rights of all things in endless particulars, as rent, surplus, profit, tithes, and all else of God, of man, and of nature. Their arrogance carries its god in its hand, the sword; and they are ever slaying Abel, because his works are good and their own evil. The good is thus ever dying to evil, and is ever living in newness of being and having being.

In this full gradation the particulars are, Cain's offering, Abel's offering, the sacrifice of all sum-substance in Abel's death, and all into the Lord's dealing with Cain, and the crying of the all sum-substance blood to the Lord from the ground. It is from the ground, or oldest and outmost, hindmost and lowest, up to the Lord and on in the ever newness of things. The ground is thus the outer sum layer, circle, or form of the all original Om; the flock is the inner layer, circle, or form of it; and the shoulder point of the field, in which Cain and Abel meet and have the all concentration of things, is that into which the all sum-substance is brought into the all Omic form and meeting with Jehovah and parting with all oldness into all newness. This meeting with the Lord is always the turning point in every Ishtar descent or transition change. Here the Ishtar stripping of all old articles of garment of old things is completed; full account is rendered to the Supreme Judge, Lawgiver, Governor, and Giver of all good; the Ishtar sum-substance of things are passed on, also the scape-goat passes on in its newness and new outer place and relations; and the all incidental oldnesses and evils are put away and disappear for ever. The Chaldean, Egyptian, Greek, and other ancient representations of this agree with what the Bible everywhere says of it. It contains the everlasting covenant in all sum-substance of Father Son substances, forces, and laws of all being and having being, in the one eternal Spirit; and is formally made known in Jesus Christ, the Absolute and the Relative Jehovah Elohim. It is confirmed by the death of the Abel-Christ Testator; and the Divine Oath is attached to it in the declaration made as to the continuity of all things in preservation, propagation, and relations of all beings in wellbeing.

The declaration is here put in the form of assurance of the safety of Cain's life. Cain's real sum-substance dies to the oldnesses of things and lives to the newnesses of them in, and with, Abel, only as outer in gradation; and the real sum-substance of the matter and meaning of the covenant, confirmation, and oath, forever accompanies that sum-substance of things, or is the same therewith, in their ever inner Abel and outer Cain, or Jehovah and Elohim, sense. The mark of this covenant belongs really and essentially to the Jehovah sum-substance; but outwardly, representatively, and officially, it belongs also to the external form and Elohim manifestation and meaning of things. So this mark is set on Cain, in its seven or tenfold Omic and Aeonic form; and this

9

seven or ten form is accordingly the measure and manner of vengeance on any killing Cain. This mark has to do with the divine image, the cross, the essential form of force in motion, and all else in nature, man, and God. Its inmost and highest form is in the Spirit or the divine nature and personality; then particularised by gradation in the Divine Name, as said to be in the Angel of the Covenant or the Father-Son Mediator of the covenant and its Angel and its all and all included; farther, as on the white stone or Ishtar substance and him that overcometh of Revelation, the Abel sense of all of all beings, as the saints and their gradation in all existences; and lastly in all outer things of Cain gradation.

Cain's curse is his natural destiny in the process of time and action. He is excluded and confined to the sphere of the older and outer forms of things. The change of renewal implied in his offering, in that of Abel, and in the death of Abel, and the Lord's dealing with him thereon, is all the way through all things from the ground's opened mouth, or original Om, and in all purifying and renewing merit, virtue, and influence of offerings, sacrifice, and divine dealing, up to the Lord. His is the whole outer course of motion and work in nature, man, and Elohim; and the strength of these is in, and derived from, the self-living and all life-giving Jehovah. In the nature and action of things as in these, this strength is forever being expended and dying out, and is being kept up and continued in them as possessed in and derived from Jehovah, or in the gradation of Jehovah, Abel, and Cain form. The outer Cain course of all cannot have this strength in selfishness and wicked and murderous opposition; and cannot have it even in any gradation of nature, but as in and derived from Jehovah, through Abel dying-living renewal. His destiny is to be the to and fro fugitive and vagabond in the earth, in to and fro tilling the ground into cultivated earth, or to and fro action with the Abel of all things; to be in the condition and relations of being ever driven from the face, or refined senses and influences, of earth, or cultivated ground or nature of things, driven also thus from the face or inner mid-line communion with Jehovah, and so hid in the exclusion and disappearance; and to be slain by every person and thing, so parting with him and putting him away in all wildness, oldness, and outness. The vengeance on these slaying him is in their gradation of Abel suffering in so far as they are of the Abel being and having being; and in their causing and self-causing suffering so far as they are of the Cain kind. Abel, or Christ, in dying as sin and for sin, puts away sin and death, and passes on in righteousness and life; thus in sum destroying the works of the devil, and advancing the works of all that is good and godly.

From the inmost and highest point of gradation in the presence of the Lord, Cain goes out and dwells in the land of Nod (wandering), to the east of Eden. Nod is the reverse of Eden in word and meaning; and the east is the outer to the left and front, into passing behind, or east and south. As the outer of the all-man, his position is continued as comparative fugitive in the earth (eree, earth in process of tillage; Adamah being more of a cultivated and fruitful earth). Being the all-outer of the all-man, his wife comes forth with him, or from him in Eve fashion, as the outer form of the all-Eve Om mother of all living. She is thus an original and virginal sister wife, or all relations wife, as is the case in the female side of each of the men of the main mid-line of Christ's Aeonic genealogy. His knowing her is in connection of creation from the beginning and in connection of distinct conception from the outcoming of things in the all-man's distinct Cain and Abel form. His Aeonic genealogy and city, or line of seats of empire, are given first, because he is taken as the elder son; and the inner and younger Abel is continued by Jehovah in the all-man through Seth. His Aeonic city Son, or first seat of empire Son, is Enoch, as name of son and city in the sense of the reverse of Cain, or ain, an eye or Om, and chain, a possession, together making Om-possession, or city and seat (of empire) of central and comparatively settled condition as distinguished from all wandering life. The term Enoch is thus related to land and city at the beginning and at the seventh, otherwise tenth point end; so it is the name of the seventh son from Adam. The Cain succession and city are the outer of the Aeonic line to the Deluge. Tubal-ain contains the sum of the whole Adamic Cain in outer relation to the Jabal and Jubal meanings of Jehovah Father God, into one whole sum-substance of all, in the summary and universal standard and type of the Tau or Tora. Naannah is the one sister of all, as Dinah is that of all Jacob's family. She is the Omic means of all in passing into a new order of things; but this is not stated here, because it is the history of the Adamic Abel which is continued, not that of the Adamic Cain.

Lamech's address to his two wives is in respect to the artificial means and ways of work and life, through which men pass into self-made beings and having being. He has thus slain a man, man as only natural, not thus artificially improved, to his wounding or dying to the old and unimproved character and condition of things, besides the deadly and destructive use made of artificial means like the sword; and a young man, the past youth of man and the world, to his hurt, or suffering and loss in parting with the simple and easy naturalness of the past in passing into the new mechanical, artificial, formal, and dry order and manner of things. If Cain shall be avenged sevenfold as a merely natural sevenfold man formation or being, Lamech shall be avenged seventy sevenfold, or two sevens placed beside each other, 77, being double seven for him as now double man, or double all-man and all world. This double state applies to all through all time to the Deluge and to the end of the world, and specially to Christ's time, to which the Aeonic men are seventy-seven in number; and on His work the seventy-seven sin of the world from the very beginning is forgiven, and the incidental Cain-Judas disappears as to the past, but has its peculiar succession of its kind and after its kind.

CHAPTER V.

THE re-appearance of the whole creation in the begetting mode of reproduction is in the Adamic all-man Aeonic son Seth, the first particular and distinct sum-son under the Abel of all things is continued under these head-sum names, ever dying to, and ever being slain by, the Cain of them. Sheth (Shin or ish and Heth) signifies appointed and given place to, or inner and Hittite man, as internal strength and continuity of the Jehovah Elohim all Aeonic mid-line. This continuity is in all-man begetting; so the next name is Enos (ain, an eye, a well, an Om, and ish, a man), the Omic and Aeonic man. He is in the position of beginning or mature in sexual, moral, religious, and all manly feelings. So it is at this level it is said that men began to call upon the name of the Lord.

Here is introduced the book of the generations of Adam; perhaps an already written document, and containing the whole of this chapter. The day that God created man here means the time when He did so. In first Samuel xxix. 3, David's time with Achish is called days or years. Man as then created is spoken of as plural, male and female, and having one name Adam. It is the representative summary all-man. As man was created in the image of God and after His likeness; so from that point the Aeonic genealogical descent is continued in that image and that likeness from God and as the Son of God through Adam, Seth, Enos, and the rest, without speaking of Abel and Cain, who are taken, not as particular Aeonic genealogical persons, but as the whole two Omic layers, as inner and outer of the Omic and Aeonic all-man, throughout the whole genealogy. The Omic layers of relations, taken from within outwards and backwards, are the Spirit as inmost and highest in all beings and common to both Father and Son, and therefore stands as sum third Person, to them as first and second, and yet is eternally the Omic One containing the three, or three in one. The onward motion and movement leave a gradation of grandfather, great-grandfather, and such in ever ending-beginning succession. But the all-sum head is in the Spirit and Father-Son, or simply Father-Son, with the Spirit as the all common, all-invisible, and all inclusive, One Being. Hence the whole genealogy consists of the successive Aeonic individual head-sum sons: each son becoming father in begetting a son, and being put in the form of son of, son of, in one

Omic and Aeonic line of son head-sum of all beings. The Spirit is the all-sum Being. In self-begetting, He becomes All-Son, and necessarily All-Father to that All-Son. He is thus the all-sum personal One Being as ever original and ever virginal Omic and Aeonic Spirit; He is the all-sum personal One Being as ever original and virginal Omic and Aeonic Father; and He is the all-sum personal one Being as ever original and virginal Omic and Aeonic Son. In Himself He is the one absolute Being; but as Spirit-Father-Son He is the whole sum of the whole possible relative, and implies and contains all possible relations. He is infinite, eternal, and unchangeable; but implies and contains all possible Omic and Aeonic ending-beginning measures and limits, days or times, changes and vicissitudes. While He is all as Self-Being, He is as nothing and unthinkable except as in the self-begetting of the self-being-begotten Son in whom the Father-Son all manifestations are possible.

As Father, the Spirit is eternally passing away and disappearing in self-begetting and self-being-begotten and in self-appearing and self-being-manifested in the Son. Hence the Son is the only and whole Logos, or personal manifestation of the Deity. No one hath seen the Father at any time; the only begotten Son who is in the bosom of the Father, He hath declared Him. Thus, in studying the cosmos, or world of these manifestations, or any formation, part, or particle, of the universe of beings, the mind finally arrives at a point, or level, at which all beyond is unthinkable, the region of no Father-Son form of manifestations, where all is as nothing, as Omic zero of non-being; yet in that whole region, in that whole zero, is the infinite, eternal, and universal Om and One of the All-Being.

The genealogical line of Father-Son succession is most expressly given by Luke; who begins with Jesus, and traces the connection through each one named as son of that one's predecessor to the words, the Son of God. The whole line is one of sons, or of the son, the son of man Son of God, or Son of God son of man. Jesus was supposed to be the Son of Joseph, but was really of the Spirit; and so is the whole line as the head-sum line of all things. Joseph is Jehovah-ish-eph, Jehovah man Father-Son. Jesus is the Greek form of the Hebrew Joshua, to which eph is added in Joseph (eph being the aspirated strong form of Abba). Each son in the line is a son in this sense of the Jehovah Father-Son all-man; and Jesus is the sum son of them all. In being so, He is the being-begotten, or self-being-begotten of the self-begetting and self-being-begotten Spirit, through the Spirit's ever original and virginal Om in Mary, the female side of the all ever dying ever living all being of beings. Mary, or Miriam, signifies sea waters, or the all bitter, or dying-living, waters, ever ending-beginning in ever being changed into living and life-giving sweet waters by the Spirit's ever creating and begetting work. The Spirit in the Father-Son Jesus is the Tree of Life;

and a branch, or the branch, the one, of it changes all waters of Marah into living life-giving sweet waters. Mary is thus the Spirit's Omic female side of all being and having being, the Spirit's ever original ever virginal sum Om, the All-sum Lady of the All-sum King of Kings and Lord of Lords, the all-sum sister-wife of each sum Father-Son man in the all Omic and Aconic line in all gradations and relations of universal being. These gradations are indicated by the words, and he begat sons and daughters.

Cain is the whole sum-substance in whole sum-son of the lower, outer, and older, of all things. So, at the Garden, the whole creation work, from the beginning up to that point, becomes distinctly the lower, older, and outer, of the middle or higher, inner, and newer or younger, Abel of all things. This occurs at the fourth, or one, four, seven, ten, point maturity or manhood of things, as at the Garden, here in Cainan, the third Aconic son or the fourth with Adam included. So is it in Ham as related to Shem, in Ishmael in relation to Isaac, and in Israel as a nation out of Egypt into Canaan. Taking all the lower, older, and outer as Elohim in relation to the middle or higher, newer, and inner Jehovah, the meaning of the words, then began men to call upon the name of Jehovah, and of Ex. vi. 2-4, may be easily perceived. In every change, great and small, the second layer from without becomes the outer with the sum-substance of the previous outer; so the Abel of the actual period becomes the advanced Cain of the new period, the Jehovah of the actual becomes the Elohim of the new period and its dispensation, the Jews of Christ's time become the Cain-Judas outer to the Christians, and the Jehovah from Moses to Christ becomes Jesus of the world's Christian time.

Mahalaleel is praise, or praiser, of God. In nature and man the time and conditions in entering the middle are specially marked and accompanied with joyous expression and jubilant outbursts of prophecy and music. So is the Song of Moses, the prophecy and music connected with the election and unction of Saul to be king, David's passing into public and kingly life through the victory over Goliath and the Philistines, the singing of him in dances by the women, and his own musical services to the king. So is the singing of birds as known in nature, and distinctly referred to in the Song of Solomon. Instrumental music belongs more to the outer layer, circle, and region of things. So the Cain Jubal is said to have been the inventor of such, the father of such as handle the harp and pipe. To have all sorts of music and musical means introduced into divine worship is a sign of oldness and outness of things and the near approach of the height and end of the period, and its customs and habits, forms, and fashions. As the male embryo passes, at a certain stage of growth and development, from the common sex form into the distinctly male; so does the voice pass at the maturity stage into the Mahalaleel character and exercise of male, and both male and female into the prophetico-musical stage. Mahalaleel consists of three singing syllables into a long fourth one, as in the crowing of the domestic fowl, Jupiter's true sum-bird; it is the one, four, seven, ten of all music.

The organs which act together in producing the voice are in action similar to the parts of a wind instrument, as the lungs to the bellows, the windpipe to the pipe, the larynx to the reed-box, the vocal chords to two flexible reeds, and the throat, mouth, and nose to the resonance or sound box. The whole vocal apparatus is nature's musical instrument.

Jared is Jehovah ruling with the sum-substance of descent and ascent, like the Chaldean Ishtar. Here is the sixth point like that of creation, at which the titans or shoulder point powers for good or ill form into full greatness, like Saul from the shoulders and upwards.

11. Enoch is composed of ain, an Om, or the Om, and a form of chain by transposition of letters, as quite common in Hebrew names. It is here related to the seventh point transition Omic line, through which the whole six points of the begetting passes in sum-substance into the head-part, as the whole of creation into the man summary in Adam. At the level of Enos it is said that men then began to call upon the name of the Lord; and this calling in continuance up to Enoch is now summed into the expression, Enoch walked with God. Here the whole lower and mid parts pass into the third or head part, which is the world-meaning of the words, and he was not; for God took him; the heaven-meaning being that he, or the Enoch spiritual substance of heavenly good of things, passed into the heavenly region and state of bliss. In the seventh point transition passage is always the great sacrificial and God man festive change, as in the works and formations of creation passing into man, in the ram sacrifice of Isaac, and the crucifixion of Christ. Enoch's walking with God, his change, and his transition and translation, are of the same nature and meaning with those of Christ; and so they are representative and prophetic of those of Christ, as stated in Jude's Epistle. Ten is the number of the Aeonic men from Adam to Noah, Enoch being the seventh. The number representative of persons and things in all full national sense, is a thousand. These ten Aeonic men, with a thousand saints of sum-substance significance under each, make up the whole ancient world summary representation and prophecy of all such in all beings through all duration and changes. The Lord comes with these sum-substance ten Aeonic men, each the head-sum of a thousand sum-substance saints, in the putting away of the ancient world oldnesses of all persons and things, as in one purging and purifying Deluge; and so does He in Christ's work at Jerusalem, and always and all where.

The third triad of the Aeonic gradation of persons and things is more difficult of clear perception in distinct particulars because it is mostly a summary triad of the lower and middle triads. Methusaleh relates to a change as if through death and hell, through the ten points summary transition by the sum-substance of all the things of God, man, and nature, from all oldnesses into a new order of things, as in a new world. This is made more distinct in Lamech, which name here indicates that the Abel and Cain of all beings are about to be, or are being, changed into newness of an improved character. Christ's crucifixion was from the sixth hour, and there was darkness over all the earth till the ninth hour, and the tenth is the summary hour. So here the Lamech (Abel and Chain) time is about the ninth ; and Noah is the summary head-sum man in time, persons, and things, from the old past through the Deluge transition line into the new world ; his tripartite sum-son substance of all being Ham, Shem, and Japhet.

The number of years is arranged and collocated in their natural three in one relative positions, and columns, of one column. The young come forth from thigh and shoulder Omic and transition absorption and sexual and rearing communications, being born and brought up in front, with special relation to east and south, in conformity to the natural shape of the body and the course of nature, particularly of the sun and the seasons. From one to four there is the opening out of every thing ; from four to seven there is the full opening ; and from seven to ten is the closing again into the one and Omic zero of the ten. The number of relative positions corresponds to the number of the Omic layers, and the relations of son, father, grandfather, and great-grandfather. When one is brought forth at the front or inmost point the outer line arrives at its tenth point and has its sum-substance, with that of the other lines, absorbed into and caused to pass through the transition line into the next new three in one form. Thus the outer numerical line can never be more than between nine and ten in number ; and so is it necessarily with the other inner and inmost lines. The beginning or birth figure is always the same as the ending figure, namely, one. The tenth point great-grandfather is thus forever being put away and disappearing ; but its sum-substance and scapegoat form pass on as renewed, while its oldnesses disappear. The grandfather line takes the place of the great-grandfather line, whenever one is born or produced in front ; the father line takes the place of the grandfather ; and the son line takes that of the father ; all just as in all Father-Son creative and begetting relations in all beings and periods of time or duration through universal space and the eternal Age of ages. The days of creation are Omic and Aeonic forms of gradation of creative action and mode of production now and ever going on in all original substances and laws of being up to the begetting mode of production as visibly known. The whole in relation to man, as the all-man, head sum is taken as one with two zeros written as one hundred. His puberty age for the lower part is about thirteen ; his manhood age of lower and middle taken together into three in one form is about thirty ; and the figure three, as standing for both, is placed after the one with a zero in the third position to mark the third line and the female side, all making one, three, nothing, and written as one hundred and thirty, as Adam's age when he begets his Aconic full seventh point son Seth. The Hebrew language is written and read from right to left, or from east to west with the course of the sun and the seasons, or the whole Aconic course of nature. The whole Aconic line from Adam as Son of God to Jesus as Son of God consists of about seventy-seven of Aconic sum-sons. This line put in arithmetical figures must be written and read from east to west and from south to north.

Cainan............... 1 4 7 10		Cainites.
3 6 9		
2 5 8		
Enos.................. 1 4 7 10		Naamah (Sister).
3 6 9		
2 5 8		
Seth.................. 1 4 7 10	Tubal Cain............ 1 4 7 10	
3 6 9	3 6 9	
2 5 8	2 5 8	
Adam................. 1 4 7 10	Jubal................. 1 4 7 10	
3 6 9	3 6 9	
2 5 8	2 5 8	
Son of God 1 4 7 10	Jabal................. 1 4 7 10	
3 6 9	3 6 9	
2 5 8	2 5 8	
Animals.............. 1 4 7 10	Lamech.............. 1 4 7 10	
3 6 9	3 6 9	
2 5 8	2 5 8	
Plants............... 1 4 7 10	Methusael........... 1 4 7 10	
3 6 9	3 6 9	
2 5 8	2 5 8	
Crusted Earth....... 1 4 7 10	Mehujael............ 1 4 7 10	
3 6 9	3 6 9	
2 5 8	2 5 8	
Chaos................ 1 4 7 10	Irad................. 1 4 7 10	
3 6 9	3 6 9	
2 5 8	2 5 8	
Gaseous Spheroid..... 1 4 7	Enoch............... 1 4 7	
3 6	3 6	
2 5	2 5	
Nebulous Ring........ 1 4	Cain................. 1 4	
3	3	
2	2	
Creator (Triune) 1	Adam................. 1	

The column from Creator to Cainan is written and read in the same way onward to Jesus the Son of God, as given in Luke's Gospel. Its outer side is in the Cainites. Things take the same form everywhere. At the feasts of the ancient Celts the minstrels sang and the harpers and pipers played, while the household and the guests sat and ate in three Omic rings, the more honoured in the inmost ring, the shield-bearers in the next or middle, and the javelin-men in the outer. All had a share of the viands without distinction; and equality reigned. This Omic character of things, among many other customs and habits to be noticed farther on, shows that their religion was that of nature, of Genesis, and really of the whole Bible.

CHAPTER VI.

Men begin to multiply, and by improvement to become doubly men. Daughters were born to them; which means that both sexes increased in all gradations. At the Aeonic shoulder point the titans appear, with implied female sides. In Dan. ii. 43, sub-kingdoms are said to mingle themselves with the seed of men; but that they shall not cleave to one another as iron not to clay. Noah is much the same as Jonah, the ending-beginning Jehovah sum-substance of all beings.

Elohim, as the outer of Jehovah, says, the end of all things is come before me; a saying evidently uttered in the manifestative meaning and form of me, in all gradations of beings. Thus the change refers specially to the things that manifestly appear, as creatures of earth and the earth itself; the creatures of the deep not being distinctly spoken of.

Ham, Shem, and Japheth, are the tripartite of the Jehovah Elohim, or the Jehovah Elohim All-man. Ham is the aspirated A, or Ja, or Jah, from the lowest and inmost origin and source of Omic opening onwards in all life-breathing to the closing-opening m; all as lower and outer in creative and begetting respects; and hence including Cain in all natural and all artificial and advanced states and stages. It necessarily includes what belongs to itself, to its position, and to its sphere, of the Elohim in a good sense or perverted sense, and so also of the inner Jehovah, only always as lower and outer of Shem. The inner, higher, and more real mid-part Son is Shem, summed into the production of man, and therefore called Shem, from Ish, man, and Ham, or the Jehovah man including Ham, or Jehovah all-man as made in the image of God. The image of Jehovah is in the Elohim; so man is made in the image and likeness of Elohim, or made as Elohim all-man. Ph is the hard and strong form of bh of Abba or Abha, father; th is the same of dh, as in Adam, or Adham, man; and Jah is Jehovah. Thus Japheth is Jehovah, and man as made and as father-son, or Jehovah man creative and begetting, or the third part head-sum Jehovah Elohim all-man, in all descent and ascent, outgoing and incoming, substance and form of all beings. The last part of Japheth, heth, is the shoulder point name for giant or titan, as in Heth and Hittite.

There is a manifest distinction between what is said of man, beast, the creeping thing, and the fowls of the air, and what is said of the earth as also being corrupt and filled with violence, which latter is said to be through them, the Elohim as evil. Both the Jehovistic and Elohistic all good is in and represented by Noah and his family, or in him in his three sons sense in generation gradations of beings. The evil Elohim, or the evil Elohistic head-sums, or generation sums, of all, is in the gradation head-sums of man, beasts, the creeping thing, and the fowls of the air, to be destroyed from the face, or all cultivable region of being and having being, of the earth or world. And through them these second, these evil Elohistic head-sums, the earth also, in the sense of all being and having being, represented by these evil head-sums, is become corrupt before God, or in this evil character of the Elohim, or of the men, means, and modes of His manifestations, and is filled with violence. The self-indulging, self-righteous, and self-deified titans, or powers that be, are the head-sum leaders in being corrupt and violent, in causing, in spreading, and in intensifying the corruption and violence, in all kind and character, manner and measure, of that corruption and that violence, in man, beast, the creeping thing, and the fowls of the air. The term earth, as distinguished from the term ground, signifies more than the physical world. It means the ground and the world, the cosmos or whole order of things, as being cultivated and civilised, improved and refined, beatified and beautified, being, with God and in God's image, likeness, and example, made all very good and very glorious.

The phrase, through them, implies that the powers that be, as evil, have selfishly, corruptly, wickedly, and violently misappropriated the things of nature, man, and God; that they have violated and perverted all good laws, beliefs, traditions, customs, and habits; that they have corrupted the minds and manners of themselves and others; that they are misusing and abusing the natural means and modes of natural production; that they are maltreating the people and denying them, and depriving them of their rights and vital interests; and that all such things in all such conduct of all such corrupt, wicked, and violent beings must be put away and they themselves in all their gradation must be put away therewith. They have corrupted their way in all manner of contrast with what is said of Enoch and Noah, namely, that they walked with God, that they were led and were leaders on the everlasting way of right and uprightness, mercy and truth, justice and righteousness, rectitude and refinement, purity and peace, good and glory. The female side is most frequently taken in Scripture as metaphorical or figurative of the really weaker side, the line of least resistance, the side of all imperfection, and all wrong, the side here called the daughters of men. In sexual communication one's substance, as Solomon speaks of it, is given away to others, and made to pass on in preservation and production, while the giver and therein the loser of the substance gradually passes to the position of the older of things until he is absorbed and disappear.

Repentance by the good Elohim is in the religious, intellectual, moral, social, sense-perceptive, all-life, and physical, sum-substance being absorbed into the Jehovah midline and made to pass on through the transition line into the new order of things; while the scapegoat Elohim passes on in scapegoat sense, and the evils and oldnesses are put away and disappear. In these absorption and transition changes the evil Elohim always makes every endeavour to take and keep all things of nature, man, and Jehovah to itself; but it does so on the Omic female, weak, and wicked side; and in the very endeavour Omically loses it and itself therein in best substance, therewith in scapegoat sense, and therefrom in incidental evil sense.

Noah is called the eighth in the second chapter of second Peter, because, as has been already repeatedly seen, the seventh or eighth is otherwise the tenth. He is one, as the head sum Deluge man, or ancient world Aeonic man into the new world; he is the fourth as the three sons, Shem, Ham, and Japheth, in one or into the fourth; he is the seventh or eighth, as the head-sum, like Adam, coming forth from the sixth through the seventh into the eighth point; and he is the tenth, as being the tenth from Adam as at the plant life tenth point at the Garden. He is thus correctly and really the one, four, seven, ten sum-man. In each of these numbers he represents the sum-substance of all beings passing through the transition Deluge into the new world. That the Deluge is universal is necessarily implied in the nature of things as in the causes, modes, and purposes of the event, in the assertions made respecting it, in the terms used, and in the law of contrast of the words and statements.

The Ark represents the Omic and Aeonic form of beings and having being. It specially represents such summaries as the world in its Omic circular layers of outer, middle, and inner; the works and beings of creation up to the Garden as continued and conducted under the begetting mode of production from the Garden to the Deluge, all under the head sum ten Aeonic men: the human body, as head-sum representative of all formations, or rather the whole all-man as representing and in the fullest sense containing all things; and, in the highest, inmost, and universal sense, the Spirit in the Jehovah Elohim all Being and all having being, all as passing through a universal renewing change. The words, before me, here used as by Elohim, denote His Being, region, and sphere of manifestations, as the region of the senses, and the having being, of man denote respecting man. It consists of three parts lower, middle, and upper, after the manner of the works of creation and begetting mode of production, and corresponding to Ham, Shem, and Japheth in Noah, as sum-sons. Each of these three contains a triad, making ten according to the ten Aeonic men. Its rooms, apartments, or chambers, imply the same and are as to all beings in all representative gradations outwards and downwards, in all parts, points, and particles. Gopher has the middle letters ph in the sense down and up, out and in, ending-beginning of the creative and begetting in all beings. It is the strong and hard of bh, as in Abba or Abha ; and means the passing as it were out of being into being, the Spirit's beginning again in all things. It is symbolic of the Spirit's original, invisible, and universal ending-beginning work. It indicates the same as the black pine of the Chaldeans. So here the colour within and without is black, or pitch. It is the ending of all colour in black, in the transition line to all colour in white, or the all-sum colour white into the all-sum colour white through the no-colour black. The common black bird, when it happens to change its colour, changes it into pure white. The black stone of the Persians is said to have been before or at the creation purely white ; but that it is black in passing through the changes that take place in time, in sin, and in all misery, while in itself it is forever purely and heavenly white. This Gopher symbol is most appropriate in passing from all life through death into all life, from all light through all darkness into all light, from all colour through no colour into all colour in Noah's natural covenant sign of the Rainbow, spoken of farther on, from of all flesh and all being through the end or ending-beginning of all flesh or all being into all forms of being and having being. The Ark is a ship, boat, or Om, the sum of the line or side of least resistance, in zero form, lying and moving like the Halcyon's nest, but containing the all Being the Spirit with the sum-substance of all beings, moving as originally, and ever originally, on the face of the waters, brooding into reproducing the world into all newness. In measure the length is three hundred cubits, the breadth fifty, and the height thirty. The height is that of manhood in thirteen, or thirty, otherwise three and ten, or three times ten. The breadth is the average age of man, the breadth of the hand with its five fingers as the circular layers of the Om in one, four, seven, ten, to the small outmost as if ever being absorbed or passing on in scapegoat sense next to the incidental and disappearing shadow and evil; the other hand side being the same right round the circle, and the two sides together making ten of all circles in all round breadth. The length is three hundred, one hundred or ten times ten Aeonic length of each man, Ham, Shem, and Japheth, somewhat like Adam's one hundred and thirty at his puberty or manhood age. Or the whole being the all-man, it has its creation tripartite division into lower to the fourth point or to the fifth and the production of animal life, the middle to the seventh, and the third to the Garden ; and in the begetting sense, with each part thereof having its respective creation part as underlying it, the lower is to Cainan, the middle to Enoch, and the third to Noah.

The whole is come to its full all-man age of a hundred, or a hundred and twenty. But it is in three parts sons, Ham, Shem, and Japheth, each being of that age of a hundred ; and the three make three hundred. The breadth is the mid-time and jubilee of each in fifty; and the puberty or manhood of each is thirteen or thirty. Taking the creative time from the beginning always to the Garden or puberty Paradise time, as the lower part, and the whole begetting time from the Garden to the Flood, as the mid-time, the third or overlapping head part of Noah all-man is from the Flood to Abraham. The third or head part is taken always as the part and time of rest and peace; and this is meant in the term or name Noah (rest, peace, comfort), and in what is said of him in the previous chapter, that this same shall comfort us as concerning our work and toil of our hands, because of the ground which the Lord hath cursed. The only way to that comfort is through the great transition change; when his sons formally take the Aeonic midline position, he goes to the overlapping and co-existent side, and they each in his respective place, as Ham keeping to the south in the westwards Aeonic movement, Shem in the midline, and Japheth in the north.

The new has always the sum-substance of the old or past, as in a new born child, and the overlapping father and God-father head part of the old and past; and both his newness and this overlapping imply peace, rest, and comfort. So this kind of entrance into, and this kind of new and youthful possession of the new land, with head and God-man overlapping, are accompanied with the command of keeping and observing this time as a Sabbath. The overlapping of the middle part from the lower begins at the fourth point, as that of the lower of Abraham towards Ishmael or that of plant life towards animal life; but the overlapping of the head part from the middle, or the middle and lower, begins at the seventh point, as that of the whole of Abraham towards Isaac, or the whole works of the six days creation towards Adam, or man as newly created. Thus there is a seventh part Sabbath implied in the rest, peace, and comfort. Also the Jubilee fifty implies a Sabbath; so all rest, peace, and comfort are implied, or an all summary of all things in this universal all-man change. The all-man, as Adam, comes forth out from the sixth day creation; the all-man, as Noah three sons, comes forth out from the sixth point, or son, in the begetting mode of production; and the all-man, as Abraham, comes forth, out from Noah's sixth hundred, or sixth and two zero marks of the three in one Aeonic line. In this form of things the whole from the beginning up to the Deluge is taken as the whole lower part, the whole from the Deluge to Christ as the middle part, and the head part and time thence onwards to Christ's next transition advent.

A window is made to the Ark, and in a cubit it is finished above. The window is the distinct all-sum Om of the cerebellum, and the one cubit is the one of the first and tenth points, or the all-sum radicle or rod of the all-sum Om in the all intellect of the all-sum man. It is the all-sum Om of the Spirit at the original first point and ever ending-beginning tenth point and all between. In the lower part head sense it is the Teraphic Om and one. In external nature it is the sun in the all-sum Om and rod; the rod being the all-sum of all rays of light, heat, and living and enlivening influences. Zohar is the Hebrew term used for light and here for window, or Om light; and it is here said to be finished above, as being the Spirit's all-Om from which all new birth is, as Jesus tells Nicodemus, from above as the highest summary of creation, and from above in relation to the all-nature head-sum, and to the all-man head intellect. Window in the secondary sense is in the cerebrum as the head and body midpart, through which the intellect receives and gives out impressions, impulses, and actions involuntary and voluntary to the outer sense region in the face or frontal part of the head and the corresponding outer sense region of the body and of nature. Window in this sense is here called chalon, as when Noah is said to have opened the window and sent out a raven. Zohar window light corresponds to the light existing before the six days' creation and to the same in the first day let there be light fiat; and chalon window opening is the sun moon planets or stars light being brought forth, or opened on the fourth day between the first or lower part from one to four, and the second or mid-part from four to seven. This agrees with man looking out at the fourth point and the outcoming of the fish and fowl life with the already out plant life, and with Noah looking out and putting out the raven is for the whole lower part life of fifth day creation in fish, fowl, and night birds, with the already out second and third days physico-plant formations. Noah's first outlooking, being at the fourth and fifth creation days, is called, after forty days, which phrase means four of ten, or four and ten as in the fifteen mentioned, or four times ten as in the forty. When Lot went out of Sodom he sought permission to go into Zoar; and the sun was risen upon the earth when he entered into Zoar. As an all-man outer of Abraham beginning a new having being, he could not flee or move forwards and upwards into the mountain of the mid-part, or come out of the mid-part of his being but by going the way of Zoar by moving forwards through his lower part way and measure of growth from one to four in his Zohar sense completed in the outcoming or rising of the sun on the earth, as at the fourth day of creation. The Zohar window is thus above the earth and man, above at the fourth point of every first part growth of the universal and all-man growth. Again it is above at the seventh point of the plants or fourth of animal life and distinct man's creation; and it is above at the tenth point all ending-beginning sum, which is the seventh of animal life and fourth or puberty manhood point of man, making in all the transition line of one, four, seven, ten, or the all ending-beginning Om and one as at the first, or the Spirit's universal Om.

The door is the Spirit's Om of Father-Son creative and begetting action. It is in the side, the south, the front, as of the human body, in the grove begetting place of the lower, the grove rearing place of the middle, and the summary grove of the face; each grove possessing a sum-inlet and outlet of all the senses, and the sum-substance line of the spirit and the intellect lying along the back up to the all-sum substance in the cerebellum, like nature's sun looking out of the dark blue ethereal sky. All new birth is in being produced on the side or face of the earth, but from behind or out of the Spirit's invisible Om Father-Son invisible action. The description is summed up in the tripartite division of lower, second, and third stories or parts shalt thou make it.

It is here noteworthy that the Ark has a prominent place among the sacred emblems of the religions of the Ancients ; and that the traditions of the Deluge are still universal through the world. The localisation of the landing and resting of the Ark, as spoken of in the traditions of each nation or people, is either within their own bounds or at what they consider to be the central part or point of the places within the area of their traditions. This implies a vague idea of a universal seat of empire with a general Aeonic impression, anticipation, and presentiment, that the Deluge is one Omic event of a succession of such Aeonic changes, great and small, in the outward course of things. Among the Armenians its resting place is supposed to have been in Mount Baris above Minyas in the land of Armenia. In the Assyrian tablets it is told how Sisit's ship went to Mount Nizir. The Greeks say that the Ark of Deucalion landed and rested on the mountain of Colhuacan. The tradition of the Fiji says that two mischievous young men had killed the favourite bird of the god Ndengei ; that on the ground of this insult and offence the god sent a destroying flood ; but that another god sent out two canoes by which those to be saved were to pass into a third big boat made of the fruit of the shaddock, which moved with eight of the Fijians on the waters till it rested on Mount Mbengga. In Samoan and Hervey groups of islands the island Rakanga of coral formation is said by the inhabitants to have been the landing and resting place of the Deluge Ark. In another one of the same islands its landing is localised within their own insular area. The tradition says that the first King of Mangaia and a few of his people escaped in safety. Its cause was supposed to be an all sexual desire between the waters below and those above for reproductive intercourse with each other. In this reproductive intercourse the Spirit acts in the Father-Son Om and one as the all line of least resistance, or female side, and the all-sum rod, or radicle ; and the sum-substance in the conceived and being begotten being must thus pass through this line of least resistance, which is the transition passage line of the change, to the landing place of the outward grove place mountain of begetting, and that of new-born rearing. In this passing through the comparatively hollow, or open vessel side, the being begotten being, while being produced or renewed through the intercourse of the Spirit's Father-Son action symbolised by that of the waters above and below, must be, as it were, ever being brought forth out of the waters and moved safely on and above the waters, to a landing and resting place on earth as a central place, or seat of empire, between the upper and lower waters, as the earth itself is between these waters, and as the mid-part of the body is between the lower and upper parts. This mid-place line of safety is symbolised by the Ark, or ship, or boat, or mountain ridge. So these Islanders held that King Rangi and his sum-substance band, or company, traversed alongside of the dip, or hollow, of Viviaunoa hub on the mountain ridge terminating at Paeru.

Resemblances between Noah's Ark and the boat arks of other ancient nations are such that they all must have been intended to symbolise the same things. The Ark of the Covenant also has its corresponding arks among the natural and sacred symbols of these nations. In all cases the number of principal parts was the natural three. The lower was of a simpler and more common form, like the Hebrew outer court; the second part contained more images and symbols, as in the holy place; and the third part contained the sum-substance sacred Tau, the universal summary symbol, like the law in the most holy place. There was a double concave broad-based pillar indicating the form of the inner Jehovistic mid-line and its outer Elohistic form. Cherubic figures were of like kind, form, place, and purpose with those of the Hebrews. There was another figure like an insect or bird, sometimes called the symbolic beetle, sacrabaeus, or Ateuchus Sacer, with wings extended, and holding in its claws a globular form as the all-sum Om out of which the spirit brings forth all kinds and forms of beings. Above all there was sometimes a canopy, with or without figures, and representing the heavens. When figures were present, they were somewhat like those in the holiest place of the Ark, being the highest head representations, as sapphires and seraphim, wings of light as of the invisible Being, and stones of fire The things of earth and the relative are copies of things in the heavens and the absolute.

Jehovah as I, even I, brings a flood of waters upon the earth, to destroy all flesh, wherein is the breath of life, from under heaven; and everything that is in the earth shall die. But the sum-substance Omic Covenant of Jehovah is to be preserved and established with the all-man Noah, and his, in all gradations of beings. The Spirit's self-begetting Father-Son action is eternal and eternally putting away the old and producing the new, containing the sum-substance of the old through eternal renewal in eternal newness. In doing so the Spirit himself is the mid-point, mid-part, and mid-line of eternal source and foundation; absolutely white, but invisible and, therefore, as if pitch dark, stone, Leucadian Rock, everlasting mountain ridge. Passing on in this action, or eternal act, into Father-Son, the eternally being-begotten Son is the same or is ever becoming the same foundation, Rock of Ages, Aeonic range and ridge of Jehovah's mountain mid-line, in and on which the all-sum life of all beings, as produced and as ever being produced, passes onwards, through the eternal chain of changes and special transition passages, in eternal Omic or covenant security and safety; while all incidental oldnesses and evils are forever being put off and away. All this finds outlet and expression in the gradation of let there be, let produce, let us make, and in the begetting mode of production ; the special form of universal sum-change being the Flood, accompanied with a removal of the world's seat of empire into an advanced place, position, and condition.

Noah is the first full era begetting man, of tripartite puberty or manhood stage and stature in Ham as lower, in Shem as mid-part, and in Japheth as higher or third part. The second or mid-part full era begetting man is Abraham, with his tripartite puberty or manhood stage and stature in Ishmael, mid-part in Isaac, and the head-sum in the six sons of Kiturah. The head all-sum full era, or fulness of time, man is the man Christ Jesus, Son of God Son of man ; who contains in Himself the all-sum of Adam, Noah, Abraham, Isaac, and Jacob, as one Joseph, or contains in Himself the whole sum-substance of all the Aeonic line of genealogy as given by Luke. The Deluge of passing out of the ancient world into the Abrahamic era is the puberty or maturity era head-sum stage change into the Abrahamic mid-part era, and both are summed into the all-head-sum part in the Man Christ Jesus. Noah is the lower part era head-sum of all-world nation of nations; Abraham is the mid-part era head-sum of all-world nation of nations ; and the Man Christ Jesus is the higher or head-sum part of all-world nation of nations. Noah's whole old world sense is summed as one lower part in Ham, the Abrahamic mid-part in Shem, and the all-sum Japhet head part in Jesus. The whole part as lower must be improved into Abraham's lower part, which is done in Ishmael, and again in Israel as coming out as national sum-substance of Egypt in the Exodus. The Red Sea of the Exodus thus corresponds so far to the Deluge. In both cases the change is that of the lower part passing at the puberty stage into the mid-part. Thus the Flood is the era puberty stage and change into the era mid-part begetting stage, condition, and action, as in the case of an individual man and woman at that age and stage of life in body and mind. The waters above and below are the universal semen of all sperm and germ of male and female in all gradation of Father-Son begetting action in all beings. The full gradation is from the Spirit in all Omic Father-Son action in all gradation of beings. This is the real and true meaning of the words of Jehovah, 1, even I, do bring a flood of waters upon the earth. As the Spirit originally moved on the face of the waters of Omic elemental seed of all creation, at the beginning ; so now, at the ending or ending-beginning of all things, there is a universal re-beginning of re-creating, renewing, and re-begetting sum-substance, as out of and from the original Om into the mid-part era new world.

Christ's reference to Noe and the Flood (Mat. xxiv.) is of this import: they were eating and drinking, marrying and giving in marriage, until the day that Noe entered into the Ark, and knew not until the Flood came, and took them all away. All oldnesses and evils are put off and away only in and by creating, begetting, renewing, and advancing the good, according to the saying, overcome evil with good. Noah in his Aeonic all-man and tripartite sons, and masculine and feminine sides in all gradations of beings, and with all sum-substance of kinds and gradations of food in semen and substance for continued subsistence, is to come into the Ark; to come in and with the All-Sum Being Jehovah. The manifestive Good Elohim is included; and so the Elohistic oldnesses and incidental evils, implied or attached, are put off and away. All Sabbatic and renewing change implies its measure of Jehovah's self-resting and refreshing, including the resting and refreshing of all beings in all gradations in and with him (Ex. xxxi. 17) This is Lamech's prophecy in saying of Noah, this same shall comfort us concerning our work and toil of our hands, because of the ground which Jehovah hath cursed. Noah is taken in the all-man universal sense into the Ark by Jehovah, as the all-man Adam in the sense of all animals (named by him) or all beings, and Eve as mother of all living, were put into the Garden by Jehovah Elohim. Every being is taken in its masculine and feminine side. Thus did Noah; according to all that Elohim commanded him, so did he. The divine dealing with him in its highest and inmost and most immediate sense is by the Spirit acting in the Jehovah sense; but, in the more outward, mediate, and manifestative sense, it is as Elohim in forms of thought and feeling, word and action. Thus internally and externally the Noah all-man does according to the internal Jehovah and the external Elohim.

CHAPTER VII.

12. Jehovah's call to all is to come to Him. Of Him, and through Him, and to Him, are all things. From the lowest and outmost ground, in the first out-coming substance and laws in lowest formations, He brought and ever brings, in onwards and upwards creative evolution, all things or beings. These He brought to their head-sum in Adam, who named them in knowing and conscious recognition of them in and with himself as the man and all-man. In and with Adam He put them into the Garden, through which they passed and ever pass into begetting continuity. In all to and fro direction He gives out and takes in, brings forth and brings in, opens and closes, descends and ascends, destroys and constructs. Here He brings all to Noah, and Noah and em to Himself, as the all and ever ending beginning Father-Son

Jehovah. His life and character must be in them as their life and character, in all orderly, natural, and necessary gradation. Righteousness is the term to express this character in man, and clean is that to express it in animals or living substance in all gradation outwards and downwards to the outmost and lowest entity. All substance has some measure of life after its kind; and so the term substance is very properly here employed. All from the Spirit in the inmost and highest sense thus to the smallest entity, or to non-being, is to be destroyed in the sense of putting off and away their oldnesses and incidental evils; while nothing is anyways essentially destroyed, nothing is lost. The Noah all-man and his house thus of all beings are called and caused to enter the Ark, the Om of universal reproduction. This All-Sum being of things is said to be before Jehovah. In the inmost and highest sense He is the eternal Father-Son begetting and being-begotten. In this Noah sum of being before Him there is His outer, like the region of the senses in man; and it forms into union and oneness with man in Son of God Son of man. In the farther outer sense it is He, Jehovah, in all self-living and all life-giving in all gradations in all beings.

Generation in the first verse stands for the whole ancient world era from the Garden to the Deluge; the creation sense underlying, or being implied therein. Beings unclean, or uneatable by man, and therefore relatively outer, are taken as outer to the clean, in the Omic and Aeonic order, relations, and gradations of begetting. In number the former are to be taken in twos, the latter in sevens. Greater preservative care is to be taken of the inner and cleaner. From the sixth, and through the seventh, man comes forth as the all head sum man, and all the rest are in him or belong to him, and are in gradation connection with him. The sacred character of the transition change numbers of one, four, seven, ten, belongs pre-eminently to the inner Aeonic line; having the Maskim or evil spirit's character as incidental to this sacred character. The inferiority and comparative externality of those called unclean are marked by counting them in twos, the two between one and four, the two between four and seven, and the two between seven and ten, making six in all. This number six is equal to the number of the creation days; and, when taken as three in one times in a horizontal arrangement, or in a square of one, two, and three Omically arranged, it makes the number of man and the beast alluded to in Revelation. These forms are 666, and

$$\begin{array}{c} 6\ 6\ 6 \\ 6\ \overline{\left|\begin{array}{c} 1\ 2\ 3 \\ 3\ 1\ 2 \\ 2\ 3\ 1 \end{array}\right|}\ 6 \\ \overline{6\ 6\ 6} \end{array}$$

Israel's number in Revelation is $12 \times 12 \times 1000 = 144{,}000$. The one is an all triad of triads, the other an all triad of triads into a fourth and mature sum, times itself, times thousand. In meaning and intention, work and effect, the whole is to keep seed alive upon the face of the earth ; it is a universal begetting renewal.

The face of the earth is its specially manifestative sphere of divine action in creative and begetting work, preserving and propagating processes in all relations and gradations. The words, yet seven days, signify the Spirit's moving of the seed waters from the original Om, as in the six days into the seventh day of creation, the deep sleep of Adam, and every begetting action and special change, forth into actual flowing for conception and new birth. During forty days and forty nights the flowing seed waters will rain or run, as living and life-giving, seed-giving and seed-preserving, waters. Each of the begetting forty is one evening-morning, or ending-beginning, Omic day like the days of creation, in the gradations of all beings. They are all three in one, or into a fourth, one sum-number, as ten in each of the three into the fourth or whole sum ; corresponding to Ham, Shem, and Japheth, into one all-man Noah. Ten is the full Aeonic number of three triads in one. Here there is this full Aeonic ten number for each of Noah's tripartite sons, making the puberty, or manhood, number of thirteen, or thirty, into one, or fourth, all-sum ten of all-man, through whom the whole old world sum-substance seed passes in Deluge seed flowing and food substance through the great transition passage between, and from, the old world era into the new world era. It is the fourth point and a zero of old world as lower part.

Noah is six hundred years old when the Flood of waters is upon the earth. The three figures represent the relative positions of sons at manhood, of son, father, grandfather. He is the sum of the Aeonic man from the Garden to the Deluge, with the head-sum meaning of six or seven, at which man was made, and at which every Aeonic mid-part son comes forth ; and he occupies the whole level of transition line of one, four, seven, ten, here at the Deluge as Adam did at the Garden. His sons are not counted in this number by positive figures ; but the two nothings are for the Omic positions of Ham and Shem read from right to left, and that of head-sum Japhet is the Noah-sum six, Noah and they being regarded as the one all-man. It is to the seventh otherwise tenth point of the all-man from the garden. Noah's overlapping, or great-grandfather, or god-sire, time, is in the three hundred years after the Flood ; being the three from seven to ten, when they are propagating the Deluge seed and replenishing the earth the new seed population. Of Noah's six hundredth year the second month is the sam of the first part from one to four of the transition line ; and the seventeenth day means the seventh point and the tenth point of the same, all indicating the passage line through which the Ark and its contents were to cross into the new world. Then the absorption of the sum-substance, in matter of seed and subsistence, of the whole old world, from the Spirit's Omic waters of the beginning to the all-ending tenth point of that whole old world order in the Spirit's Omic waters of the Flood, begins. The absorption is thus in sum-substance from the waters of the beginning and the end, of the above and the below sexes, of the Spirit's Omic underlying and Omic overlying, into and through Noah's three in one sum-sons generations for renewed seed and substance in the new order of things, in all gradations of all beings. Each of the Aeonic men from the Garden to the Deluge implies a seat of empire. All these ten are now formed into the Ham, Shem, and Japhet three in one Noah all-man of all-world; Ham in the south, Shem in the middle, and Japhet at the shoulder (tropics) and northwards, the renewal and advancement of which into another advanced stage of world seat of empire being in the Abrahamic era in parts and into the Christian era in all-sum.

The shutting in of Noah by Jehovah is similar to that of Lot by his visitors, in separation of what is to be absorbed and made to pass on from what is to be put off and away. In such an act the thoughts, feelings, and senses are comparatively closed to all else. It implies an Ishtar universal descent and ascent through the past and continued creation and generation into this regeneration; the creation always underlying the generation and both underlying the regeneration and renewal. All the high hills, that are under the whole heaven, are covered. These hills are of Omic and Aeonic character, and so is their being covered in the Spirit's regenerating and renewing action and the influence of the Omic waters. Five cubits as the half of ten agree with animal life coming forth on the fifth creation day; and fifteen agree with the three Aeonic sum-sons in the extent and measure of the regenerating change. The titan mountains are levelled by their sum-substance being absorbed, the scapegoat substance made to pass on, and their oldnesses and evils pass away; and the Aeonic mountains advance, by which process the low places, lowly persons, and every thing of right and rightful being are exalted and advanced. The waters prevailed upon the earth a hundred and fifty days; a jubilee or honeymoon fifty days answering to each of Noah's tripartite sum-sons, and a matter finding distinct recognition in the laws of Moses respecting persons newly married.

All the oldnesses and evils, in all gradations from titan personalities to the minute shades of the most minute beings, are ever being cast off and away; while all of the Spirit are ever being re-created, regenerated, and renewed and caused to move onwards and upwards in strength, beauty, and blessedness. The titans become Beelzebubs (lords of flies and beasts of prey, cannibals and kennel-keepers); and they call Christ Beelzebub, and all good and Christian persons and things by kindred appellations. In their insane and evil selfishness they madly succeed in their self-destructive work of separating themselves from the sum-substance of all good and putting it away from them, and so unwittingly doing much of the Spirit's will and work (Acts 13, 27-29). Their process of perverting and profaning all things sacred and secular culminates and terminates with themselves and their self-destruction. Their Judas-like bag keeping and Master-betraying, their sixth point and shoulder position, and their practices of consummate evils, are peculiarly related to the drying up of the Euphrates, the preparing of the ways of kings and the frog-like unclean spirit of the dragon, the beast, and the false prophet; for such are the spirits of devils, working miracles, which go forth into the kings of the earth and of the whole world, to gather them to the battle of that great day of God Almighty.

The Spirit underlies and prevades every thing. He creates, controls, and carries on the whole course of the world. In every thing there is a shady side of dark, selfish, mimic form of rivalry and opposition to Him. The ancient Chaldeans had their own way of describing this. The spirits, or these rival representations, were too numerous to be named. So they were spoken of as legions, or hosts, or specified classes, or combinations of beings; one general name being Anunnaki. Those selfish mimics of spirits in the outer and overlapping parts culminating in the titan point, and those in the hollows, or parts and points of the transition lines, were called Maskim. They were in the hollows of the ocean, along the rim of the ocean stream, the rim of boat-shaped earth, of the sun's other side transition line. They were also in the hollows of every smaller transition line, as of rivers, and all else. In the sky they were in every change atmospheric or other-kind, from calm to storm and tempest; also on earth in every change of formation, most conspicuously in all catastrophe, convulsion, and commotion, inundations and earthquakes. They are never submissive to Mulge, lord of the abyss, or to Ziana, Ana, Spirit or Lord of heaven, or to Zikia Ea, Spirit of earth. In sum they are foes to Ea. In the outer world, or outer titan line and formation, they are present at every part and point, and mimic the Spirit's perfecting and completing work, as if to continue on and up the outer titan form to heaven in all opposition to the Aeonic midline of Divine Empire. At the end of every period and era, and in less conspicuous gradation outwards and downwards, they appear as if working for the dethronement of the supreme Ruler, like the Greek representation of the conspiracy against Zeus. They are mules of no substantial sex. They are neither right men nor women; and they have neither Omic wives nor Aeonic children. They heed no progress or supplications. They have no real law or order, and do no real beneficence. They are out of way beings, yet by every wayside, but not for safety. They are zero throne bearers to the gods and imagine themselves gods. They stick as incidental evils to all essential good. They are parasitic unrealities and empty non-entities on all substantial realities and positive existences. Their accomplishments are in contrast, their perfection in opposition, and their deity and doom in selfishness. As in the Babel disorder and confusion, they disappear at the end of every thing and vanish. So be it always to the selfishness of such that are such enemies to themselves.

CHAPTER VIII.

God remembered Noah and all in the Ark. The inmost and highest point of transition is in the term remember, the central point of the Spirit's cerebellum Om and conceptive Father-Son action, and issuing in Elohistic manifestation. The Aeonic number of from one to ten begins and ends in one with the Omic zero; and the whole is the full Aeonic length of the one of triad of triads, or nine, otherwise ten, otherwise twelve, making the full one of ones length of the one as produced in creative and begetting work. This one with its Om is the one cubit and its window above the Ark as the figure ten, or one and zero, at the beginning and end of the full Aeonic number of triad of triads. According to this is the measuring by the three triads of nine inches, as the natural and normal measure of the conceptive one, but into a fourth triad as the one sum of the three, and taken as twelve, to make one foot, and a triad of feet into one yard. This, like everything else, shows that the naming and numbering of things in Genesis and through the whole Bible are the same in all nature, among all nations, and at all times. The whole Om is thus brought out in its triad of triads of full length triad, or whole one, in the six otherwise ten days of creation; and then in the begetting sense in each of the ten Aeonic sons from the Garden to the Deluge The whole shows that the whole history of all beings is in these two modes of production, the creative and begetting, and in triads and triads of triads, tens and tens of tens, with one window and one cubit, or one whole Om of one and its zero form, as above and below, ending-beginning, and all through, one Spirit's work.

The Ark is the original, ending-beginning, and universal Om. Its contents are the all beings of the world as absorbed, or brought back into it, in Ishtar descent way back through the creation length of seven or ten, to be re-created or stored up in Ishtar return way, for being again, anew, and newly begotten in a new order of things. Its Gopher wood is, as it were, the Spirit's muscular and tissued coverings of the whole Om and its Omic rooms, in seven or ten Aeonic numbers summed in three parts, as in the triads of the days of creation. Ishtar's descent and ascent of seven, or ten, steps each make the fifteen mentioned, or five each for Noah's parts sons. The Om or Ark is thus ever being emptied and filled, or emptying-filling, closing-opening, ending-beginning, like a vessel or valve, like the seasons, like plants, like the moon, the tides, and the monthly courses; like man's life's stages and those of nations and the seats of empire, like the setting and the rising of the sun, in short like all changes in nature, in man, and in all of the Spirit. In no change and in no work or one act does the Spirit, or the Lord

God, destroy, or put off and away, in simple and sole revenge. He causes, controls, and conducts His works in righteousness and love, truth and mercy, purity and peace, or in the harmonious exercise of all His perfections; and the revenge is incidental to His works, as sin is, and because sin is so. In and through His working He is ever putting off and away all the sin and the suffering, all incidental evils. And the all-man Noah only remains and they that are with Him in the Ark, that is to say, all the sum-substance of all beings preserved and to be reproduced in a new order of things. The flowing of the waters is this filling of the conceptive Om in conceptive action, to be followed by the new birth. The Ark moves on the face of the waters as the Spirit does at the beginning; the face being the begetting change region.

In the growing up of the seed, as in creation, or in the womb, Jehovah is coming forth and the seed is coming forth and out in manifestative Elohim manner and character, to re-appear on the earth, as new world new seed beings, in substantial continuity, identity, and overlapping scapegoat. The completion of the conceptive intercourse, or the opened space, as by the withdrawal from each other of the two objects already called the above and below, as in relation to the beginning firmament, is marked by a wind or air passing between them, or over the earth. Then the waters assuage, their flowing ceases; the fountains of the deep and the windows of heaven, or the Om below and that above are stopped, and the ozone or sperm rain from heaven, or the above, is restrained. The presence of the wind, in addition to what has already been said of it, implies that all the elemental substances, conditions, and relations, necessary to life and living are present. It has already been observed that when the sap in plants descends the buds become Oms and serve as such at the beginning of the next season when the sap has returned upwards to pass in one sense forms through into new shoots. In every Aeonic ten form the one at the tenth point makes its Om for farther or begetting advance by the Adam deep sleep return all the way of the past to the original Om, which is really its tenth point Om and its one. In the embryo of separate bodies of different sexes the growth is in the universal to and fro action, as the descending and ascending sap in plants; in which process the difference in sex is formed by that in one case and at a certain point becoming fixed as feminine, and that in another becoming fixed as masculine. Generally the first issue is masculine, and those that follow are alternate.

Notice has already been taken of the hundred and fifty days. The Ark rested in the seventh month, on the seventeenth day of the month, on the mountains of Ararat. Here it is moon measure of time that is meant. The seventh day of creation is the Sabbath or resting transition day of God and all-man, into the eighth and full and formal stage and condition of things in the one, four, seven, ten level line of the Garden. At this seventh into the eighth point many children, and all-Aconic sons, or men, or sons of man, are born; but the full natural and normal time of childbirth and puberty of Aconic men is at the ninth point, otherwise one whole sum tenth point. So here the seventh month is put with seventeenth, or seven and ten, as a compressed and contracted form of man's time of creation, the birth time of children, and more especially the puberty or manhood fourth point of Aconic man for the level stage of Ark landing or Omic man birth in new order issued on Ararat. Ararat means curse or incidental destiny of travail connected with child-birth, as expressed in Jehovah Elohim's address to the woman in the Garden. The term literally is a tongue rolling articulation of Adam into the hard form of d as last letter t, and indicating a to and fro desire (to husband) and action, pleasant in receiving and conceiving, but painful in delivering and giving forth the ever being begotten man.

The mountains of Ararat are thus the high grove place and head-sum point of the whole lower part of all beings taken in one sum. Here the whole creation work and time, and the whole begetting work and time from the Garden to the Deluge, are taken as one whole lower part to the Abrahamic middle part, which again is on to the Christian era, the all head-sum part. This Ararat point is, therefore, appropriately spoken of as that of the tenth month, the first day of the tenth month, when the tops, or head-sum points of the mountains are seen. Tenth, first, and tops here denote the universal Om and one of the grove point, or the above, of the whole old world now as Aconic lower part, like the window and one cubit above the Ark. That the term, mountains, is plural is because it stands for the Aconic mountains of the old form in one ending sum substance, and the beginning entrance in one sum of those of the new.

At the end of forty days Noah opens the window of the Ark which he had made. Noah stands for the whole midline meaning as the all-man, in the sense of ending-beginning Jehovah, or the Spirit in the Jehovah Father-Son sense, already explained. He is, therefore, spoken of as doing everything. He is the one of the Om, or window; and, as such, he opens it by beginning to move forth in the new or Abrahamic world sense; which, though middle between the old and the Christian era, consists of the usual three parts of lower, middle, and higher. He does so at the end of forty days. The Om is in three in one, or into a fourth, layer or circle; the first being the one, and the fourth being the tenth, of the Aconic one, four, seven, ten; so that the first and the fourth are the same ending-beginning Om, or one and its zero. This three in one, or into a fourth one sum, of Omic level, or closing-opening point, is the closing-opening point between the preceding and succeeding tens or eras; and is, therefore, the four of tens (here translated forty), and the Deluge transition line of passage from the old into the new world. It is the same of creation passing into the begetting period of from the Garden to the Deluge, through which both are now passing into the new world.

At this point he sends forth a raven, which goes forth to and fro, until the waters are dried up off the earth. Also he sends forth a dove from him, to see if the waters are abated from off the face of the ground. The dove is specially symbolic of the Spirit in peculiar relation to the sacred numbers one, four, seven, ten, and the sacred Omic and Aeonic places and passages; hence it is spoken of in the Song of Solomon as being in the clefts of the rock, in the secret places of the stairs; the same being true of the saints as holy Oms and filled with the Spirit in Christ. Christ's spouse is the one Om of her one mother Om of all (Song vi. 9). Christ's eyes, Omic eyes, or Oms are as those of doves by the Omic rivers of waters (v. 12). In the Spirit's Jehovah Father-Son forth-coming is His creative and begetting work, orderly distributed and communicated at all passages, notably at the sacred numbers, as with Jesus at the Jordan Baptism, and here at the one, four, seven, into one tenth sum numbers. All this has its outer in the raven to and fro force and action in the three pairs of twos occurring between the sacred numbers, and making the 666 Revelation number of all outer beings and works. All these outer beings and works have their internal Jehovistic gradation of matter and mode of being, with the manifestative Elohim and attached incidental imperfections and evils, which stand to the Jehovistic sense as the Raven to the Dove, Cain to Abel, Ham to Shem, Esau to Jacob, and so of others, all into being as Judas to Jesus. The raven to and fro force and work are going on continually from one to ten, or until the waters are dried up from off the earth, from the lowest and outmost point of ground to the highest and inmost point of earth, or ground wrought into a cultivated condition. The raven work is done in necessary connection with, and dependence on, the dove action. So the dove is put forth at each sacred number in Omic communication and to see as to the raven work from the lowest and outmost verge of ground sense. At each sacred number the Spirit absorbs the sum-substance and does the work of change together with a creative or begetting communication, both which are made to pass on in renewed and advanced being and having being.

This raven and dove work is the embryonic and unborn infant growth in the Ark Om and the head-sum grove Om of the old world, new taken as the whole lower part; out of both which Ark and old world Om the new all-man and all-world order is to be born and to emerge. It is the same process of work as in the beginning when the Spirit was moving on the face or Om of the waters, or elemental seed region of Father-Son creation and begetting work. It is the same process as in the six, or ten, days works of creation, and in the obstetric process of bringing forth the young of all beings in actual delivery. Nature's process in the young unborn being is taken under the symbol of the raven to and fro work, which continues until the waters are dried up from off the earth, or until the Omic elemental substances are absorbed in the process of growth into the completed young being mature for delivery. The elemental waters in mother nature's womb at the beginning of creation and all continued creation are taken as being the same as those in mother Eve's womb, and each distinct mother's womb; the Spirit and His Father-Son action as the same in both; and the raven and dove work the same in both. The gradation and order in the process of being, action, and growth are also the same. The head-sum tenth point contains the sum-substance of all things of all or of each being; and the same ten sense obtains through the whole being, to the outmost points of trunk and limbs, as the fingers and toes, grass and hairs, horns and hoofs, and all parts and points of all seed and system. The raven and dove work begins at the Om or head-sum, which is also the foot-sum as implied in the dove finding no foot-rest. The head and its number are also the foot-sole sum and number; and both are the point at which the raven and dove outgoing and work begin. Water process of abating and drying is downwards from the hill-tops of the earth and the head-top of the young being; and the seven days of water abating are to the level of the shoulder point of each, where the embryo has grown up to its fourth point as the waters have, by absorption in nourishment and growth of the young, abated from the head-top to the shoulder point. Here the dove brings in a leaf as plant life passes in inner sum-substance into animal life through the dove fourth day into fifth day animal life. Here plant life and animal life are in dove or secret and sacred fourth point union and oneness of seed, substance, and life, symbolised by the olive tree; and the head-sum substance of this is formed by the creative and begetting action of the sacred dove and the common raven of the spirit into one Omic formation of tongue and mouth or whole Omic face, into breast formations at the shoulder level, and into the sexual organs at the lower part head; the whole process of work being simultaneously carried on within and without in the young all-man and young all-world. Another seven days part in being and work completes the process into maturity and fulness for the new all-birth, when the dove like young being, or the all-man all-world comes forth in the dove or divine image and likeness, though not yet formally born by actual delivery.

The time of the process is a triad of sevens into a fourth, or a month form of time. Here in the six hundredth and first year, in the first month, the first day of the month, the waters were dried up from off the earth; and Noah removed the covering of the Ark, and looked, and, behold, the face of the ground was dry. Noah as tripartite all-man has three figures, which he also has as having all-sum relations, six and two nothings. Being the sum of all the Aeonic men from the Garden to the Deluge, he is the six-sum, otherwise ten-sum, man. He has now also passed into the all-man young being, matured for delivery into the new all-world order and era ; and is, therefore, the new one at the top or above the six hundred years, as the one cubit of window or Om is above the Ark, whence the number is six hundredth and first year, month, and day, of him as all-man into new and young all-man being, and of earth as all dried up and mature young world. The words, the face of the ground was dry, mean that the new world is renewed to its lowest and outmost verge. The new all-man and all-world are as yet taken as being of seven months stage and age. Now other two months are added, making the normal and usual nine. During these two months the unborn young being ripens in all kinds of life into fitness for outward enjoyment and exercise of all kinds of life ; so that, in actual forth-coming, there is the all combination or all-sum of all kinds of life, in wife, sons and wives, every living thing, of all flesh, fowl, cattle, every creeping thing, as in the first creation and the bringing all living things to, and being named by, Adam.

The covering of the Ark removed by Noah is the sum of the oldnesses attached to the Ark as the outer couch, Om, or Omic sum of old all-world covering, and of the oldnesses attached to the Ark as the inner couch, Om, or Omic sum of old all-man covering. The womb in which the new world is conceived, and renewed and out of which it is brought forth, is the old world order ; and that in which the new man is conceived and renewed, and out of which he is brought forth, is the old man order. The renewal is from within outwards to the outmost skin of things, and from without inwards to Jehovah and the Spirit. It begins with the Spirit and Jehovah within in the Jehovah repentance, and is outwards to the Elohim outmost ground covering ; and again inwards to the Jehovah smelling a sweet savour, and saying in His heart I will not again curse the ground any more for man's sake. It reaches outwards to the outmost evil in gradation from the inmost spirit and heart, the very imagination of evil in any thought of intellect or feeling of heart. Absorption inwards of sum-substance causes the process of drying to be from without inwards ; so the ground is said to be dry before the earth is said to be so (vs. 13, 14). The eyes are the highest sum-substance of the senses ; so at the removal of the Ark covering Noah is said to look out. This is the outward beginning of formal outward moulting, which in all beings begins at the head-top. It is a species of new birth. Delivery in birth, in the coming forth of beings in image form, in moulting, and in putting off and away of oldnesses, is much the same ; and its process is by universal to and fro action in all-sum of gradations and relations. This to and fro force is the two mid-wives of Egypt, in all states, steps, and stages of force and motion, being and having being.

Mabbul is the Hebrew of Flood, the middle part of which is Abba (father), the first letter m being for ending, emptying, or closing, and the termination of meaning rolling in on-flowing. The whole term signifies emptying-filling, as an all-sum ebb and flow all ocean tide. It is an all-man and all-world Father-Son begetting sense into a new order of things. Heb. xi. 7 says, that by faith Noah, being warned by God concerning things not seen as yet, moved with fear, prepared an Ark to the saving of his house. This fear began at the shoulder point of titan and giant position from the seventh to the tenth point, or of Enoch to the Deluge, at which points there is always the Hittite fear, terror, or death, and the head-sum of faith and intellect to pass through the transition line into a renewed condition and character.

1 Peter iii. 18-22 speaks of the Flood as the change through which the old all-man and old all-world passed into newness, and as the lower part into the moral part; and that, in like manner, the moral passed in Christ's time and work into the higher or head part in which is implied more than the putting away of the filth of the flesh as in the lower sense, even the essential implication of conscience and intellect, and heaven to which Jesus Christ has gone, all in change upwards and inwards into Jehovah and the Spirit.

It is not said distinctly and separately what becomes of the Ark as such; but, throughout all that is said of it and of all things connected with it, it is implied that, in whole and each being's form and sense of it, it passes on in, and with, the sum-substance and scapegoat of all things, while the incidental old-nesses and evils attached to it and to all beings are put off and away, and made to disappear. It is the all-Om and one of all Oms and ones; and it is renewed and made to pass as such in all gradations and relations of beings.

Noah builded an altar unto Jehovah: and took of every clean beast, and of every clean fowl, and offered burnt offerings on the altar. Altar is from the Latin altus high, and means the inmost and highest form of the sum-substance of any or all being, the inmost and highest form from which it comes forth and to which it has returned. Like the term Ishtar of the Chaldeans, it is the inner and real being of the beings, or all being, or any being. Hence theologians correctly teach in respect to Jesus Christ, that He offered Himself in His human nature of all-man-all-world sense on the altar of His divine nature. He does so as Jehovah in the manifestative Elohim. But the inmost and highest sense and sum-substance even of Jehovah is the Spirit, as it is said that Christ offered Himself by the Eternal Spirit; and therefore, the altar, the sum-substance of all that the divine or all being is, is the Spirit, in His absolute sense. In self-being, self living, and self-acting, or self-being and self-having being, He is eternally modifying Himself into being the Relative, and eternally returning from that All-Relative into the All-Absolute. He is the eternal All-Absolute in the eternally being modified Absolute, or the eternal Relative. The Absolute as self-modifying is Father to the self-modified Absolute or Relative Son. The self behind, indwelling, and underlying, the self-modifying, is father to the self-modifying, and grandfather to the son, who is ever becoming Son in ever becoming Father, or is eternally being begotten in Father-Son or Jehovah action by the Spirit, in the absolute and the relative. The comparatively outer is forever having its being and all from its comparatively inner; and again forever returning, in sum-substance as offering on the inner of that sum-substance as altar, to the comparatively inner. By thus forming into, and returning in, sum-substance, the all-being builds an altar, as it were of high and holy heap or mound of self earth in the sense of cultivated, refined, and sanctified substance, or of stone or heap of stones in the sense of substance, like the Rock of Ages in Jehovah Himself, or in the eternal Spirit. Hence the ancient custom of taking mounds of earth, or stones, not cut or carved, hewn or hammered, by any instrument. Thus the sum-substance of the all-world all-man is built as altar in its inner and more divine nature, and is offered as sacrifice in its more outward and common nature, on that altar, to Jehovah; or it becomes to be as Jehovah, and passes to the Spirit or becomes Spirit: and the worship is in Spirit and in truth in and to God, who is a Spirit, or the All-Spirit.

Similar to all this is the process of all outgoings from the cerebellum and intellect through the whole body, and all the ingoings, in impressions, informations, and impulses and all else, to the cerebellum and intellect. So are all outgoings and ingoings in nature and all beings. So is it at the growing up of any and everything, and all things, into a head-sum, as at the one, four, seven, ten points, and all points. So is it markedly at the creation of man in the divine image, in the Garden passage of becoming as gods, the Jehovah Elohim double begetting, and the all-representative offerings of Cain and Abel, and in the Enos stage and meaning of men beginning to call upon the name of the Lord. The sum-substance of all the beings from the outmost point is implied in the offering of all the clean beings; for the sum-substance of the outer is taken in the usual absorption. It also means the being begotten self-substance.

It must not be forgotten that the whole, from the beginning to the Deluge, is taken as representative of the all-world and the all-man through all duration as one sum, and yet as in all gradations of beings and summaries of beings; and also as the Aeonic lower era in relation to Abrahamism as middle, and to the Christian era as head. Both as head-sum in all duration, and as head-sum of all as lower era part, it has an Om or grove head form, which is built in the lower part sense of organs of generation in one and zero, sacred mount, bones, and testicles, of nature's altar kind. The passage bone, or bones as one, or bones and testicles as one or together with the Omic one, have the significance of the Leucadian Rock, the Rock of Ages, for all conception and birth, all outlet and inlet, all being and having being. In the middle part sense the altar and offering are at the seventh or titan point, otherwise the tenth, or the one, four, seven, ten at that ending beginning passage ; and the head-sum of all is at the head into the cerebellum and the intellect.

Jehovah smelled a sweet savour. Noah, as the all-man and the all-world, is built up and builds up into the highest and inmost form of head-sum substance, and passes to Jehovah and to the Spirit ; and therein becomes Jehovah and Spirit, as it is said that Adam and Eve became as gods. This is the sum of all pleasure and profit, sense and satisfaction, as to the all-world, the all-man, Jehovah, and the Spirit ; the all fruit that is good for food, and that is pleasant to the eyes, and a tree to be desired to make wise. The all sum-substance is matured into being Jehovistic.

13. Jehovah said in His heart, I will not again curse the ground any more for man's sake ; for the imagination of man's heart is evil from his youth ; neither will I again smite any more everything, as I have done. Incidental lower side, or line of least resistance, evil, and destiny or doom of curse, have their relation and connection with all beings from the inmost heart in gradation outwards to the outmost of Cain ground, and summary or personal evil. So the address about the eating of the Garden fruit is by Jehovah Elohim, in the order of the actors in the action, with the implication of the promise or covenant in what is said to each. The woman's Omic and Aeonic Son is to be all-prevailing in absorbing the head-sum, and nothing lost, of all the outer into the inner, by which the serpent's seed is caused to disappear ; and the serpent's seed in bruising the woman's seed's heel is in incidentally killing it by both dying to each other in the absorptive separation. The woman is to continue to bring forth children in all being and action with and under, or in continued relation to, her husband ; all which implies continued preservation, propagation, and all relations, though with incidental evil and sorrow. Adam is to have all the days, years, eras, and ages, and Age of ages, of his life, in the eternal ending-beginning whence-whither of elemental seed dust.

Thus the curse is expressed as incidentally attached to the ground, in the sense of the doom or end of every thing, from the inmost Spirit and heart to the outmost point, having its outer, weaker, worse, and wilder, dark, dying, and disappearing side ; and things are to continue so until man returns to his whence-whither elemental dust. This returning is to the original Om of the Spirit, or to Jehovah and so to the Spirit. It is the returning from the outmost and outer in gradation to the inner and inmost Jehovah and the Spirit ; and, therefore, from the incidental evil and curse, with faces towards the Spirit. The perfection of becoming as the Spirit implies the name of God being in and on one as really as the names of all the animals were in and on, as well as by, Adam, and that there is no more curse. And there shall be no more curse ; but the throne of God and of the Lamb shall be in it; and His servants shall serve Him; and they shall see His face; and His name shall be in their foreheads (Rev. xxii. 1-5). The duration of the curse is the duration of the connection with the outer Elohistic Cainism; whether in the sense of the eternal Aeonic course of the Age of ages, as represented by the time and course of things from the beginning to the Deluge, or in the sense of that time and course, as the lower era to Abrahamism, and the Christian era, or in the sense of any other period, person, part, or particle. The ending of things represented by the Deluge, in the comprehensive sense of the Age of ages, implies the end of the incidental evil and curse; because it implies things having been built up in Noah altar and offering to Jehovah and the Spirit. Noah's offering is a burnt-offering as of the nature of the fire of the head-sum of all things in their comprehensive sense, and in that of the head-sum of things as the lower era part era; and also in the sense of having now entered into the middle part era of comparative heart and blood as distinguished from the lower part water. This second part will have its great ending-beginning in heart-sum blood shedding in the death of Christ; and this again in the purification of things by head-sum fire. Each time is a virginal time, or once; each Aeonic son is a virginal son.

The term, because, expresses the causal connection of the curse with the incidental evil incidentally attached to beings and the actions of beings; and not that the evil or the curse arises from the divine will, or from what any being or act is in itself or as essentially considered. Both are for ever being put away by the Noah returning and absorbing, advancing and building of all things into the altar of their character, merit, and efficacy of Jehovah and the Spirit; and into the offering of them in their outer or Elohistic character changed, as by fire on that altar of burnt-offering, into the character of Jehovah and the Spirit; to whom they so become a sweet smelling savour, or Jehovistic and spiritual substance in everlasting light and life. To say that He will not again curse the ground any more for man's sake is tantamount to saying that He will evermore bless all from the inmost to the outmost ground for man's sake; for man, as the representative head-sum of whatever is contained or implied in the all-man and the all-world. It has been repeatedly noticed that an act of imagination is necessary for an act of perception, followed by the exercise of the other capacities. Nothing can be given out or received by the intellect without some form or image. So everything in the relative is in the image necessary for communication between itself and the absolute, as well as for having being in the region or sphere of the relative itself. The whole relative is the outer and lower of the absolute, and implies an incidental comparative weakness, imperfection, and evil, which are ever being put off and away in its ever being renewed, reformed, and newly imaged in the likeness of the reality of its inner substance; and these changes are being made in all Aeonic gradations. So is incidental evil attached to the all-man and the all-world ; and is yet being put off and away by the building of the altar of the inner Jehovistic and spiritual substance, or in being re-created and begotten again into partaking of the divine nature in the divine image. The New Testament writers speak plainly and clearly of this doctrine of being partakers of the divine nature and being re-created and begotten again in the divine image, that image as in the son. This course of changes will continue in man and in nature, through the duration and alternations of day and night, times and seasons, eras and ages, and the Age of ages ; while the earth remaineth, seed time and harvest, and cold and heat, and summer and winter, and day and night shall not cease.

CHAPTER IX.

THE course of these times and seasons pass through the Aeonic changes of the usual three in one or into a fourth, as spring out of chaotic winter, followed by summer and autumn, and again through winter, in endless rotation ; and so, as to the three parts in one of night, of day, of man and every being, and every combination of beings. Noah's three parts are his sons in gradation through all beings. All these are to continue in having their being, and having being in the divine blessedness and goodness, and therein to be fruitful, to multiply, and to replenish the earth. Among these universal beings, taken as one whole, the Jehovah Aeonic midline is in man, as distinct from the inferior creatures ; but that midline has its gradation also among all men and among all the inferior creatures, and in each of both, down and out to the lowest and outmost being. Accordingly, the fear and dread of Jehovah are to be, in gradation from the highest and inmost point, the Spirit, upon man and all beings. It is of particular importance to observe that there is a distinct and great difference and distance between man and all the other beings ; such distance and difference that fear and dread of man are to be, as imposed and fixed by nature and the divine will, upon all these other beings as being outwardly in and under the all-man, as man's body is under his head, and summarised in his head, and in gradation inwards of head-front or face, cerebrum, and cerebellum; the last containing the sum-substance of all in the intellect or spirit. Thus all go out from the intellect, as all beings go out from the Spirit, and again back to the same ; and so do all go out from man and back again to man.

Thus the substance, forms, and laws of all beings have their whence and whither in the Spirit ; in Him we live, and move, and have our being ; and yet all beings stand also as outer form to the Spirit. Thus the substance, forms, and laws of all beings have their whence and whither in man under Jehovah and the Spirit, or the Spirit as Jehovah. In Him they live, and move, and have their beings; and yet all they stand also as outer form to man. Service and worship are implied in the fear and dread spoken of; and they are rendered from the lowest and outmost in gradation of all beings, through man, the all-man Noah, the Man Christ Jesus, up and in to the eternal Spirit. So is it in the Psalms, as in Psalms 104 and 148; so is it in all the Bible, in all man, and all nature; and all beings are blessed in this all-service and all-worship. Natural distinctions exist among them, and are formally recognised and expressed in what is here said respecting them. The statement is much the same as respecting them at man's creation; for here is the ending-beginning of the new world, as there is that of the old, and as is ever in unbroken continuity of world of worlds and of man of men.

All things are thus common to all men, to each, and to every man; and all things have a distinctiveness in themselves, and in the manner in which they are to be possessed and enjoyed by each and every one. Original equality of original rights is universal, and also distinct. Community and equality of rights to the Spirit, to the Father-Son Jehovah-Elohim as Creator, Father, and Governor, to one another in being and having being, and to all nature, or all beings, are true of all men. To deny this is to deny one his right to his very being, and all that is implied in his being, to his having being, and to his God, in whom he lives, and moves, and has his being. Here the all-man has, and each individual man has, in his God the Spirit, in the Jehovah Father-Son creative, begetting, and governing works, in himself or his being and fact, matter, mode, and meaning of his being, in nature, and in the manifestative Word, his original, inherent, and inalienable rights, statutory title, charter, and magna charta, as to all nature and all things. To act contrary or in opposition to this is to usurp and arrogate the all of God, of man, of nature, and of the course and government of things. It is ignorant and wicked, presumptive and practical self-deification, all leading to self-destruction. It is all true of all tyrants and all titans, monstrous formations that always become peculiarly conspicuous at the outer Aeonic shoulder point, rendered notorious in the world's experience and history by the Gorgonic giants and the Hittite sons of terror and of death. Inequalities do exist everywhere; force and motion are in all things related to the line of least resistance, as the masculine is to the feminine, the one to the Om; and nature leaves no vacuum unsupplied, God liberally supplies the wants of everything that lives, or has being. Inequalities in nature and in man are caused not by selfishness on the part of the divine Being, but by self-denial and self-sacrifice; and the changes made by absorption are the harvest ingathering of the sum-substance in all things to pass through their Omic transition passages into a renewed and advanced stage, state, and character. The Spirit, peculiarly dwelling in the inmost, highest, and most holy place of every being, in the original cell or Om of every being, evolves into full form that being as the one, the radicle, or the budding germ, in that cell, by the absorption and assimilation of the original sperm and of continued supply of congenial substance from its environments. The Spirit is the inmost being, source, and energy in all this begetting and creative process; the evolved and grown-up formation being the outer and temporary part of the being. No selfishness is implied; it is a to and fro supply and absorption, or supply and demand, according to and limited or qualified by the nature, necessities, and capacities, of the being and of the process of action. Incidental evil, sin, or selfishness, is attached to everything in the way of indirect necessity, and not as directly caused by the divine will or the essential nature of things.

Elohim is outer and eternally temporary to Jehovah; so is the outer part or form of everything; so is every titan formation or being; and all these outer forms or beings, in becoming selfish, are being for ever put off and away in their incidental selfishness, sin, or evil; while their sum-substance is absorbed, and their scapegoat form passes on in outer relation to the mid-line all sum-substance in the Jehovistic and spiritual being. Out of the Spirit's original, virginal, and universal Om of all Oms come forth all beings to be fed and formed in the inexhaustible gradation of surrounding goodness, each growing to a mature stage at which, with an Omic helpmate, it repeats the begetting, absorptive, renewing, and advancing process. To this all-man all-world process all things render service by to and fro giving and receiving, closing and opening, ending and beginning, dying and living; every moving thing that liveth shall be meat for you; even as the green herb have I given you all things. All-zero, in all gradation of feminine side or line of least resistance, is eternally self-emptying and self-filling; everything moving on, as it is moved on, in fruit-seed and food-substance, through a zero Omic vessel shell or covering, of outer form. In its forward movement, in Om and one being and action, it matures and begets a seed and sum-substance son, or child form, after its kind, to whom or which it, in doing so, becomes a father, an outer part being, an overlapping, or scapegoat. Every being thus exists in its Omic vessel, boat, or outer form; and passes on from vessel to vessel, still and ever having its original and inmost being of Om or cell and one with the Spirit. Every being is thus self-existent, having its being out of itself, Neith-like coming from itself, yet living and depending for all things on all other beings. Its sum-substance is ever in and from itself; yet it has it also in and from all else. It is thus made, and ever being made, in the divine image and likeness in having an inmost spirit, a Father-son Jehovah, and outer Elohim. All this is caused and given to be so by the Spirit, Jehovah, Elohim, as dwelling and acting therein.

Flesh is not to be eaten with the life thereof, which is the blood thereof. To eat any thing is to put it to its highest and utmost use and end ; but it must not be to the end of extinguishing or finally ending its highest and inmost life, or its tree of life. Parallel to this is the saying, lest he put forth his hand, and take also of the tree of life, &c. The tree of life, in its inmost being and Spirit, and in the essential meaning of the divine image and indwelling of the divine Spirit, is not to be eaten ; for it would mean universal annihilation. Allied to this is the prohibition of taking and killing a dam and its young. It should be remembered that the Deluge whole ending-beginning, with its Omic Ark and contents of all-man all things, and the coming forth of all these into the new world order of things, are in whole and parts similar to the creation work from the beginning to the Garden and onwards. So the passage here is parallel to what is said of Cain and Abel. Force is in to and fro form of motion, which necessarily implies to and fro negative and positive, resistance and impulsion, competition and concurrence, accumulation and distribution, and other laws; the negation being first, as night is before day, yet ever in endless alternation with the positive; the one being brother to the other, the outer being the Cain to the inner Abel. Hence all substance and law, and all being and having being, are positive and come forth positively, but yet in and through their negative form. All things move on in a course of progression in and through antagonism. The one forbids or prohibits the other; yet each supposes, and is necessary to, the other; and both must be true of all being and action. In the Decalogue the commandments, excepting one, are put in the negative or Omic form, yet also with all positive implication.

The Garden all-fruit is forbidden ; but it must be eaten in gradation from the lowest and outmost verge of being in, and up to, Jehovah and the Spirit, with, and in, the all-man. In the eating all beings pass on in progression through antagonism, and through the renewing and refreshing line of transition. All things thus renewed, and thus passing into the new order of things and begetting mode of production, must pass in consecrated substance, as an offering in the same natural gradation, through the outer Cain fruit form and inner Abel blood form to Jehovah and the Spirit. There must be the offering, or all transition sacrifice, in gradation from the lowest and outmost ground into Cain full fruit offering, and that with Abel flock offering must pass through the Abel shed blood to Jehovah and the Spirit ; without shedding of blood there is no remission. The offerers must be brothers ; and so must their offerings be, the all elder and outer, and the all younger and inner, as Elohim is to Jehovah.

Here the prohibition is of eating the flesh with the blood. The blood must be shed and poured out and down to reach to the outmost and lowest point of beings, which is the same as the sum-substance of all the outer passing with that of the flesh through the blood, or through the water of the lower part and the blood of the midpart, to Jehovah and the Spirit; water and blood poured forth out of Jesus Christ's spear wound. This is as putting an end to the life, the divine image, the Jehovah and Spirit, or all being, yet really in the sense of all renewing and refreshing ending-beginning transition into the new all-man all-world order of being and having being. Resisting force is necessary to impelling force, antagonism to progression, absorption and ingathering to filling and forth-giving; both serve for the continuation of force in Omic and Aeonic form. So are the absorptive eating and feeding and transition changes to the preservation and propagation of all beings. The course of nature, or the divine will, is thus fulfilled in onward mid-line movement in every thing and all things, directly and indirectly, essentially and incidentally, and as all very good, notwithstanding the all incidental evil, and even through the indirect necessity of incidental evil; and all the evil is ever being put away in and through the very process of fulfilling God's will in nature's course. Negative and positive are thus the to and fro forms of force in things physical, in plant life, in animal life, in social, moral, and religious life. In motive, rule, and end, the divine will is to be performed; and no evil is to be committed in order that good may follow. In doing good evil is incidentally present; but it is put off and away in the Jehovah mid-line fulfilment of the divine will in the all onward course of things; I thank God through Jesus Christ our Lord. So then with the mind I myself serve the law of God; but with the flesh the law of sin.

Surely your blood of your lives will I require; at the hand of every beast will I require it and at the hand of man; at the hand of every man's brother will I require the life of man. Whoso sheddeth man's blood, by man shall his blood be shed; for in the image of God made He man. The words, blood of your lives, are the sum-substance of them all, of all beings, as passing in to Jehovah. It is to pass in to Him in natural order of gradation from every beast, or living being in which there is blood; then with man's blood-life substance to Jehovah, and lastly as spirit to the Spirit. Of course the sum-substance of physico-plant life is implied as being contained in that of the every beast, and so on inwards. Again the whole is divided into two parts, the man and the outer man, or the Abel and the Cain of the all-man all-world. A special distinction comes in here, as also in verse three, inasmuch as this new world stage is the Abrahamic mid-part of the Aeonic all-man. Water stands peculiarly related to the old world as lower, with physico-plant as outer Cain to the animals and man as inner Abel, as now and here blood stands peculiarly related to the mid-part new world, with the beast or animal as outer to the every man or human life. Verse three indicates this advance in giving flesh and all things to the all-man for meat; because his mid-part nature implies the sum-substance of flesh and all things, and so needs all such as food.

The words, at the hand of, signify at the outer, as the hand is the outer sum of one's body. So to say, at the hand of every beast will I require it, is to say, of or from every beast as the outer to man will I require it; then at the hand of man, or of man, or from man, as the outer man ; and, lastly, from the man next inner, with Jehovah and the Spirit as inmost, will I (Jehovah) require it. Whoso sheddeth man's blood, by man shall his blood be shed. Here the whole is summed into two parts, the man whose blood is shed and he who sheds it ; and the latter is to have his blood shed by man. He whose blood is shed represents the whole inner, as Abel, containing the animals, or the sum of Abel's offering in, and with, himself, as the whole inner of the all-man, like Jesus and the Jews. He who sheds it represents the whole outer, as Cain, containing the physico-plant life, or the sum of Cain's offering in and with himself as the whole outer of the all-man. The blood shed is the sum-seed of all and every one of the old all-world and all-man ; and it is shed by a begetting act, or process of conception and birth, in and by which it passes from the old into the new order of things. This is implied in Abel's blood crying to Jehovah from the ground, that is, from the lowest and outmost points in gradation upwards and inwards to Jehovah and the Spirit, as Jesus commits His spirit to the Father's hands and the Eternal Spirit. It is the same in Onan's spilling it on the ground. The order of the steps of gradation in the shedding of it must be all from the lowest and outmost to the highest and inmost ; and all the steps must be taken in immediate relation and connection, as brother to brother ; all beings in the one Aeonic all-man being all brothers to each other. All beings are brothers as from the one Spirit in the one Jehovah Father-Son ; and are begotten anew in that common relation, as Christ's disciples are all brothers in and under one Lord and Master. So here, at the hand of every man's brother, or of all as brothers, and in the natural gradation of immediate succession from the lowest and outmost, after their kind, their age, and all distinctions. So sat Jacob's sons in their natural order with their common brother Joseph in Egypt ; so are all the parts and particles of one's body, of every formation, all in one all-man all-world.

Each offering must be, and is, a self-sacrifice. Every begetting act is a whole-man self-sacrifice. The outer titan's offering and all manner of action are self-sacrifices to himself ; and therein is self-destruction and yet the passing of the sum-substance inwards, upwards, and onwards, with the all Aeonic line of movement. For in the image of God made He man ; all things in the all-man, and he as one whole, must be continued in the divine image and likeness, and be, as gods, God-like. Thus all beings are to be fruitful, and to multiply ; to bring forth abundantly in the earth, and to multiply therein. Earth is here taken as the renewed and advanced sense of the old world, as the cultivated earth was under the old world to the uncultivated ground.

Jehovah establishes His covenant with Noah and his sons with him, as tripartite whole, and with their seed after them; also with the all other beings; and all flesh shall no more be cut off by a flood, nor shall there any more be a flood to destroy the earth. The covenant is the Spirit's all Om of all Oms into which the all-man and the all-world, and each being with its respective part Om, are brought into the Omic Ark by begetting action, and out of which, as in new birth, all come forth to propagate onwards, and multiply, and fill the earth. The Spirit's Om is to continue with them as established with them, as all-man and all-world, and as in gradation of all beings. It is an all dying to the old and all living to the new; confirmed by the all death through the all self-sacrifice in the all self-begetting into the all new life of the all new man in the all new world. The usual oath is implied in the pronoun I as attached to the blessing, the command, the promise, and the all-sum Omic covenant, of which Jehovah Spirit Himself is the All-One Being, who in eternal Father Son action begets and brings forth all seeds of all beings and each seed of each being (Is. liv. 9-10). Hab. iii. 9 says, The bow was made quite naked, according to the oaths of the tribes, even thy word. The Hebrew term translated tribes really signifies rods, or Omic ones, the singular being the rod or one of the Om. The tribes are the seven, ten, or twelve points, or ones, in the one whole man Israel. Literally rendered the passage would read, The bow was made quite naked, the oaths of the rods, the word. Oaths taken as a noun of multitude would mean the Omic summary of beings, or of things, in full Aeonic number of seven, ten, or twelve, of Oms and their ones or rods, established or ratified through their death, or transition through death, into life, all forming into one head part or word; the I or Jehovah Spirit, together with the all-man and all-world, as the all-sum in the one, or rod, of the all-Om. Thus also the old all-man and old all-world for lower, and the new Abrahamic all-man and all-world, would form into one head world, or Jesus Christ in the Christian era.

The one, or sum-arrow of the bow or Om, is the Spirit, or the Spirit in the Jehovah Father-Son action; and the arrow as coming out of and from the bow, as one whole Om and one, is the son of the bow. The words of Jesus, who is the personal word or Logos, are Spirit and Life: the inmost in them is the Spirit, and that Spirit in the Jehovah Father-Son or Jesus, the gradation being through believers, and all beings. It is said that the bow shall be seen in the cloud; also that God shall look on it that He may remember His covenant, which is between Himself and all beings. Looking is one's highest power, as the eyes are the highest organs of sum-sense, corresponding to light and truth as to sensation and intellect. Eyes are the Oms into which all Oms are summed up, with light as that into which all rays, or rods, or ones, are summed up into being the all one of that all eye Om. Thus the Spirit, Jehovah Father-Son, all-man, and all beings in all gradation, are together, in all sum sense of light and look, in the one covenant Om of Oms, or eye of eyes, and one oath-ray of oath-rays, or light of lights, of all life, of the all-man and all-world, as said of Jesus Christ, the Logos.

It has been already explained that Noah means the Jehovah Spirit's ending-beginning of the old into the new world; the all passing through the Deluge transition into the peace, rest, and comfort of the advanced state. The bow is the sum-sign of all of the covenant; hence theists have associated it with the new world reign of peace and plenty, all good and all comfort. In ancient forms of religion the gods are spoken of as descending and ascending on it, as on Jacob's ladder; which in meaning is quite correct, because it is a summary representation of all matter, manner, and meaning of Omic and Aeonic work. Its colours are related and unfolded in due prismatic proportion, from the red to where the violet falls into the sky. Many of the Ancients spoke of it under the name of the goddess Iris. Iris is associated with Osiris much as the moon is with the sun in nature and all natural production; Neith being associated with him in his Apollo or more divine sense. Iris is again associated with him in the combinations of these productive forms and principles in actual conceptive intercourse by these, as in light, heat, moisture, air, and earth, or as often called by the Ancients, fire, air, earth, and water. In such Father-Son action is the actual outcoming of any and all things from the Spirit or the gods. Hence Iris was associated with the rainbow, as bringing messages, productions, or all kinds of issues from the Spirit, or the gods. Elithuia is a secondary agent of Herè, and is, as such, included with Iris in the obstetric or midwife part and sense of productive work, as in actual birth. Herè is the all sum female side. So Iris is always present in the Olympian Court, is at the disposal of Zeus and Herè, and, possessing such god-like nature and offices, will not sit down with the winds or worldly inferiors to banquets. Herè, Demeter, and Iris are much the same.

From the bow's representation of the production of all beings and all good, came the idea that wealth is concealed under the ends of the arch where they touch the earth, but is difficult to be found either in labour production or treasure-trove. The production of the rainbow is by the refraction and reflection of the parallel rays of the sun falling on spherical water drops of rain. By a law of refraction, a ray of light passing through one medium, as air, and entering a denser one, as water, is bent back somewhat, as is well known in the trick of the porcelain basin and the silver coin, or any basin and any coin. By a law of reflection, a ray of light, falling on a spherical or plane surface, goes off at the same angle to the surface as it fell to it. The parallel arrangement and relations of the rays correspond to the onward Aeonic lines of every formation, and the circular form and layers of the bow to those of the eye and of all Oms. The bow seen by the one eye is not that seen by the other; each ending-beginning Om has its corresponding ending-beginning Om at the other tenth point, and the Aeonic succession of Oms between both. Out of, through, and from the Omic sun all sun rays come as the all sum one of the sun, and are shed on their onward way as multiplied sun-sons, entering all things of sea and sky and earth in their refractive mode of sexual intercourse, and issuing forth in reflected birth of all new light and life, being and having being. On the fourth day of creation is the all-world morning sun rise, enlightening, enlivening, and reddening, or prismatically colouring, all things in passing into red and all colour blood in animal and human life. This sun-rise is three points from the first behind, and has its rainbow at the seventh point man-rise, which is three points before the other end, or tenth point at the Garden. The fourth point sun-rise has also its all old-world bow at the Enoch seventh point, or three points before the Deluge. When the sun is at man's creation point, the bow is behind at the fourth point, and indicates by natural and prophetic course that the sun and all things will have similar relations at the fourth point after the Garden level. Prophecy has special (sun) connection with the fourth point, priesthood with the seventh, and kingship with the tenth.

It is the same in the morning and evening of every day and all days, every season and all seasons, every era and all eras, in one's body or person and life, and all else; so that it is the Omic and Aeonic sun-sign in all things. It holds in its form and meaning equally in things social, moral, and religious. It contains an epitome, whenever and wherever seen, of all nature, in all the light, life, and glory of all nature, arranged in nature's Omic and Aeonic constitution, impressively marked in nature's all colours of one whole white (implied in the spirit's dark and invisible centre point of the Om), in three parts of red, yellow, and blue (or Ham, Shem, and Japhet), in seven points of red, orange, yellow, green, blue, indigo, violet, and all tints and shades of modified combinations. It is formed and seen in its three into a fourth parts; each layer, circle, or line, being an ending-beginning transition line of the universal one, four, seven, ten, as the light at the beginning or first day, the sum-light at the fourth, the man-light at the seventh, and the tenth point ending beginning like the first. The point of refraction is its entrance into the (drop) transition line; its point of reflection is its ending-beginning turning point of darkening and dying into lighting and living in touch with the spirit; and out of that nothing point, or point of peculiar touch with the absolute (Leucadian Rock of Ages and of all issue of all being), come forth anew all things of all-man and all-world.

It exists everywhere in the all-man and the all-world, and the all-man and the all-world exist in it. It is in some or all form the mark on Cain, and now on Noah and his tripartite sons, and on all things whatsoever. Its evening form is in the crucifixion, with the Omic Mary of Marys at the foot of the cross and Jesus as the one passing through darkness and death and the grave ; and its morning form is in the resurrection, with the Omic Marys again at His feet. In every case the sun is behind the observer, and the bow is before him in all its forms and meanings, beings and their having being ; the spirit being behind, and in, the sun, the observer, the bow and its all, which order and gradation are those universal and invariable in all beings. The semi-circular arch supposes and implies its counter-part and complemental other side arch ; so that in representing the heavenly hemisphere above it bespeaks also the complemental heavenly hemisphere on the other side of earth and every hemisphere, arch, and arc, all round heaven's relations to earth, and so of all possible horizon over the whole earth, and over each and all beings, as the Om is round the one. The covenant or bow is thus universal ; Jehovah accordingly saying, between Me and you and every living creature of all flesh that is upon the earth ; and these beings in relation to the waters which are not to become a flood to destroy all flesh, in relation to earth and heaven as being in the cloud over the earth, and in all the bow's own meaning and manner of having being in all beings. It is also everlasting, inasmuch as it is the Spirit's Om in all Father-Son action, in all gradations of beings, in all duration of durations, or Age of ages.

All things are taken as one tripartite all-man and all-world, and as moving on in being renewed and advanced in one great midline of all-man and all-world seats of empire. What is thus true of the midline is relatively and by gradation true of every being in its own place, its midline, and its all. When it is said that of Noah's sons, that go forth of the Ark, the whole earth is overspread, the meaning is that the change of renewal and advancement is universal over the earth. Elohim says (6. 13), the end of all flesh is come before me ; for the earth is filled with violence through them ; and behold I will destroy them with the earth. But here the Omic covenant is with all these, or all heaven, earth, and all beings, as beginning anew. The ending and the beginning spoken of are equally extensive and comprehensive. The change in ending is from without inwards from and by Elohim ; that in beginning is from within outwards and onwards from and by the Spirit in Jehovah's Father-Son. That in ending is in putting off and away the shoulder point titan oldnesses and evils in gradation inwards.

Noah, or the all-man, consists of the three parts sons, Ham, Shem, and Japhet. Ham consists of the lower in all beings into one head sum ; Shem consists of the middle of all things ; and Japhet does so of the head-sum of all in one head-sum form ; and the three make up the one all-man Noah. The all things before the Deluge are essential to the Noah summary said to pass through the Deluge change, and also necessarily so to the same summary as re-appearing in all new birth after the Deluge. The locality of the all things, or all beings, before the Deluge, is the locality of them after the Deluge ; it is where they, in their old-nesses, overspread the earth before, and in their newnesses after, the Deluge ; with an improvement and advancement in themselves, and a farther step in their forward march of seat of empire. Each periodic step marked by the precession of equinoxes, as already explained, is a progressive step in the great all movement of the seat of empire from east to west, and in universal relations as to heaven and earth and all beings.

14. Noah began to be a husbandman. Adam's outer side in his ending-beginning at the Garden is physico-plant life, his middle in animal life, and his third in human life. His outer sum-son is Cain, his middle is Abel, and his third is man-sum into Jehovah and the Spirit. Cain goes forth a to and fro fugitive on the earth, the Abel man is a keeper of flocks, and the third is in man Jehovah and the Spirit. Now all things come forth into an improved and advanced condition and character. Instead of the all physico-plant into one head fruit in the Lord-God-planted Garden, there is the vine-sum fruit in the man-planted vineyard ; in which form the man Ham-part is outer with Elohim, in place of the serpent to and fro kind. Jehovah Elohim planted a Garden is in relation to the Noah planted vineyard, as the let there be formula is to the let there produce one. Special notice should be taken of the word began, which indicates the Deluge actual beginning, issuing, or coming forth as in birth, out of the Deluge actual ending of all things. This actual beginning implies the planting of the vineyard and the distinct forthcoming of all things in the tripartite order and under the sum-son heads of Ham, Shem, and Japhet. The vineyard is the being-born new all-man and the being issued new all-world. The vine is symbolic of the first sum-point, and, in the same sense, the tenth sum-point of the improved and advanced physico-plant lower and outer part, instead of the same as unimproved in the Garden : and corresponds, in its mature fruit, to the maturity and headsum grove of Ham as lower part of Noah, which is the lower part from Adam to Cainan of the ten Aeonic men from Adam to the Deluge, and the whole sum of these ten in the sense of the whole sum of the old world as lower part to the Abrahamic and the Christian eras. At this Ham grove point is the beginning forthcoming of the vine and its fruit as new and of the Ham all things as new ; and it is followed in order and gradation by Shem and Japhet, in their covering the nakedness of their father, which is the forthcoming of each in his respective distinct new part. In this forthcoming process, or father-son action, Noah is expressly called their father. That process in and by which they become

distinct new sons is essentially and necessarily that in and by which he becomes their distinct new father, and takes the overlapping place and position in relation to them.

Instead of the mid-part animals of creation is the Shem mid-part, from Cainan to Enoch ; and instead of the head-part man as created is the Japhet head-part from Enoch to Noah all-man ; each of the tripartite sons being the head-sum of his respective part of all beings of the all-world. Noah's tent is the Spirit's Om, as the original womb out of which he as all-man, or all things, are to come forth anew. In his Deluge Ishtar descent all coverings of created forms of all beings and each being are put off and away in the ending sense ; and now in the beginning sense he, as the all man all beings, begins to come forth in new birth and must be re-clothed in re-created and re-begotten forms. The first of his parts to come forth is Ham, then Shem, and thirdly Japhet. Ham comes forth in the sense of the universal lower part as the physico-plant life of the six days' creation works, as the lower part of the begotten Aeonic men from Adam to Cainan, and as the whole old world to the Deluge taken as the lower part in relation to the Abrahamic and the Christian eras ; all this in one sum forming the all lower part of the Noah all-man and all beings. Every being's lower part is the Ham of that being. So is the lower part of the tripartite manhood, or up to the puberty of that being. At this puberty point comes forth the next inner and middle or Shem part of that being. Then all these form into the third or Japhet part, or shoulder and head part, as from the fourth to the seventh, and from the seventh to the tenth of creation, and from Cainan to Enoch, and from Enoch to the Deluge, the comprehensive sense being from the Deluge to Christ's time, and thenceforward in the Christian era.

Noah drank of the wine, and was drunk ; and he was uncovered in his tent. The waters of the Deluge are the elemental seed from the windows of heaven, or the masculine in all beings, and the fountains of the deep, or the feminine side in all beings, flowing as seed sum substance of all beings into the Spirit's universal Om of every Om in all beings. In this Father-Son process there is a universal purification by the seed parting from, and dying to, the all oldnesses ; each being thus returning, as it were, to its original Om, and yet moving forward in so doing, as through its natural transition Omic passage, to the turning point of death into life in the mid point of that passage. At that turning point the waters from above and below, or of the masculine and feminine, unite in their beginning new life, and hence called by the Ancients the waters of life, and here called wine. It means also the turning of the maturity of the young of every being in the womb for actual delivery into the air and all else of outward living. Generally taken, it is the Cana of Galilee wedding water changed by Jesus into wine. The Noah all beings are thus being re-begotten into the all new order of things. Wine is the symbol of the Spirit's one, four, seven, ten living and life-giving sense of all seed waters passing into all stages of all kinds of the life of all beings; and the state of things at each turning or transition point is symbolised by drunkenness. It is in this sense that the Ancients spoke of Noah, the ending-beginning Jehovah of all things, as Bacchus (Abba-Chain-Ish, Father-Son absorbing and issuing all-son beings). Wine's most comprehensive sense here is in being the head-sum sense of water as in the beginning, in the Garden rivers, and in the Deluge. It and honey are specially related to the head part, as blood and milk are to the mid part of every thing.

Noah is uncovered within his tent, in the seed sum-substance being bare of the past, and not yet grown into new forms and formations, and in the young while yet in the womb not being born or brought forth into the fitness or environments of the external world. Ham, the father of Canaan, saw the nakedness of his father, and told his two brethren without. Ham through the Deluge change comes forth as the new lower part and sum-son of all beings. As lower part of Noah passing through the Deluge change he is father to what he is now in coming forth in his new, improved, and advanced form called Canaan of all-man and all-world lower part. The Aeonic men lower part from Adam or the Garden to Cainan Son is father to this lower part Son Canaan. Cain is, in the lower and outer physico-plant or creation sense, the father and predecessor of Cainan, and Cainan is the father and predecessor of Canaan; the relative gradation being Cain as Adam's lower and outer part as great-grandfather, Cainan the grandfather, Ham son the father, and Canaan the new son. So is it with Shem midpart as in Abel, Enoch, Shem, and his after Deluge Son being, and so likewise with Japhet as shoulder and head son. Noah, as father of Ham and his two brothers, is thus the all-man sum of all great-grandfather relation, but continues with Ham, Shem, and Japhet as their father, and as grandfather to them in their sons sense of coming forth anew. It is in this father-son process or action of coming forth anew that Ham passes into being Canaan son, and the two brothers likewise pass into being new sons; while therein he and they become fathers and Noah becomes grandfather and so in gradation backwards.

It is also in this action that Ham sees the nakedness of his father. To see implies the eye or eyes, as the highest or tenth point, and therefore the lowest or first part, Om. The Noah all-father is identical with Ham himself in lower parts from the beginning and in all-sum of all from the beginning to the Deluge as lower part of the Abrahamic and Christian eras. So in coming forth into being son he comes forth from and out of himself and his eye of eyes, or Om of all Oms; which is self-begetting and therein begettingly seeing or knowing the Omic fatherhood of Noah, that is, of himself in the very act of becoming father, which means seeing or knowing the fountain-head of begetting action in its most secret and sacred form next to the divine let there be. He begins with knowing or being known by the Spirit and His let there be and himself in his self-begetting sense of let produce. All this is in the original, virginal, and universal point of action. It should be remembered that, in the Ishtar descent, the garments or coverings of outward and circumstantially acquired forms are gradually put off and away till there is perfect nakedness of the sum-substance in reaching the Omic midpoint passage ; and that the re-clothing is again gradually performed in ascending, or new birth, forth-coming. Ham, as lower part of all beings of physico-plant forms, animals, and human beings, is thus, by nature and necessity, comparatively naked. It is his natural and necessary destiny, here called curse, that he is the lower part, and has the place, sphere, and function of servant to all the middle and upper parts and beings. He is not very capable of improvement and advancement apart from Shem and Japhet beings ; but with them he will make improvement and advancement in indefinite correspondence with theirs, a fact which all Christian philanthropists ought to study very carefully and make the best and utmost use of.

He tells his brothers without. To tell is to use the mouth as the inlet and outlet head-sum Om of the whole person, or the leading sum-substance Om of absorption and communication at the shoulder and head parts. He sees the nakedness within the tent, comes forth at the first point, and grows to the fourth point, where the sub-substance absorption of the Ham lower part, here called telling (told), passes into the forth-coming Shem midpart to grow up into sum-son at the seventh point, where the sum-substance of Ham and of himself, again under the same word telling, comes forth into the head-sum from the seventh to the tenth points. The all Ishtar ascent of the all-man thus comes out, as in creation, from the naked Om and one of the first point, next by the absorption and issue at the fourth point, and again in like manner at the seventh point, all into and out of the tenth point. Shem and Japheth cover the all-man being thus newly created and begotten by laying the garments on their shoulders, or the Omic and Aeonic parts of four, seven, and ten or to ten, at which they come forth and take outward Aeonic all-man form. They do so walking backwards in the sense of their Ishtar ascent from the lowest and inmost turning point in the Deluge Om to which they and Ham and all had Ishtarly descended. So does all nature descend and become naked in the winter season and ascend, or turn and walk backwards, in the spring season ; in which all things reclothe themselves each and all in connection with the shoulders or change points in all formations. So is it at the change or transition points in man and all things. That Shem and Japhet do not see the nakedness of their father means that they come forth at the transition points between the first and the tenth and under the self-formed covering together with Ham as under and outer side. The covering or clothing at the Garden is by Jehovah Elohim; here it is by Shem and Japhet as the improved and advanced form and sense of the Jehovah Elohim in the new all-man all-world. Ham is naked and darker as natural lower part from one to four.

The under and outer here is Ham instead of the physico-plant outer side at the Garden. Shem is next or middle part, and stands for the full form Jehovah Elohim, with h-em for h-im; the term Shem being Isha-hem, the Jehovah man Elohim, or Jah-Ish-em, Jehovah Son Elohim, the Lord Son God, the Son of God son of man, Jesus in the midpart all comprehensive sense. Hence the words conveying the blessing of Shem are, Blessed the Lord God of Shem, or blessed be the Jehovah Elohim Shem. Ham is Jehovah Elohim though as under and outer and so a servant, or the all-sum servant, to the Shem higher and inner Jehovah Elohim; and all beings have thus their being and having being in the Jehovah Elohim and His blessedness, in all gradations and relations. Japheth is to be enlarged by Elohim as acting in the under and outer spheres, and Canaan shall be his servant. Japheth is J of Jehovah, ap the hard and utmost form of Abba, and heth the aspirated hard and utmost of d in Adam and of h-im in Elohim; all making Jehovah Father-Son man God in the highest and utmost midform and meaning, as the sum-substance of Ham and Shem. He shall dwell in Shem's tents, in every Omic sum-substance point of ending-beginning summary, which comes forth and passes on in new enlargement. A special one of these points is the titan shoulder point, that of the Hittites or the sons of Heth. He is the head-point of the one in every Om and foundation. Abraham is composed of the sum of all these names in their etymological forms and meanings, and in their gradations and relations of great-grandfather, grandfather, father, and son.

Noah's years contain the sum-substance of all from the beginning to the Garden into the number of Aeonic men from Adam to the Deluge, the titan point of which being at Enoch, the seventh from Adam. Each Aeonic man stands in the place of the great-grandfather, with two places for grandfather and father, the last for ever passing into son, followed by the others to the ever disappearing of the great-grandfather. This in arithmetical figures is six and two nothings, 600; which with another triad make nine hundred, all into the one tenth point Deluge from the old into the new order of things. The Deluge is the passage into the Jubilee era of peace and comfort, marked by number fifty; the whole making nine hundred and fifty, which is Noah's whole number of years. There are three triads corresponding to the three sons, or sum-sons, of Noah, passing in all-man all-world through the Deluge from the old into the new order. It is a triad of triads and conveniently marked three with two nothings, or three hundred; the Jubilee being marked by fifty, makes, with these, three hundred and fifty of Noah all-man all-world coming forth out of the all-Om Deluge. This means that the all beings that lived, or existed, before the Deluge passed through it as through death into the after Deluge new life. There is always an overlapping of from the seventh to the tenth point prolonged with the renewed for that length of points, which here, with the fifty, make three hundred and fifty.

CHAPTER X.

THE tripartite sum-sons of Noah now come forth into the midpart era, and representing all beings in renewed, improved, and advanced condition and character, are Shem, Ham, and Japheth. Under each of these is a ten-form number of sum-sons as being born, or come forth, after or out of the Deluge. Shem is mentioned generally first, because he is the main midline son. In mentioning their sons, those of Japheth are here given first, because the head part is foremost in conception, birth, and moulting, or passing out of the old into the new condition and character. Seven of these are given in their Aeonic gradation, corresponding to the creation days and the concentration of the senses in the head—Gomer, Magog, Madai, Javan, Tubal, Meshach, and Tiras. The first and fourth points sons are Gomer and Javan, the first giving forth the sum-sons, Ashkenaz, Riphath, and Togarmah, and the fourth giving birth to Elishah, Tarshish, Kittim, and Dodanim. The isles of the Gentiles into which these are divided are the Omic head-sum centres, each being a representative head-sum mouth and tongue, or Om and one, in Spirit and Father-Son relations and process of begetting in gradation of families and nations of all-beings, continued as renewed, or re-begotten, through the Deluge change, and to be continued in onward preservation, propagation, and universal correlations. Taking these sons of Japheth in the absorptive order from the face into the cerebellum, the seven, otherwise ten, are regarded as four, or one, four, seven, ten, of the face, passing into three in the cerebrum, and again into one in the cerebellum.

One, four, seven, ten, of every being form the layers or circles of the Om and one, and are the same as great-grandfather, grandfather, father, and son. Here in the order from the centre outwards, they are Javan, Gomer, Japheth, and Noah. In the Japheth Om and one they are Gomer, Magog, Madai, and Javan (in order of age). Likewise in the Gomer form, they are Gomer, Ashkenaz, Riphath, and Togarmah. And in the Javan form, they are (in like order of) Elishah, Tarshish, Kittim, and Dodanim As the sum-substance of the lower passes into the improved and advanced higher, so also the nature, or character, and name of the lower pass into and under those of its higher. This has been seen under what is said of Shem and Japheth in covering their father while walking backwards in doing so. Thus every being is, and is regarded and spoken of, according to what it is in its higher or head-sum part. The tree is known by its fruit, its head-sum substance. All beings of creation are so known by their head-sum man, Adam; all the animals, or living things, are so known and named in and by him; and all beings eat of themselves in the all eating of the all forbidden fruit, and know their sum feminine side in so eating and self begetting action in ever onwards creative and begetting generations. Every being is a Jehovah Elohim, and is so known in and by its head-sum. At the same time it continues its kind, character, and identity in its scapegoat form. The Javan form is at the Japheth head-sum level; and, therefore, contains Jehovah Father-Son Elohim in the names Elishah, Tarshish, Kittim, and Dodanim.

Ham's four points sum-sons are Cush, Mizraim, Phut, and Canaan. Those of Cush are Seba, Havilah, Sabtah, Raamah, Sheba, and Dedan. In a more direct way is Nimrod a sum-son of Cush, wherefore Cush is said to beget him. In this Nimrod is the greater outer side of Ham, containing the improved and advanced greatness sum-substance of the Cainites, as represented in the names here terminating in im. He begins to be a mighty one in the re-appearing new earth, at the Deluge Om. He is a mighty hunter in the sense of a begetter, or generative organ, before, or in the begetting side of, Jehovah. At this highest level, and therefore the lowest beginning level, of the Omic full-formed layers, or circles, of Cush is the mature, or manhood, Jehovah Elohim of Ham's outer side head-sum from the old world. The old world being the all-sum lower part of the all-man, the Deluge ending-beginning of things is the puberty of the all-man. So it is here said that the beginning of Nimrod's kingdom is in the renewed being of his Omic level of Jehovah Elohim; the particular points in this beginning being, Babel, Erech, Accad, Calneh, in the land of Shinar. Shinar land gives forth in renewed sense, Nineheh, Rehoboth, Calah, and Resin. Under the sum-name Mizraim are the ims, Ludim, Anamim, Lehabim, Naphtuhim, Pathrusim, Casluhim (out of which is Philistine), Caphtorim.

It should be borne in mind that the four points sons are always summed into the fourth as the one whole midline Aeonic son, as Judah is the one son summary of the same four of the sons of Jacob. The four are the sum-substance in the all-Om from the past; and the fourth is the sum-being of the four, through which fourth the Aeonic line is begettingly continued. So, in the previous chapter (v. 18) Ham is summarily said to be the father of Canaan, as including all of Ham; and, in vs. 25-27, Canaan is taken for Ham. Here, then, Canaan is taken in the new sum-substance which is to be the lower part and servant to Shem and Japheth. His sum-son points are in full sum tens, with the eleventh as the sum-one of the Ham sense of the Deluge Om in its new all-man all-world beginning, namely, Sidon, Heth, the Jebusite, the Amorite, the Girgasite, the Hivite, the Arkite, the Sinite, the Arvadite, the Zemarite, and the Hamathite. The outside layer, or circle, of the Canaan sense of the Deluge new all-man all-world Om is here called the border of the Canaanites, marked by Sidon, Gerar, Gaza, Sodom, Gomorrah, Admah, Zeboim, and Lasha, in their Omic relations. Such are Ham's sum-sons in the sense and order of their tongues or head-sums, families in tribal issues, and nations as all beings under each of all sum-parts and points. The term land is used in the summaries of Japheth and Shem; but not here, because it is implied in Canaan itself, as the new and advanced midearth seat of empire. Cainan is after the Garden, the midline inner and advanced of Cain; and Canaan is that of Cainan.

Shem is the midline Aeonic all-man Son; Japheth is the elder, because the shoulder and head-sum son; and Ham is the lower part son. Shem is the father of all the children of Eber. This term Eber signifies passage, or transition; and all the children of Eber are the children, or the ever being begotten beings, of the great midline movement of the all-man all-world of universal empire. Eb denotes the ever forth-coming from Abba (father); er is the rolling and repeating of d of Adam into El; and H of Jehovah prefixed to the full form Eber makes Heber, or Hebrew, the Jehovah Father-Son Elohim. Eber in its original or etymological form of Abba, to which Abel is allied, and taken with Ham, makes Abram, changed at the Melchizedek and Isaac transition into Abraham. Eber represents the all Jehovah Father-Son sum-substance from the beginning to the Deluge, and now coming forth in the Abrahamic midpart of the Aeonic all-man all-world. Abraham thus contains all from the beginning to Jesus Christ, and is so taken by Matthew in the genealogical table prefixed to his Gospel. In short Abraham is the Abracadabra of the all-man all-world from the beginning to Jesus Christ, and in Him onwards Abraham's whole Aeonic lower part is from the beginning to the Deluge; but the lower part of his whole midpart is here from the Deluge to his call out of Chaldea, consisting of ten Aeonic sum-sons, Sem, Arphaxad, Cainan, Seba, Heber, Phalec, Ragau (Reu), Saruch (Serug), Nachor (Nahor), Tera, himself being the eleventh, or re-beginning, one, as called into the public life of his midpart.

This succession of ten Aeonic sons are given in the next chapter. What is given in this chapter is a summary of the head-sum parts and points under each of the sum-sons of Noah in their representative relations in the all-man all-world, all as coming forth out of the Deluge transition. Ten days, like the creation days from the beginning to the Garden, are taken in that Deluge transition as the recreative time and process. The all-man all-world being in three parts under the names Ham, Shem, and Japheth, a sub-duration and process of ten days are implied in each, making a triad of tens into a fourth ten, which are called forty days. Otherwise put the forty days are the one, four, seven, ten, which are the four points of ten time and process of creating and producing again, or of renewing, the all-man all-world; all being now represented as so renewed under summary names. In continuation of such names, under Japheth and Ham, are now given those under Shem, namely, Elam, Asshur, Arphaxad, Lud, and Aram; of Aram, Uz, Hul, Gether, and Mash; of Arphaxad, Salah; of Salah, Eber; of Eber, Peleg and Joktan; and of Joktan, Almodad, Sheleph, Hazarmaveth, Jerah, Hadoram, Uzal, Diklah, Obal, Abimael, Shela, Ophir, Havilah, and Jobab. It has been observed that Eber denotes an ever forthcoming from Abha. This causes one becoming two, and he is said to have two sons, one of whom is named Peleg, for in his days the earth was divided. The Eber, Hebrew, or Abrahamic Aeonic being of the all-man all-world, begins to grow forth and on in new nature and character, condition, and cultivation, and in distinct parts and points.

Joktan holds the Jehovah midline parts and regions, while the Peleg sum-sons occupy more of the farther out regions. Shem thus moves along the Aeonic main midline of seats of empire from the east towards the west. Ham, as lower part, occupies mainly the south, though generally in land and people, with Shem and Japheth. Japheth, as shoulder and head-part, is regarded as mainly occupying the tropics and northern regions, though generally dwelling in the tents of Shem, with whom he has Ham as lower part and servant. Mesha is moving force, as in the great Aeonic movement. It is referred to as the all-man all-world Aeonic high way from east to west, from behind onwards, being the all-midline of the world's seats of empire. Sephar is a marked, or written, roll, or scroll, here rendered mountain. It is the ever ending-beginning mountain of creative and begetting Omic maturity in the all high way of life. The words, as thou goest, signify the Ishtar descent and ascent in relation to the Sephar all historical and all history giving mountain in and from the east. All beings have their being and having being in their relations to it. The way of it is the all good old and new way; the history of it is the history of all; and to write all that history, the history of Jesus, would be to write more books than the world could contain (John xxi. 25). Noah marks the old world's last, and the new world's first, seat of empire. The names stated in this chapter as standing on the Omic one, four, seven, ten, after the Deluge level, under Noah's three sum-sons, are representative of all the divisions of the all-man all-world in parts and points, lands and peoples, or beings in all gradations, regarded first in their limited distances and relations to this particular seat of empire, and then also in their universal distances and relations over the whole earth. So are the words, and by these were the nations divided in the earth after the flood.

CHAPTER XI.

AND the whole earth was of one language, and of one speech. Israel's all-man all-world seat of empire comes to the pinnacle of its greatness, grandeur, and glory, in Solomon's head-sum wisdom, excelling that of all the children of the east country and of Egypt, or of all the preceding seats of empire. In 1 Kings iv. the David all sum-substances of him and his, as the all-man all-world of the time, is given and brought into the one tongue, the Om and one of the all in all; being also prophetic and representative of Him who is greater than Solomon, the Logos all in all. He spoke of all beings and having being from the hyssop and the creeping thing to the cedar of Lebanon, and all the kings of the earth. The whole earth in this sense was of one language, and of one speech, that of Solomon at Jerusalem, the all-man all-world seat of empire of the time. So was it on the day of Pentecost (Acts ii.), when there appeared unto them cloven tongues like as of fire, and it sat upon each of them. And they were all filled with the Holy Ghost, and began to speak with other tongues, as the Spirit gave them utterance.

Eastern nations had the custom of cleaving the tongue or facial part of their Teraphim, placing the head in a niche of the house wall, setting lighted lamps near it, and consulting it as an oracle. Rachel took with her the Teraphim of Laban; she always does. It has been already explained that the Teraphim, taken in the plural, or as one sum in the singular, represents the head sum-substance of the whole lower part, in the sense of the grove Om and one. While the whole from the beginning to the Deluge forms the lower part to the Abrahamic and Christian eras, and is suitably represented by the Teraphim; it also has its head of all meanings in the Ark and Deluge summary, which implies the mid-part Cherubim, and head or intellect part Seraphim, in addition to the lower part sense of the Teraphim proper. Thus, the Teraphim must be regarded as including all of the Teraphim proper, of the Cherubim, and of the Seraphim, in one all ending-beginning head-sum, in the sense and form of the Noah all man all-world. The mouth and tongue denote the grove Om and one of the lower part physico-plant and animal natures for the reproduction of all beings, each after its kind; being in such respects to the whole body or being as the mouth and tongue are in all respects to the whole being, the all outlet and inlet, the all way of Ishtar descent and ascent. In the strictest and most original and universal sense the Teraphim represents the Spirit's Om and one of the lower part, also summarised in the face; the Cherubim that of the mid part, also summarised in the cerebrum; and the Seraphim that of the head part, also summarised in the cerebellum or intellect. Hence in Acts ii. they were all filled with the Holy Ghost, and began to speak with other tongues, as the Spirit gave them utterance. So here all things come forth anew, or are being born or issued again, as out of the Spirit's original all-Om and one, one mouth and tongue, one speech.

They journey from the east, find a plain in the land of Shinar, and dwell there. Shinar signifies double man, ending-beginning man, man and world being renewed and restored (Is. xi. 11; Zech. v. 11). Plain in the land of Shinar signifies the same as field in Gen. iv. 8. Every living being in being brought forth into the world finds the field, or sphere, of existence before it as at the beginning, when the all-man, or all living beings, and the all-world are together and to each other as out of their oldnesses into and in their newness of existence. Adam, the all-man, comes forth and out of his Cain outer and older creation character; bringing with him, and containing in him, the sum-substance of that outer and older in Cain's offering together with that of Abel. In this, his Abel new sense, he dies to, or Abel is slain by, Cain, who passes on in his scapegoat sense and disappears as to his oldnesses, while Abel passes on in newness of sum-son Aeonic Seth. This field or plain is meant as the representative all-world Omic dwelling place, formed in the image and likeness of that out of which all beings are brought forth.

Their journeying from the east is their passing from the preceding seat of empire into this new one. Cain talked with Abel his brother, as they here say one to another, go to, and so on. The original Om and gradation of language are the same as in all other things. The connections from the lungs, through the larynx and the tongue to the lips, are in Aeonic gradation, as previously observed. In gradation from within to without is the debarreem or debarrim (words) as the outer Elohim to the Jehovah Father-Son Saphah (mouth and tongue). The last sounds of language are its first, all centred in the all ending-beginning Abba. Gradation in language is from the deepest breath and guttural sound to the labial closing-opening contact, with breath motion surd, sonant, or aspirated; and all and each, even every vowel having that gradation. The same gradation is in accents in pronouncing, speaking, and reading words and sentences. Language is milder and softer in its beginning and ending, and stronger and harder in its midpart of public life and use. Every new and advanced form absorbs and carries with and in it the sum-substance of the languages which it puts aside and leaves behind. Cain's talking and their saying here are each the exercise of the one tongue spoken of, in the new life action of each being in the one whole all-man all-world. In its first sense it is go to, equivalent to let there be an all Omic motion and action; then let produce takes the form of let us make brick, a city, and a tower; and for let us make man, there are the words, let us make us a name. It is the all-man all-world creation coming forth anew; all from the absolute and the spirit's original Om, to the tower-top reaching into heaven, or the human intellect, at the Melchizedek level of eternal perfection; and having as here its central representation in the world's central seat of empire.

What is to be built is a city in the sense of each new born and reared up being in Aeonic formation over the whole world; but the all-city of cities, the capital city, the metropolis, or head-sum city of the new world being at its new seat of empire. The outer of the world's Aeonic line of cities from the Garden to the Deluge is Cain's city; and the outer here is in Nimrod's city. Nimrod is formed by the transposition and perversion of Dornim, or Tora-im, the outer form or Elohim of the Jehovah Father-Son, or Omic and Aeonic, Tora of universal being. This ever ending-beginning, yet ever unbeginning endless, Tora is the true Spirit and Father-Son kingdom, the all one eternal kingdom of the All One Eternal King. Both in its inner Jehovistic and outer Elohistic forms this universal kingdom is inherently, inalienably, and necessarily that of the eternal Father-Son Divine Being. By essential nature, organic law, and intransferable rights, the only and eternally being begotten Son is, by eternal decree and appointment, placed in perpetual occupation of its throne and perpetual sway of its sceptre.

Its outer manifestative Elohim is intended to be what it really is, so far as it is good, the working out of its Jehovistic Being. Its Elohim is the actual and acting body and limbs of its Jehovah; it is its Teraphim, Cherubim, and Seraphim. When only two Cherubic figures are used, as in the Tabernacle and Temple, they stand for the whole two sides of the whole being. But this outer Elohim or Toraim has ever a measure of incidental Cain character of outerness and oldness, of Nimrod wildness and wickedness. The name is said by some to mean two enemies; and it does mean an enemy to all good, and so an enemy to all itself outwards to final self-destruction. It is said by others to mean the ruler asleep; and it does mean the want and the perversion of, and opposition to, all good rule of real rights and righteousness, laws and action. The higher than the highest of them does not always seem as one asleep. Awake, O Lord, and plead the cause that is Thine own.

They have brick for stone, and slime for mortar. The brick materials are burnt thoroughly. Being a new creation it must be reared up as at the beginning; having all its materials reduced as by head part fire, which is as the original fire, or the fire from heaven, to their original state at the lowest level of Ishtar descent. All things of earth, and sea, and sky, are thus being reproduced and re-begotten, from the elemental means of original substances, protoplasm, ozone, and all Omic seeds, to the full-form tower of each being reaching to its heaven height, everywhere over all the earth, with the all central representation on Shinar's plain. In each being there is union in diversity; so is there one leading seat of empire of the whole world, corresponding to the unity of the

Divine Trinity and trinity of trinities of all beings. There is a natural kind of necessary competition between the to and the fro of all to and fro force, motion, and action. The one cannot exist and act without the other. Hence is the forbidding of the Garden fruit; and hence here it is said, lest we be scattered abroad upon the face of the whole earth. They must be reared up in whole being; but they must also be diversified and scattered. Their name is all beings in one, as all come to Adam, or go to compose him as sum-stance of and as the universal being. The face of the earth is the Om of all Oms over the whole earth, or its whole life means, its sphere of existences.

Jehovah comes down to see the city and the tower which the children of men are building. The forbidden fruit of the Garden is the all sum-substance of the whole works of creation from the beginning to the Garden. Eating it is all Ishtar descent in reducing all to the original point of the Spirit's moving on the face of the waters, that as Shinar plain; and the eating is also the Ishtar ascent in re-creating all in the begetting mode of production. The gradation of the process of the work is from the serpent to and fro action, like the Spirit's moving on the face of the waters, upwards and inwards to man, and his coming forth in the Divine image, and therein in the coming forth of Jehovah. Adam is brought to be as gods, but not to take Jehovah's place of tree of life; and hence it is said, lest he put forth his hand, and take also of the tree of life, and eat, and live for ever, and so forth. So here it is said, now nothing will be 'restrained from them, which they have imagined. Jehovah Himself must come down to see, to use the eyes, the head-sum Oms of light and life, as in the whole works of original creation, and specially as in the coming forth of man in the Divine image as the head-sum of all with Jehovah. In the process of the original creation the mid-line unity is fully and for ever kept; but the beings, as they come forth, are scattered over the earth, or are brought forth over the whole earth, though in special relation to one whole world seat of empire. So here Jehovah is constantly coming as the light and life-giving Life of all. He, like the sun, gives light and life and motion everywhere; and the light and life spread and are scattered everywhere. Things are forming up and in to the Jehovah level, position, and character.

15. The children of men do all things according to some ideal; not one thought can be formed or perceived without an act of imagination; and the all standard ideal is the divine image. They are right in imagining to do all things and everything to reach to heaven, in creating and begetting intercourse with heaven, and to perfect conformity to the ideal and image of the All Father and All Creator. Jehovah makes an eternal Ishtar descent in and with all beings in changing and being changed, in stripping and being stripped, of all oldness and incidental evil, and an eternal Ishtar ascent in creating and begetting all beings anew, as at the

beginning. He descends in and with them; He ascends and grows up in and with them; fear not to go down to Egypt, I will go with thee; Jesus Christ formed in us is the hope of glory.

Go to, let us go down, and there confound their language, that they may not understand one another's speech. So Jehovah scattered them abroad from thence upon the face of the earth; and they left off to build the city. Here the creative work and growth come to completion and maturity. The Om as a city, or whatever other form, has its one as tower in full form and fitness in every being at the puberty or manhood of that being. At this point, as at that of originally moving on the face of the waters, the Spirit in Jehovah Father-son head-sum action is necessary for begetting action. The confounding of the language is in passing from the creative into the begetting mode of production, which takes place in the gradation of all parties, from the lowest and outmost, as in eating the forbidden fruit. Christ is the head of every man; and the head of Christ is God. In all force and motion, creation and begetting, the head-sum is foremost; but it does not come forth in the highest and inmost form and sense till the full length of the formation or work. The fruit of every tree appears through the Omic blossom at the level of maturity. Man, as the head sum-substance of all creation, appears last, and Jehovah in whose image he is made. Jehovah and man appear in every and at every step and stage; but there is a special appearing of them in the head sum of every being, and the all head sum is in the last head summary as all-man all-world. Adam, as all-man, in eating the fruit, begins to take the sum-substance of all creation, and re-create it in all the variety of beings of creation each after its kind, through the begetting mode of production; and therein he becomes and acts as gods, next to being Jehovah and the Spirit. At this point it is Jehovah's part in the gradation to act; and He does so in the Spirit all Father-Son into universal begetting, which is universal scattering of all seed-beings. The mid-part comes to appear as united to, and after the lower part.

The struggle for existence begins with existence. It is essential and necessary to all to and fro action and all laws of substances, and all beings. It is essential and necessary to all force, motion, and life; and the sum of it is in unity in diversity, in all one and each triad in one, and all triads of triads. So here it is all one tongue and one speech, yet all confusion of language and all scattering of all seeds and all beings over all the earth. The old world with all its beings must pass into the new creation and new birth in becoming the all world Abrahamism, and it in turn must so pass into Christianity with its Gospel change among all nations of all beings.

They leave off building the new creation, because it is completed as at the Garden; the new midpart Abrahamic seed being sown, as if scattered, over all the earth. So do the sun and seed in spring time; and so do all beings, each at its maturity and in its mode of life and living. Strictly taken, the meaning of the implied confusion is sexual intercourse, conception, and birth, sowing, sprouting, and springing up, in the newness of the new season, as in the Abrahamic era. It here takes place at the age and stage of maturity of the old world as forming the Aeonic all lower part re-created, renewed, and grown into the new all-man all-world fitness, capacity, and action of begetting mode of reproduction. It should be observed that all beings are thus reproduced in the original and virginal sense of Aeonic sonship.

The name of this universal Aeonic city is Babel, because Jehovah does here confound the language of all the earth, and from hence does Jehovah scatter them abroad upon the face of all the earth. The plain, or valley, in which they build, and out of which they are scattered, is the Shinar begetting grove, like the Cain-Abel field, like Israel's Succoth at the maturity point of their exodus out of Egypt, like the Jordan plain and clay ground between Succoth and Zarthan (1 Kings, vii. 46), and like the Jordan valley of the baptism of Jesus and His forthcoming into public life. At each of the one, four, seven, ten transition points there is a forthcoming or tripartite ten points, all making the number forty so often noted. On the fourth day of creation work the sun, moon, and stars appear, with full day light, heat, and clay burning into fifth day animal life and formations. Unlike the physico-plant formations of the preceding days, which are comparatively fixed and unfitted for locomotion, these animal life beings are brought forth to be scattered and to move over all the earth. They contain the sum-substance of the preceding days beings, and belong to the middle part from four to seven, being the Shemites of the creation ten days. On the sixth and seventh days the shoulder (Shechem), or Hitite, absorption takes place into the eighth day appearance of the Japheth, Jehovah all-sum man. Then the whole from the beginning to the Garden is taken at the Garden as one whole lower part, like the first three days into the fourth day as lower part. Thus the Garden point in beginning the begetting mode of production to the Deluge is like the creation first day, then like the creation fourth day, and it is really the seventh and tenth, all making one, four, seven, ten, in one. So is it here at Shinar grove plain. It is one, four, seven, ten, valley. As fourth point transition sum of things it is that of the rising sun, when all living beings move forth over the whole earth.

The Deluge Ark is spoken of like a huge vessel, with the sum-substance and seed of all living beings, sailing with the sun, the window above, round the whole globe. As it moves farther and farther on its ocean way, the earth seems at the same rate to sink behind, or, which is the same, the waters seem to rise until they cover the whole, even the highest parts, with a depth of the Aeonic height of creation, or one, four, seven, ten into one head sum Garden Om of all as lower fourth point of forthcoming living beings, as contained in the Ark, otherwise fifteen cubits. In beginning to rise again the first part is formed in the first day dawn light up to the fourth day point of Mount Ararat maturity, which has been shown to be the same also as the Garden all tenth point, and in both respects the level, plain, or valley, of the forthcoming of all living beings over the whole earth. This sun circling holds in day and night, in moon measures of time, in the seasons, in the ages, eras, and all changes of all beings, from the most minute and short-lived to the most mighty and long lived (Ps. 19 4-7 ; Ps. 104).

Babel is a contraction of Abba-Abba-El, or Abel-Abel, and signifies a repetition in a renewed and advanced form of the Jehovah Father-Son Elohim, a new and farther stage in the all Aeonic progression. The Aeonic city or kingdom is ever being transmitted from father to son in the great Aeonic line of Father-Son genealogy. Okeanos and Tethus have been consigned to the deep abyss of ocean bed ; Kronos and Rhea or Rheia are confined to the now past underpart world ; and now from the Deluge to Jesus Christ is the reigning era of Zeus and Here, or Abraham and Sara. The Son is ever being begotten by ever becoming Father in the Spirit Father-Son action, as the future is ever being begotten out of the present as the present is ever becoming the past. The ten Father-Son and Abel line Aeonic Sons and city from the Garden to the Deluge are here passed into the Abrahamic lower part of sons and city. Babel is Abraham's lower part city with the ten sons, Sem, Arphaxad, Cainan, Sala, Heber, Phalec (Peleg), Ragau (Reu), Saruch (Serug), Nachor (Nahor), and Tharah (Terah). It is free to all to be prophets, priests, and kings in and with Jesus ; and to be so in and with Him is the only right and rightful way of being so at all. Any other way of divine right to such cannot be. Any other way of human royalty to exist is from the ignorance of the people, a diseased state of society, and the ignorance, arrogance, fraud, and force of the usurper and his associates. The Lord is King, the Lord is One.

It has been seen that Cain's city is the outer of Abel's city from the Garden to the Deluge. So here Nimrod's city is the outer of this Abrahamic lower part city. In this inner or spirit Jehovah Father-Son all-man all-world city, or kingdom, Jehovah or Jesus is ever, ever speaks, and ever acts, as He that serveth, while He is its only and eternal king. But its outer manifestative Elohim form has ever so much of Cain or Nimrod wildness, perversion, and selfishness incidentally attached to it that its improprieties of self-indulgence, self-righteousness, self-aggrandisement, and self-deification grow as it grows in age and greatness ; the remedy of which being always in and by the shoulder point absorption of the sum substance of the contained good, the scapegoat of its Elohistic kind and form, and the self-destruction of its evils and oldnesses.

Shem is one hundred years in the sense of ten in each of the ten men from the Garden, when he begets Arphaxad two years after the flood. Ar is the rolling and repeating form of Ad in Adam ; Pha is the farthest ending-beginning of bha in Abha or Abba ; and xad is the utmost ending-beginning of Chain man, the whole name being the renewal of the all-man as Adam-Abel-Cain, into Arphaxad of Abraham, or the Abracadabra of the Abrahamic era. The three columns of figures denoting the ages of the Aeonic line of genealogy have already been briefly considered. The highest figure of the outer column always becomes a fourth column point, or great-grandfather point, by the forthcoming, or begetting, of a new son on the other, the east and south, or front, side. But its sum-substance is being absorbed, with that of the others, in the same process that gives birth, as well as being, to that son ; while its scapegoat passes on as a farther overlapping, and its incidental oldnesses and evils vanish and disappear. Each of the list here given is about the thirty manhood age at begetting a new son. The figures of the outer line, or column, denote the steps of the Aeonic line of seats of empire ; the stages being at the one, four, seven, ten of the same whole ten steps of this lower part of Abraham. No figure in any column can go beyond nine into the ending-beginning ten form of Om and its one, or one and its Om. Cainan is given by Luke as son of Arphaxad, but is omitted here. Eber here is named Heber by Luke. It is unnecessary to go more minutely into the analysis of these things here.

The ten names here are the renewals of the ten names from the Garden to the Deluge. Noah, as the all-man sum of the men from the Garden to the Deluge, and as passing into the overlapping position at the Deluge, when his midline is taken by Shem in ten form sons into Terah, this overlapping by Noah co-exists with the Shem new lower part of Abraham, and is finally absorbed in Nahor into the maturity point of Terah as sum lower part of Abraham. Thus the name Nahor signifies Noah-tera, Noah-ham-tora, or Noah all old world sum and new lower part sum of Abraham formed into pure, perfect, and middle part Abrahamism, or Abrahamic lower part head-sum Teraphim. The letter n is the inmost ending-beginning Jehovah Father-Son of the old world in the new Shem lower part of Abraham, and now it is that ending-beginning of overlapping and all into Nahor full-form Tera, Teraphim, or Teraphic Abraham. The name Nahor indicates the Spirit Father-Son sum-substance of all passing into the Teraphic Abraham ; but the scapegoat form of the same must also be indicated ; and this is done in and by the same name as brother of Abraham. Hence the name is sometimes spelt Nachor, the c being put in for Cain scapegoat sense, the termination hor being really Ham-Tora, or Ham Teraphim, as lower part of Abraham.

Tera, or Thara, is a contracted and reversed form of Ararat, for Tarara ; Ararat being the rolling articulation of Ad in Adam, meaning the ever re-making and re-begetting of man and all things. Mount Ararat is thus the high place, or maturity grove propagation. Sin, bush or grove, from Ish (man), Isha (woman), with the ending-beging Omic n, is much the same; and is, hence, formed in such words as Sinai, Senah, Sivan, Shinar, Senacherib. Sin is the Chaldean name for moon. Zeus means Omic action from Father-Son to Father-Son, from Jehovah Father-Son to Jehovah Father-Son, in gradation of from Ish to Ish, from Sin to Sin, and so on; and hence Jehovah appears in its other cases after the Nominative, as Gen. Jovis, Dat. Jovi, &c. These things, in their names and meanings, are contained in the Chaldean Ziggurat. It means the Spirit Jehovah Father-Son mode of formation by creative and begetting action. It was constructed on the model of the Aeonic mountain, or midline formation, in stages, all forming up like a pyramid to the shoulder point. A sanctuary, or shrine, formed the top. One of the oldest and most famous known was in the city of Ashur, and was called the House of the mountain of countries. So did the Israelites speak of the Tabernacle and the Temple. Nebuchadnezer's Ziggurat at Borsip was known as the Temple of the Seven Spheres, built on the foundation of a previous one; as Israel's Temple succeeded the Tabernacle, and was built three times.

The lower part of a Ziggurat consisted of a high platform; and, including this, the whole was about a hundred and sixty feet in height. Of its seven stages the second three into a fourth receded equally on three sides to the top sanctuary, which contained the third three from seven to ten, with the sanctuary in the head form of the face as outer court, the middle or cerebrum part as holy place, and the back or cerebellum part as most holy place, or all in the form of Om and one. The platform part represented the foundation on which every being or formation is built up. The most original, virginal, and universal foundation is the Spirit as the Eternal One Absolute Being in the Eternal Om; then the Spirit in Jehovah Father-Son Being and action in the whole relative; and this foundation is represented and symbolised in all the relative in and by every thing on which any formation is begun and built up as the flint, metals, precious stones, all rock, and the solid and crusted earth on and around which all beings and formations are forever being created and begotten. It means also the past as the foundation of the present, and both as that of the future. So are the gradation points in force and motion, joints in plants, jointed bones and valves in animal and man, past dynasties to the present or actual dynasty, and all summaries of steps and stages and every step and stage in relation to its next one or succession of ones. It is the same in the steps and stages of the formation which is being built up, created, or begotten. Every measure of force and formation has its sum-substance and sanctuary, or temple, in its head-sum point, part, or Omic centre, as in the valley, or plain, grove, the lower part head-sum grove, the mountain stages and head-sum top temple of the gods, the flowers and fruits in plants, the gradation of parts and points in all things, particularly in all animals and man and summed up into the head part; man being the head of all, Christ the head of man, and God that of Christ. Each has his head-sum something as his top of Ida and his God; often not so high but far below. Each being has its line of removals of seats of empire in the steps and stages of his course of existence, with corresponding outward signs. The world's (French) Diamond has gone for a time to the New World (America); and Demos is making rapid progress from Demonocracy and Nihilism to Panocracy and Christian Socialism. All men, like all nature, will have themselves and their all, as Ziggurats raised and reared in Aeonic and holy fashion, as altars on which sacrifice and offering of all sum-substance are ever being presented to the One Jehovah. The Chaldeans ornamented and decorated their Ziggurats with images of all kinds of beings from water and slime and clay up to man, and presented all as bearing God's image to the Supreme and Eternal One Being, the One and Om; of Him, and through Him, and to Him, are all things.

Nahor is twenty-nine years when he begets Terah; not thirty, because all things are being completed into, and to come forth out of Terah; and because of Nahor's character of female side, which must be counted by the moon of four sevens or weeks in the one, four, seven, ten sense. His overlapping time is a hundred and nineteen, not a hundred and twenty. Terah is seventy when he begets the three sons, Abram, Nahor, and Haran. The number seventy is man's age allotted span. Seven are otherwise ten; so seventy are otherwise one hundred; and seven are to ten as seventy are to one hundred. Both seventy and a hundred are each taken as man's full age. The Aeonic men in the Aeonic genealogy from the beginning to Christ are about seventy-seven. Jacob went down to Egypt with seventy. Christ sent forth seventy disciple evangelists. The short form of seventy is seven otherwise ten, as from the Deluge to Tera; and the long form is seventy times seven which is in begetting renewal, as in increasing and multiplying to pardon, and as in woman being saved through begetting offspring or children.

Abram, Nahor, and Haran are the improved, advanced, and Abrahamic mid-part forms of Shem, Ham, and Japheth. Abram is the eldest son of Terah. He has not yet any son, yet he is high or great father, indicated even by the name. The r is the rolling and repeating form of d in Adam, and Abram is the contracted form of Abba-Adam, Abba-Adam, or Adam (man) become great-grandfather grandfather, and is father in having Isaac and descendants in great multitude of nations in his loins or Om of lower part maturity head-sum grove here implied (Heb. vii. 9, 10). The dynasties of Okeanos and Tathus, Kronos and Rhea or Rheia, and Zeus and Here, or of the sum of all elementals to the six days' creation, of all thence to the Deluge, and of all from it to Christ, all as three in one, while the Son Christian era are in the loins or Om thereof. Thus he stands in, has in himself, and is coming forth in, universal relations of the all-man all-world, or the whole universe. He is verily the very Zeus of his dynasty. He sees the days of Jesus, and greatly rejoices. He comes out and down from the level of Melchizedek and works all up into tenth point tithes of all sum-substance to that level; and is in all made blessed in the blessedness of Melchizedek, and made glorious in the glory of the likeness of the Son of God. He is actual father Abraham in having Isaac Son.

His brother Nahor is co-extensive with him in his lower part of Ham form and sense of the old all-world, the past dynasties, and the present from the Deluge to Tera, or his own actual midpart, all in universal gradations and relations of beings. The east and lower being peculiarly related to the left and front in feminine and other respects, Nahor has the natural, native, and necessary element of special feminine character; of which Isaac and Jacob have in due course to avail themselves. The Om all-sum of feminine gender and character is in Sarai, the Spirit Jehovah Father-Son female character, or the Spirit's original, virginal, and universal Om, in Jehovah Mother-Daughter character. As Abram is the Zeus Apollo, Sarai is the Athenè Herè, or Rachel Leah. The r as usual marks the rolling and repeating of d in Adam in the feminine side of the three dynasties in one. Sarai is composed of Isha, ara, and i as the first letter of Jehovah; the rest of Jehovah being added when her name is changed into Sarah, as it is introduced at the same time and in the same circumstances, into Abram in the h of Abraham, to indicate the stage of actual Father-Son transition. Sarai, as the all-sum feminine side of Abram, as the all-sum masculine side, is by nature, necessity, and all propriety, the sister and wife of Abram; or she is the all-sum feminine relations to him as he is to her the all-sum masculine relations. How she is the daughter of his father, but not the daughter of his mother, will be seen further on (Gen. xx. 12).

Haran is the right side of Abram, and Nahor his left, and is specially related to the front or south and lower (as well as to the east or left). The syllables in Nahor and Haran are the same; but the arrangement of them in the one differs from that in the other; and o in Nahor being the same as a, all the letters are the same, only the o wants the one (masculine). Haran has more of place and meaning of the im in Zeraphim and Elohim. That Nahor is to the left or farther in is implied in his wife being the daughter of Haran. Her name is Milcah (queen), from Melech (king), with the feminine termination; another form of the same being Michal, the name of Saul's daughter given to David. Melech is a corruption and reversal of Jehovah Elohim. It takes the forms of Molech, Moloch, Malluch, Malchus, and Milcom, and is compounded with many other words, as in Melchizedek. Every one becomes king, or queen, at the highest or head point, as at the shoulder head point of the outer line or side, when the form becomes mingled, and is turned in and on in the process of absorption and sacrifice, of scapegoat advance, and of disappearance of oldnesses and evils. The sum of this point is in Heth, or Hittite, as highest of under and outer Ham brought into, and included in, the Japheth shoulder point of the whole of the three parts, Ham, Shem, and Japheth, all comprised and compressed in the one term Heth. What of it is being absorbed, as its sum-substance, is called the son, or younger part, as son or sons of Heth ; that which is left being called Heth, Hamor, Hiram, Haman, and such like, as Shechem, the son of Hamor. The sum-son that is thus absorbed is sacrificed in dying to the oldnesses and evils of the past Father-sum.

A female, or Om of some form, is always taken as means of carrying this son-sum, or sum-substance, in gradation from the outmost point, inwards to Jehovah midline, as whole sum-sacrifice and offering, followed by the usual covenant, confirmation by the implied death and divine oath, and return of all present and promised blessing. Milcah is the female so acting here ; her sister being Iscah, in relations somewhat as Rachel and Leah. Haran dies in the oldnesses and evils of things being put oft and away in this all transition change ; but, in the process of his so dying, he begets Lot, in whom he passes on in son-sum with Abraham. This is said to happen before the death of Tera, or the full completion of the Teraphic change. Haran dies in the land of his nativity, the Shinar land of the ten Aeonic lower part men from the Deluge to this Teraphic level. Ur is used now as the name of this land (Gaelic, uir, land or earth, and ur, new), and signifies land of light and newness, as the head-sum of all. It also signifies valley or maturity grove, in which sense it is the first part of Uriah (the Hittite), as ur and Jehovah, for new land of head-sum light and life of Jehovah Father-Son. This level is the head or fourth point of the whole lower part, as at the fourth day of creation ; and the sum-son of it, in its character of Chaldea, Egypt, and all world new lower part, is in Ishmael. The Chaldean and all world midpart sum-son is through the king-sum Chedorlaomer ; all which will be seen farther on.

The t in Lot is the hard and strong form of d in Adam, which is the same as the t of Teraphim, and the Lo is for Elohim, all making the outer side of Elohim of the Jehovah Father-Son of inner Abram. Lot as such becomes formally distinct from inner Abram in separating from each other, when Lot goes and grows into the state and form of Siddim. Stephen speaks of Abram as being in Mesopotamia before he dwelt in Charron, which is quite consistent with the account here given. Mesopotamia is from mesos, middle, and potamos, a river ; and signifies the land or valley between the rivers Euphrates and Tigris. The Hebrews called it Padan-aram ; Padan signifying a palace, or grove place in a valley, and aram signifying high or advanced, all making the ending-beginning head-sum grove. This place is spoken of as the locality or seat of Eden. The ending tenth point of every thing being like its beginning first point, this place as the ending-beginning seat of empire between the old and new all-worlds, was regarded as the original Eden, or that which possessed the greatest known resemblance to it. Thus it is taken as the seat of Eden, Shinar, and Babylon. Out of it come the characters in and related to Abram; also Rebekah, Rachel, Leah, and Jacob's family. Out of it came Balaam to curse and altogether bless Israel. Here reigned Cushanrishathain, the first oppressor of the Hebrews after their settlement in Canaan. Out of it has lately been explored the sum-substance of all-man all-world ancient records, collateral with, and confirmatory of, the Biblical records, and forming the centre point with the Bible amongst the many forces and influences which are at work in producing the present Omic and Aeonic change over the whole earth.

The ending point of every thing must be also its re beginning point. Here the Teraphic ending point is at Haran's death; and the first place at which they dwell and out of which they formally start on their journeying to Canaan is at Haran. The first-mentioned Haran is spoken of as the Haran all-man person; the second is the Haran all-world place. Both are the same ending-beginning point; and at, or in passing through, that transition point. Tera dies out of the old, in living into the new, all-man all-world. The days of Tera were two hundred and five years. Man's full age is one hundred years. Terra stands for the full and mature lower part of the second man, or the midpart man, like the first man coming out of the Garden. At this maturity or fourth point he comes forth out of Chaldea, like the forthcoming of creation on the fifth day, and like the Teraphic forthcoming of Adam out of the Garden (being the head-sum of the whole creation as lower part), which is also like the forthcoming at Cainan stage. This last makes the forthcoming and starting for Canaan most express; Cainan being the Aeonic man point corresponding to the Canaan land point, at which point the Abrahamic mid all-man and mid all-world appear in full and formal manhood maturity, for the socio-moral and public being and having being, in the really proper sense.

At this point Abram, and those in him and with him, become as gods, in the all sum Tera or Teraphim transition point out of the lower part into the midpart. Now and here Jehovah calls Abram out of the Chaldean all-man all-world Teraphic form and sense into the all-man all-world Cherubic form and sense; through which form and sense of transition point Tera passes, in his sum-substance out of his Teraphic sense into his Cherubic sense, out of Haran into Charron, as Stephen calls it. Here is the same as Jehovah Elohim sending (calling) Adam out of the Garden, and placing Cherubim at the east of the Garden. Adam was one hundred years as the first one all-man, and thirty years of manhood maturity, at the Garden. Tera, being the second all-man at the same Garden or Teraphim point, is marked by two hundred for the second all-man full hundred; and his manhood maturity is marked by five for his outcoming fifth point, which is the same as thirty years.

Sarai is barren; she has no child. This is here said because she is about to have the sum-son of the all-man lower part, through Hagar the lower part feminine side. Her barrenness is again spoken of at the conception and birth of Isaac. Abram and she are respectively king or prince, and queen or princess, of the one, four, seven, ten, in relation to all beings. Melech is the reverse and absorptive form of Jehovah Elohim; and it belongs to Abram and her to act in Jehovah Father-Son Elohim sense as to all son-sum outcoming and incoming at these points, in all beings and each being of the all-man all-world. At these points they stand at the level of king-queen. At the first point they come forth as the original One and Om. Thence to the fourth point they work all things up to the Teraphic king-queen. From the fourth to the seventh they work all things up to the full-form Cherubic or Melchizedek king-queen. And from the seventh to the tenth they do so into the head-sum Melchisalom king-queen. In the most original, inmost, and highest sense there is no succession of different individuals, no substitution, no change, and no imperfection. It is the eternal order of the Spirit Father-Son, the Jesus order of Melchizedek.

At each of the four great transition points the sum-substance of the past or lower part passes through into the next or higher, as every thing is meat and drink to its higher. But there is a divinity in every thing which implies that the kingdom of God is not meat and drink; but righteousness, and peace, and joy in the Holy Ghost. The all sum-substance is in the joy in the Holy Ghost, as in the first and tenth; the gradation being in Melchitera, Melchizedek, and Melchisalom. The whole of nature and the whole of the Bible are inspired by the Holy Ghost, and are infallibly true in themselves and in man. That which is inner and higher is meat and drink to the outer and lower; the one is and ought to be a sacrifice to the other. Sarai is barren, but she is fruitful; she gets Isaac, and she gives him. The placing in the Garden and the sending forth out of the Garden are universal; the call, the mission, and the blessing of Abram are also universal.

www.ingramcontent.com/pod-product-compliance
Lightning Source LLC
Chambersburg PA
CBHW020934230426
43666CB00008B/1672